The Common Problem

BY THE SAME AUTHOR

(with Roy Lewis) *The English Middle Classes* (1949)
and *Professional People* (1952)
(with Enoch Powell) *Biography of a Nation* (1955)
Good Learning (1964)
South Asia (1966)

THE COMMON PROBLEM

by Angus Maude

The common problem, yours, mine, every one's,
Is not to fancy what were fair in life
Provided it could be, – but, finding first
What may be, then find how to make it fair
Up to our means – a very different thing!
No abstract intellectual plan of life
Quite irrespective of life's plainest laws,
But one, a man, who is man and nothing more,
May lead within a world which (by your leave)
Is Rome or London – not Fool's-paradise.

ROBERT BROWNING, *Bishop Blougram's Apology*

Constable London

First published in 1969
by Constable & Co Ltd
10 Orange Street, London WC2

SBN 09 456520 1

Set in 11 on 12pt Monotype Scotch Roman
Printed in Great Britain
by The Anchor Press Ltd, Tiptree, Essex
and bound by Wm. Brendon & Son Ltd

For

BARBARA

(at last)

with love and gratitude

Contents

Introduction

The quotation on the title-page of this book summarises its theme. It is about the 'common problem' of the peoples of the Western world, and particularly of the people of Britain.

The book is intended as a contribution to a small body of thought and literature that has in the last few years begun to question some of the fundamental assumptions of modern economics and sociology in terms other than those of pure protest. I have also tried at the end of the book to translate some of these ideas into the practical stuff of British party politics.

There is, as Browning was at pains to point out, no text-book 'solution', no all-embracing theoretical panacea, for the worries and frustrations of mankind. It is, I think, precisely because so many people have for so long been promising us one that pessimism and frustration are today so widespread.

When the head of a Cambridge college begins his series of Reith Lectures with the words, 'Men have become like gods . . . Science offers us total mastery over our environment and over our destiny . . .',[1] it is no doubt time to remind him that each of us is still 'man and nothing more'. But it is also salutary to remind ourselves that we are nothing less. It is a simple paradox – although one which the Provost of King's College appeared to find bewildering – that after a period of unprecedentedly rapid scientific and technological advance ordinary men and women are less confident, perhaps even more afraid, than they used to be. The reasons are not far to seek.

The fear is that the oracle speaks with a forked tongue, and that the price to be paid for plenty may be too high. There is nothing godlike about a commonwealth of conditioned automata, manipulated in a state of synthetic euphoria by sociologists for the convenience of the mass-producers of consumption goods and services. Besides, many of the things which science promises – or threatens – to do are just plain frightening.

Already, however, the conditioning process has gone far. Traditional guidelines and centres of authority have been weakened, institutions denigrated and depreciated, and personal and family responsibilities eroded – all in the name of 'progress', of 'welfare', of 'social justice' and 'equality'. The tax-collector has conspired with the technocrat to make the independence which ought to be the reward of individual enterprise and endeavour virtually impossible. That the rewards of success should be limited in order to reduce the penalties of failure is not in itself unethical. It is the deterrents to *independence*, rather than to the accumulation of great wealth, which are serious. To many people it scarcely seems worth while even to try. Again, it is one thing to mitigate the penalties of failure, another to remove the deterrents to irresponsibility.

To the large-scale administrator, as to the technologist, the human individual is (in the words of Jacques Ellul[2]) 'a source of error', a creature with a dangerous predilection for making unpredictable choices. There was a time when this was considered rather a good thing than a menace, since it was believed that out of the diversity of human endeavour almost everything that was worth while was created or evolved. Men made mistakes – sometimes costly and painful – but they achieved great things too. In the vain hope – and it is, and must remain, a vain hope – of avoiding the mistakes, our rulers and thinkers seem content to deprive us of the chance of greatness. Moreover, despite all the promises, nothing seems to work quite as well as it used to, nor is quality maintained.

This book attempts to describe how all this has come about, and makes some suggestions for remedying the situation. If I had to define what I have tried to do, I could hardly do it better than by quoting Newman's definition of the 'logical faculty':

> Though it does not go so far as to ascertain truth, still it teaches us the direction in which truth lies, and how propositions lie toward each other. Nor is it a slight benefit to know

> what is probable and what is not so, what is wanted for the proof of a point, what is wanting in a theory, how a theory hangs together, and what will follow if it be admitted. Though it does not itself discover the unknown, it is one principal way by which discoveries are made.[3]

This is of course no small undertaking in itself, and I am aware by how much the results fall short of the model. Yet if this book helps to alert a few more people to the dangers of present trends, to expose the theories and the interests behind the trends, and to persuade them that these trends are neither inevitable nor irreversible, it will have served its purpose.

'I believe,' said Junius, 'there is yet a spirit of resistance in this country, which will not submit to be oppressed; but I am sure there is a fund of good sense in this country, which cannot be deceived.'[4] In this lies our hope: indeed, no matter how abundantly we are set about with social scientists, technologists and computers, it is in the long run our only hope.

Chapter 1

Illusion and Disillusion

I go back from age to age up to the remotest antiquity, but I find no parallel to what is occurring before my eyes; as the past has ceased to throw its light upon the future, the mind of man wanders in obscurity.

Alexis de Tocqueville, *Democracy in America*

Doth any man doubt, that if there were taken out of men's minds vain opinions, flattering hopes, false valuations, imaginations as one would, and the like, but it would leave the minds of a number of men poor shrunken things, full of melancholy and indisposition, and unpleasing to themselves?

Francis Bacon, *Of Truth*

One has only to settle down for an evening with the Old Testament prophets to realise that there is nothing new about social pessimism. Gildas was the first exponent of the genre in Britain, and exactly a thousand years after him John Knox was still carrying the torch handed down by Jeremiah. In this tradition, both diagnosis and cure were simple. What was wrong with society was wickedness, the abandonment of the spiritual principle for material concerns. If people would only obey God's laws, all would be well. The solution was essentially backward-looking, a demand for a return to the first principles of religion. If these did not seem to the vulgar immediately relevant to the troubles of society, that was obviously what was wrong with society, which must reform itself before it was too late. There was no question of adjusting the principles.

There are still those, and not only among churchmen, who argue along these lines. Their solutions are not always religious, nor even purely ethical, but they all involve 'going back' to a set of principles the abandonment of which is believed to have been responsible for the crucial troubles of society. What is demanded may be a religious revival, a return to the 'traditional' morality of sexual continence and honesty and hard work, or the 'restoration' of free enterprise and the competitive market economy.

On the other hand, there has been since the Enlightenment a quite contrary tradition which maintains that principles need to be restated from time to time to take account of change, if only of changes in the meaning of words and thence of the ideas these purport to convey. The tradition cannot be precisely described as 'forward-looking', since the restatements and new syntheses of principles were seldom intended to do more than adjust to the conditions of the present, but it was in no sense backward-looking.*

The essential difference between the two attitudes is, however, more than that between a 'reactionary' and a 'progressive' orientation of the mind. The old attitude looked to principles which were either assumed to have been 'revealed' or believed to have acquired the sanctity of prescription from immemorial usage; in both cases to alter the principles was unthinkable. The modern conviction was that human reason and/or experience, even unaided by divine revelation, was capable of devising principles in accordance with which society could be efficiently organised at any stage of its development. It followed that the antiquity, or the alleged sanctity, of currently accepted principles in no way guaranteed their relevance to present conditions; it was essential to test them from time to time, and if necessary to modify them.

The comparative difficulty and complication of the problems presented by the new system are obvious. Indeed, under the old dispensation there was scarcely a problem at all. Individuals might wonder whether the traditional principles were still adequate and relevant, but at least everyone knew what they were and that society was bound by them. Even questions of interpretation presented no public difficulty so long as there was a single, established and authoritarian Church. But with the Reformation and the Enlightenment certainty began to disappear. There can be no half-way house for religion in society; either there is a single, comprehensive Church, claiming a unique and divinely instituted authority

* Even churchmen have been affected by the change. John Knox wanted to go back to the Bible, whereas Dr. John Robinson wants to get away from it.

for its dogma and teachings – which must be enforced by the State if they cannot secure voluntary general assent – or there can ultimately be *no* limits to the number of sects and the variety of ways in which men will interpret the Scriptures by the light of reason and conscience. Satisfying as this is to the intellectually adventurous, and exciting as it may be to immature or volatile minds, it can also be both bewildering and alarming to the many who prefer security and even the mere illusion of certainty (and who, paradoxically, may actually feel in sum freer when they are operating within these imposed limits). The end may be a widespread and total scepticism, or a marked susceptibility to claptrap.

In the secular field the Enlightenment greatly widened the range of discussion and choice in ethical, metaphysical and political philosophy; this, Augustine and Aquinas notwithstanding, had not advanced by much since Plato and Aristotle. Yet here the results, though significant and indeed profound, were for many years much less obvious than the effects of the Reformation on popular religion. While a non-religious system of ethics became once more possible, and controversy ranged freely over the alternative bases and linguistic terms of ethics, the philosophers did not immediately promulgate any moral principles or imperatives that for *practical* purposes differed very much from the traditional Christian ones. This was presumably in part due to the fact that the philosophers themselves – even the most sceptical among them – had been nurtured in a Christian tradition which had itself absorbed the Aristotelian ethics. But it must also have been the case that the traditional moral code, however much or less honoured in the observance, yet remained adequate and relevant to the needs of a society still largely organised on the traditional lines and still deeply conditioned by the Romano-Christian heritage. Philosophers might, and freely did, avail themselves of the new liberty to discuss why men should be moral, whence the imperatives of morality are derived, and in what morality consists. But when it came to telling men what to *do* to be good, the English philosophers found little new to be said in the conditions of the time. With the French *philosophes* it was different.

Nevertheless, it is a matter of history that during the 18th century there was in Britain a marked tendency towards more humane and tolerant social behaviour. This was not the result of a movement away from Christian ethics, but the product of empirical study of social facts. It did not at that time amount to quite the same thing: after all, the inhumanity and intolerance, though they may have been countenanced by the Church, were certainly no part of the accepted Christian message. It is not to be supposed – and cannot have been supposed by English people at the time – that the Christ who exorcised devils and saved the woman taken in adultery would have approved the burning of witches, or would have considered hanging a punishment appropriate to the crime of stealing food for a starving family. It was not that Christians believed these punishments to be 'good', and that secular philosophers showed that they were ethically wrong; it was simply that people who were willing to consider facts objectively and make rational deductions from them succeeded in convincing society that it could *live safely* without these sanctions. Once the cruelty could be shown to be *unnecessary*, it was willingly abolished. This was not yet a new ethical code telling people how to be good, but the result of empirical study to enable people to live together more comfortably as social beings.

It was, however, a logical sequel that more recently the moral code has been challenged *per se*, both by the determinists and on the utilitarian ground that it no longer conduces to the 'greatest happiness of the greatest number'. Whether you believe morality to be a matter of reasoning, of intuition or of the voice of God speaking through conscience, there can be little left of it to be codified if man is as thoroughly predetermined by antecedent causes as the 19th century scientists considered that matter was. And if there is no absolute morality, but only conventions designed to ease the frictions of social living, then not only will these conventions need to be altered as social conditions change but they can scarcely be usefully derived from Divine revelation manifested nearly 2,000 years ago.

There was no sudden break, nor was much of the new metaphysics of the Enlightenment atheistic in its implications. Even the conclusions of the sceptical philosophers were for the most part capable of co-existing with a belief in God. Descartes, the first of the great rationalist philosophers and the prophet of doubt, was actually driven to postulate the existence of God in order to prove the objective truth of mathematics. Moreover, he asserts, 'I could not possibly be of such a nature as I am, and yet have in my mind the idea of a God, if God did not in reality exist'.[1] This assertion, which probably amounts to as much 'proof' of the existence of God as most believers demand, is of course not a rational deduction *a priori* at all, but a declaration of faith – and by no means a specifically Christian one. In the event, the Cartesian philosophy led many thinkers away from revealed religion towards the deism which was so influential in Europe in the 17th and 18th centuries.

As the implications of the Newtonian physics began to become apparent, philosophers set out to try to square them with their beliefs about the existence and nature of God, which involved some re-thinking about the nature of man. Abandoning the dogmatic Cartesian belief in the primacy of reason, the great British empirical philosophers founded a new school of thought which was to establish a long tradition. Though each produced a rounded system of his own, Locke, Berkeley and Hume were links in a chain of experiential philosophy that led to the utilitarianism of the Philosophic Radicals and on to the pragmatists. It can also be truly said that Locke and his successors foreshadowed modern empirical psychology. Meanwhile on the Continent the rationalist tradition culminated in the critical philosophy of Kant and the idealism of Fichte and Hegel, which in turn inspired a new idealist school in late Victorian Britain.

None of this directly affected the lives and thoughts of ordinary men and women at the time, although (as we shall see) the leading philosophers proceeded to work out the implications of their metaphysics and ethics in political terms which were to have profound effects on governments and societies, and thus on individual lives. Yet it is also important because it provided the background to the drama of the scientific revolution. This, in its later stages, not only completed the destruction of religious authority but threw the philosophers as well as the churchmen into disarray. Scientific determinism led the materialist philosophers and the psychologists in one direction – towards the reduction of ethics to the status and techniques of a natural science such as the discoveries of the anthropologists appeared to make possible. This provoked a counter-attack by the idealists, and philosophy was for decades absorbed in a sterile and largely meaningless controversy over the possibility of 'free will', in which the scientists themselves joined with enthusiasm. Since scientific determinism has appeared to be discredited and materialism obsolete, we have been addressed at large by philosophical scientists and scientific philosophers – to very little purpose, as it seems to me. Each appears so deeply conditioned by the categories of his own discipline that he throws but little light on the rest.*

Yet the whole process has been crucially important in its influence on popular notions of morality and of the place of the human individual in the world. Bereft of the certainty and authority derived from religion, men were offered no comparable practical guides to put in their place. Science for a time appeared to offer a kind of certainty, but not one which provided any guide to conduct or enabled the individual to feel himself possessing a meaningful relationship with the world. It is all very well to be told you are 'conditioned', but it does not help very much in dealing with life's problems; on the contrary, it seems to suggest that there is little point in trying to cope with them at all.

Much was promised for the future. Now that a science of mind and behaviour was possible, scientists assured the world that a properly conducted programme of research and experiment would not only free us from the tiresome unpredictability of human behaviour but also reduce the complications of social living and organisation to an orderly pattern of scientific laws which could be interpreted and acted upon by experts for the general good. The popular reaction to this was that it might or might not be so, one could only wait and see,

* An honourable exception must be made of the late Professor L. Susan Stebbing, whose *Philosophy and the Physicists* was refreshingly perceptive.

but that in the meantime things were very difficult. Enlightened intellectuals tended to be excited by the whole business, dismissing as romantic reactionaries those other intellectuals who viewed the onset of the new dispensation with some alarm. It was fine 'for the multitude of the educated, who have wearied of the formulas of a stereotyped theology, but still demand free indulgence for the appetite which that theology supplied with a regulation diet',[2] but the mass of the people were unsettled, disturbed and confused. It appeared that they were genuinely interested in knowing whether they had a free will or not. They had always assumed (or felt) that, under God, they had; now nobody seemed to be able to tell them for sure. Through the medium of the newspapers, popularised science and philosophy met an avid demand, from the educational crusades of T. H. Huxley in the 1870s to the outpourings of Jeans, Eddington and Planck in the 1930s. Indeed,

> Myself when young did eagerly frequent
> Doctor and Saint, and heard great Argument
> About it and about: but evermore
> Came out by the same Door as in I went.

When even the limited certainty that science had purported to offer dissolved into relativity and waves of probability, the wheel seemed to have come full circle. The ordinary man, seeking the support of certainty and authority, was no further forward than his ancestors had been when Galileo knocked the props from under them. In many respects, indeed, he was much more radically disoriented.

It has been said that the modern age began with the realisation that the earth revolves round the sun, which is contrary to the evidence of men's senses. And it was Galileo's telescope that precipitated the crisis, as the Church authorities immediately perceived. The Copernican system was harmless enough as an undemonstrable speculative theory. Purporting to prove something was another matter. It is true that Giordano Bruno had been burnt at the stake in 1600, but his fatal heresy lay rather in his pantheistic philosophy than in his Copernican science. Galileo's was the crucial case, and '*eppur se muove*' the first stroke of the death-knell of religious authority, completed everywhere when the fundamentalists rejected the conclusions of Darwin and Wallace. It is one thing to impose dogma with authority when the contrary can only be argued rationally without being proved, quite another for authority to be seen to beat an ignominious retreat in the face of what appeared to be demonstrable facts. Newman, in the most persuasive apologia for the attitude of authority in the Galileo case, argued that the Church is right to seek to avert the damaging effects of novelty on faith so long as it can be held to be no more than hypothesis, but equally right to modify its dogma by the assimilation of the hypothesis when it attains the status of proved fact.[3] However, leaving aside the question of whether Galileo's discoveries had not attained that status long before the Church accepted them, this argument ignores the immense damage done by the *volte-face* not only to religious authority but to religion itself.

The more authority is weakened, and the more rationalist the climate of thought becomes, the more hopeless is the dilemma. Nothing can prevent men of speculative mind from questioning dogma and applying the tests of reason and experiment. All that can be done is either to persuade them to make the vital leap from reason to faith, or to deter them by authoritarian sanctions from making their objections public. This is of course the same dilemma that confronts temporal totalitarian regimes based on ideology, where the object is similarly to avoid upsetting the unreasoning mass of the simple faithful. It is probably true that faith must, in the last resort, have *some* grounding in reason. It may take the form of the kind of rational intuition already quoted from Descartes, or of the more or less logical process of assent described by Newman[4]; for the great majority of people, the rational basis of faith will lie in the acceptance of authority. Their reason cannot justify their faith, but it may persuade them to accept the authority that purports to justify it. It follows from this that the most likely and important direct cause of a widespread loss of faith will be, not rational doubt nor the rational demonstration of the improbability of what is believed, but the discrediting of the external authority which has hitherto 'guaranteed' the faith. Then the validity of the creed becomes tarnished by association with the authority, and not vice versa.

It is not unknown for a believer to abandon or change his religious faith because of repugnance to the worldly corruption of his church. Many communists abandoned communism, not because they suddenly and spontaneously recognised dialectical weaknesses in the Marxist-Leninist creed, but because the Russians bloodily repressed a workers' revolt in Hungary. Some people have 'lost their faith' in science since the invention of nuclear weapons. Faith in democracy can be destroyed by a succession of incompetent elected governments. Of course, apart from such extrinsic causes, the discrediting of authority through a successful rational attack on one article of the faith it upholds may bring other articles, or even the whole, of the faith into disrepute.

Thus over a long period faith (which is a kind of certainty) and certainty (which is a kind of faith) were progressively weakened among the mass of the people, together with the idea of an infallible and unquestionable authority. For a long time nothing was put in their place. Religion was temporarily strengthened in particular places and among some kinds of people. The Counter-Reformation, Puritanism, Methodism, the Oxford Movement and the Evangelical cult each had its passing effect, but the long-term trend was unmistakable. Rationalism and scepticism spread among the educated and education, as well as government, became progressively secularised. In England the habit of church-going was permanently weakened by the Reformation; even in 1552 Parliament was complaining that the Laity 'do wilfully and damnably abstain and refuse to come to their parish churches'. Later, the established Church was to be decisively rejected by a populace which saw it as an institution dominated by a gentry which seemed to have become a functionless anachronism. The non-conformist sects were similarly fatally compromised by their association with the entrepreneurs of the industrial revolution and after, who interpreted the Protestant Ethic as a doctrine of hard labour for their employees in this world to be rewarded by favours in the next: the workers naturally reacted against a theology which condemned them to be paid in a kind of spiritual 'truck' while the bosses accumulated material fortunes on earth.

Even the triumphant efficacy of reason and experience, among the intellectuals themselves, was not to be perennial or unchallenged. Reason was destined to suffer an apparent limitation of its scope, as had happened with the physical senses. It must be supposed that the greatest shock ordinary men and women have ever suffered was the discovery that they could no longer trust the direct experience of their own eyes. And Galileo's telescope did more than administer the shock of discovery that the earth was not the centre of the universe; it abolished 'that inverted bowl we call the Sky' (and, by implication, Heaven), pushing back the frontiers of space to infinity. Exciting as this was to those who find that kind of thing exciting, it was profoundly disorienting to ordinary people. Certainty was on its way out.

Worse was to follow. After all, the Galilean system was – despite the mathematics – for the most part verifiable by the senses, provided the range of the senses was extended by mechanical aids. It was, with an effort, comprehensible. The Newtonian physics was markedly less so, but still retained the comfortable conviction that most things were, in the last resort, mensurable, and that at least matter behaved in an orderly fashion in accordance with strict laws of nature. Man himself, however, seemed fated to become less rational as these triumphs of his reason and perception mounted. Not only did Darwin (aided and abetted by the archaeologists) push the frontiers of prehistory back to infinity, leaving men dwarfed and isolated in a vast wilderness of time as well as space; he also made it clear that Man was no exception to the general rules governing nature. Deprived of his benefit of exemption, Man was promptly arrested by the scientists and clapped into the prison of determinism. He was deemed by experts to have forfeited the privilege of free will for the duration of his sentence.

When, many years later, the physicists discovered that they had been getting the nature of the universe substantially wrong and had to try again, they decided by a majority to release Man on parole. They could hardly restore his free will, since no one now knew what – if anything – this meant; however, if it was any comfort to him, he was no longer to be wholly determined by iron laws, but only conditioned by his heredity and environment (in unspecified proportions).

There was little point in men wishing that the scientists would make up their minds once for all and stick to it; it now appeared unlikely that anyone was ever again going to be able to do this about anything. The scientists had hedged certainty into probability. Moreover, the physicists seemed to have taken leave not only of their senses but of reason as well. Logic and causal laws seemed to be on the way out, to be replaced by statistics, while mathematics had abandoned the idea of spatial extension. Two straight lines, it seemed, could even enclose a space. Space and time had ceased to have any ordinary meaning, and had become (at least temporarily) fused in a four-dimensional continuum. Well might the philosopher Whitehead exclaim, 'Heaven knows what seeming nonsense may not tomorrow be demonstrated truth!'[5]

Physical measurement was ceasing to have anything to do with the senses, becoming a succession of messages received by instruments. It even began to seem possible that it might be as logical to say that the sun revolved round the earth as that the earth moved round the sun, which prompted a question as to what all the fuss had been about. Later still, particles started to play up, and time threatened to run backwards. But the physicists had, it appeared, lost contact in their advanced work with any semblance of what had once been called reality. They were dealing with things they could not see or even imagine, with ideas that could not be expressed in any language but that of increasingly complicated mathematical symbols. Chaos, it seemed, was come again, and *l'homme moyen sensuel* was adrift in it without pilot, map or rudder.

That he did not appear actively to resent what the scientists had done to him – and indeed continued for a time to regard them with at least the vestiges of an almost superstitious respect – perhaps calls for some comment. It was in fact not until after the military implications of nuclear fission and fusion had become apparent that there was any general revulsion against the scientists, although there had always been thoughtful men who saw the dangers implicit in their increasing dominance. It was as if people were desperately unwilling to abandon a faith in science that had seemed for a time to offer them a certainty and authority to replace those lost with religious disillusion and the passing of the hierarchic structure of government. Although the certainty had proved illusory, while the promise of a 'scientific' ordering of society now seemed either unlikely to be fulfilled or even actually undesirable, what was there left if even science failed? Democracy provided no answer, for it seemed to rely itself more and more on the assumption that in the last resort only science (or scientific method) could produce an orderly functioning of the society it had created. It certainly looked as if the science god had failed, but since there was not another one in sight there seemed no alternative but to hang on and hope for the best against all the odds.

And after all science did appear to be capable of working miracles of a sort. Even the nonsensical incomprehensibility of some of them added to the aura of divinity. 'As a matter of fact, no supposedly suprarational divine revelation and no supposedly abstruse philosophic truth has ever offended human reason so glaringly as certain results of modern science.'[6] And therein lay part of their superstitious appeal. Moreover, some of the miracles were of an almost biblical kind (of both the Old and New Testament varieties). Man had always sought to control and use the processes of nature – indeed it is a profound (if paradoxical) truth that this *co-operation* with nature is among the most natural of human activities. But the scientist's ability to *start natural processes* on his own is something quite new and very different. It is a thoroughly unnerving phenomenon, opening up a whole new vista of uncertainties. As Dr. Hannah Arendt has pointed out, this acting *into* nature, this breaking down of the boundaries between 'natural elements and the human artifice', means that we are carrying what most people still (and probably rightly) regard as the essential unpredictability of human behaviour 'into that realm which we used to think of as ruled by inexorable laws'.[7] Nothing could be more disturbing; but it cannot be denied that the ability to destroy life on a vast scale by synthetically contrived natural processes, together with the imminent ability to create life and produce a man-made pattern of evolution, has something traditionally god-like about it. It might seem that the new gods would have to be pretty strictly controlled when their creative or destructive whims threatened to get out of hand, but that they had something of the supernatural about them now seemed merely a literal statement of obvious fact.

Nor were miracles of the New Testament variety lacking, and the current popular insistence on talking about 'wonder drugs' shows clearly enough the turn that people's thoughts had taken. Disturbing and unreliable as the scientists might be in many ways, they were undeniably useful in others. It has been charitably assumed that this was their intention, although Dr. Arendt (I think rightly) bids us 'rid ourselves of the current prejudice which ascribes the development of modern science, because of its applicability, to a pragmatic desire to improve conditions and better human life on earth', adding that 'it is a matter of historical record that modern technology has its origins . . . exclusively in an altogether non-practical search for useless knowledge'.[8]

Nevertheless the 'wonder drugs' existed, in the form of antibiotics, tranquilisers and even television. There were also airplanes, motor cars and washing machines. It was therefore possible and even necessary to tolerate science, although the old faith was now on the wane. The 'glad confident morning', even if it had not declined into the 'glimmer of twilight', was perceptibly misted over.

Meanwhile *l'homme moyen sensuel* was facing other troubles. Not the least of these was that the psychologists had got at him. It seemed that not only could he no longer trust the evidence of his own senses, but his mind and body were at the mercy of an 'unconscious' which could not be controlled or influenced in the first instance by himself, but only by techniques which themselves raised alarming problems and possibilities. While Man was yet in thrall to the physicists, the psychologists had been building a new prison for him, and they hounded him relentlessly until they thought they had him in it. The wretched fugitive could do nothing right: how could he, indeed, since 'right' and 'wrong' no longer existed? Insisting that they were only trying to free him from his feelings of guilt, they persuaded him that he indeed did – or at least ought to – feel guilty. Even loving his mother now seemed to be dangerous and vaguely discreditable, while the apparent innocence of children was clouded with sexuality. The abnormal had become normal and the irrational rational – but also, of course, vice versa. Man did his best to live up to it, but the psychologists were never satisfied. Whatever he did, said or thought, it seemed that he must be a slave – to his unconscious, to his environment, or to the psychologists themselves. If he tried to ignore the whole thing, he was suffering from repressions. If he tried to enjoy the freedom they assured him was his for the taking, he was sure to overdo it and show symptoms of something deplorable – and moreover the conventional would strongly disapprove of him. If he tried to hide in a crowd, he was self-alienated; if he tried to get out on his own, he was alienated from 'society', and possibly an exhibitionist or worse. Finally they decided that he was alienated from the world – as well he might be, after what had happened both to him and to the world.*

Meanwhile the science of physical medicine had been advancing rapidly, with results almost equally unsettling to the traditional order. Improvements in sanitation, hygiene and midwifery raised the survival rate among children to an unprecedented height. Among those who now survived were many who would never be physically or mentally capable of making their way in the world unaided; this imposed new problems and strains on parents, and in the end the State was forced to make communal provision for the victims. At the same time, advances in medicine and surgery progressively reduced the number of disorders fatal to adults, so that the proportion of old people in the population increased and more and more people survived into a condition of physical dependence on others. It became increasingly difficult for people to die, even when they wanted to; sometimes bodies were kept

* Needless to say, the above is in no way intended to belittle the very real achievements of psychiatry in the treatment of mental illness. Despite some rough early passages when over-confident practitioners occasionally did real harm (with shock therapy, for example), an immense amount of good has been done and much tragedy prevented. What is here in question is the psychologist who diagnoses and pronounces at large, especially in the field of sociology, on the basis of what purports to be a deterministic science but is in reality of dubious scientific validity and backed by the sketchiest experimental data.

alive after they had degenerated into almost inanimate objects. Doctors, brought up in an ethical and professional tradition that taught them to save and prolong human life, often had to take a deliberate decision to end it.

This was by no means the whole story, of course. Many people were enabled by the advance of medicine to live useful and happy lives for many more years than would otherwise have been possible, and much pain and suffering was averted or mitigated. Nevertheless, the institution of the family was subjected to strains with which it had never before had to contend on a similar scale. At the same time the development of the National Health Service gave rise to problems of priorities which are today as far from solution as ever.*

The family was being subjected to other strains as well. Its intimate relationships were tainted by the Freudian psychology, while the religious and conventional sanctions cementing it had been greatly weakened. Yet this does not explain the philosophical vacuum in which this institution was left, while all kinds of new social machinery were erected around it and began to influence it in important practical ways. Theories of social organisation abounded, as did practical plans for 'social reform'; but the sociologists, enthusiastic for their new 'science' and tending at first to take 'society as a whole' as their laboratory, seemed to have no time for a new theory of the family which would place the institution formally in its new setting. Indeed, they sometimes talked in Marxian terms as if the family was no longer of prime significance and was destined to 'wither away'.

The reason is probably not far to seek. It was not just that philosophical theories were out of fashion among 'practical' people: it was not thought necessary to provide a new theory of the family because it was not realised that there was any urgent demand for one. It is easy to see how the misunder-

* To grab but one fleeting example from the passing stream, the following editorial footnote to a newspaper item is suggestive. 'Our Health Services Correspondent writes: The great and tragic lack is of kidney machines. People are dying because too few can be afforded.' To those who are familiar with the condition of the hospital services, the first sentence may appear to say either much too much or much too little; but the comment is here reproduced in its entirety, and (even allowing for the possibility that a sub-editor had emasculated a longer piece) the number of questions it begs is almost infinite.[9]

standing of the situation arose. The experts were no doubt aware that the famiy had once been firmly grounded on a philosophical and religious basis; but this basis seemed to have been eroded so long ago that the question of replacing it had become purely academic. Families had, after all, gone on existing, philosophical basis or none; after so long a survival *in vacuo*, it appeared reasonable to assume that the institution could get along without any theoretical justification. What was needed was practical therapy.

This, however, seems to reveal a misunderstanding of the psychology of ordinary men and women. Sociologists may be confident that they themselves can operate scientifically without any philosophic basis, but ordinary people are seldom at at ease without one. It is presumptuous as well as inaccurate to assume that, because they are often inarticulate as well as unlearned and 'don't bother their heads about philosophy', they can exist comfortably in a metaphysical and ethical vacuum. It is precisely because they are often inarticulate and unlearned that they need the implicit support of a philosophy. The medieval peasant can seldom have had a deep grasp of Catholic theology or of the theoretical basis of the ancient Roman hierarchical structure, but there is abundant historical evidence that their authority did sustain him and give some measure of meaning and certainty to his relationship with the outside world. I have suggested earlier that it is not always necessary for people to have a complete and explicit understanding of what it is that sustains them and why; so long as they know that there *is* something there, they are capable of accepting its authority implicitly until it becomes too obviously irrelevant to the conditions of the time.

That, surely, is exactly what people in this country did in the case of the traditional basis of the institution of the family, long after they had abandoned its religious framework* and after social and economic changes had made its relevance

* It is interesting (though probably fruitless) to speculate on the causes of the phenomenon which worries so many conscientious parsons—that of the apparently pagan couple who insist on being married, and having their children baptised, in church. Is it a mere vestigial reflex? Is it, as some sociologists suggest, regarded as a conventional guarantee of social respectability? Or is it perhaps a kind of superstitious insurance policy taken out 'because you never know, after all'?

minimal. It was not, as the experts seem to have parents were managing to get along without a attitude to the family at all: they were still desp to cling to the last recorded tradition, handed c by their own parents from yet remoter generati

That this was so at least until the last war is su of knowledge. That the dilemma is still keenly deduced from the expressed complaints of some of today's parents and the obvious bewilderment of others. Moreover, it seems to be felt in all social classes, though possibly more in some than in others. In most working-class homes parental attitudes have traditionally been – at least superficially – more relaxed and permissive than in middle-class families where the virtues of order and discipline have often been made a fetish. Nevertheless *some* conventions were even more strongly adhered to in working-class than in middle-class homes, and the idea of ultimate parental authority was much the same in both.

Several factors have combined to strain relations between parents and children at all levels. Not all parents have adjusted themselves to the implications of the earlier physical maturing of today's children, or to the often surprising amount of money they can earn on leaving school. The popular (in the newspaper sense) 'cult of youth' has perhaps not been taken quite so seriously by the young themselves as its propagators like to believe, but it has not been without its effects on them. You cannot be told continuously that the world is yours without beginning to assume some proprietorial attitudes towards it, and parents tend to be the most immediate obstacles you encounter. The young do seem to have become markedly more gregarious of late, and to have assumed more distinctive group *mores*. The traditional cry, 'You don't understand!', has become less of an agonised outburst of individualist protest and more of a confident assertion backed by communal authority. Confident enough, at any rate, to inspire some twinges of doubt in the breasts of many parents.

It is obvious that the intensification of publicly provided education and the increasing concern of the State with child welfare have impinged pretty violently on the family circumstances of less responsible parents. However, new conceptions in education, coupled with the increased conformism of the ng to what the sociologists would no doubt call 'the norms of their peer group', have presented all parents with new problems. Not only has school discipline become more permissive, but the conventions of the 'peer group' tend to be set by the children from the most permissive homes. There can be few parents who have not been tormented by the cry that 'everyone at school does it'. However deeply rooted the instinctive parental desire to assume responsibility and exercise authority, parents cannot help being influenced by the fact that authority is distinctly out of fashion and by the tendency of 'society' increasingly to extend the area of its responsibility. It is scarcely surprising, then, that some parents are genuinely baffled by the problem of where their own responsibility ends and that of the school-teacher – or even the policeman – begins.

Ironically enough, the school-teacher can now be heard voicing much the same complaints in reverse. 'How can I be expected to make anything of them when all the good I do is undone at home?' (But it may be noted that this frequently heard question seems to imply an assumption that the real responsibility for the children's development *is* the school-teacher's, not the parents'.) Attempts at regular consultation, either informally at 'open days' or formally through parent-teacher associations, are unquestionably useful in increasing mutual understanding and settling practical details: but they are no substitute for a philosophically grounded definition of who actually ought to be responsible for what.

It is, of course, not only parents who have been disoriented by the uncertainty into which the family institution has been cast. Relationships with, and responsibility for, old people now present a problem which is admitted by everyone to be serious. What is perhaps less well appreciated, despite the reams that have been written about the 'problem' of the young, is the extent to which young people themselves are suffering from the uncertainties of family life.

When parents can neither muster the confidence to exert parental authority effectively nor bring themselves to abrogate it altogether, it is even less easy for the young to know where they stand than for the parents. The atmosphere created is often one of complete uncertainty, producing continual friction in the home and provoking attempts by young people to assert their adulthood and independence. This is especially provoked by the inability of some parents to recognise that physical maturity now comes perceptibly earlier; and while it is true that mental maturity and poise develop little, if any, earlier than they did, the situation is often complicated by the fact that many children have now received a more intensive and sophisticated education than did their parents.

The desire to assert adulthood and independence – which has been further stimulated by the cult of youth flattery promoted by press and advertisers for purely commercial purposes – leads inevitably to early marriages. Marriage not only means escape from home (if you can get a house); it is the unmistakable sign of adult status. It is also often a desperate attempt to build something private and meaningful for yourself in a mass society. And of course early marriage is made easier by full employment, high wages and the ability to furnish a home with luxuries as well as necessities on hire-purchase.

All this is obvious, well-known and frequently commented upon. So is the fact that marriage, which is a difficult and testing business even for mature couples, imposes often intolerable strains on the immature. But the whole thing is made much worse by the complete social vacuum in which the family as an institution is now suspended. It is not simply that the teenage married couple are ill prepared for the problems of living together and adjusting to each other. They are starting a new family without the slightest idea of what a family is and what it is for (apart, of course, from some elementary and unsophisticated ideas about love and children). About what is the status of the family and the sphere of its responsibility, what is its relationship with 'society' as a whole, they have no idea at all. And they have no idea because no one else has either.

We turn now, in the next chapter, to a survey of the political, economic and social developments which have provided the environment for the individuals and families whom we have seen being directly influenced by the increasing uncertainties of life. It is, in a sense, the same picture seen from a different angle.

Chapter 2

The Apotheosis of 'Society'

The great and chief end therefore of men's uniting into commonwealths, and putting themselves under Government, is the preservation of their property; to which in the state of nature there are many things wanting.

John Locke, *Second Treatise of Civil Government*

The whole history of civilisation is strewn with creeds and institutions which were invaluable at first, and deadly afterwards. Progress would not have been the rarity it is if the early food had not been the late poison.

Walter Bagehot, *Physics and Politics*

I very clearly discern two tendencies; the one leading the mind of every man to untried thoughts, the other inclined to prohibit him from thinking at all. And I perceive how, under the dominion of certain laws, democracy would extinguish that liberty of the mind to which a democratic social condition is favourable; so that, after having broken all the bondage once imposed on it by ranks or by men, the human mind would be closely fettered to the general will of the greatest number.

Alexis de Tocqueville, *Democracy in America*

If there is one thing above all others that distinguishes the thought of the Western world today from that of its ancestry, it is the idea of 'society'. It is this, rather than aberrant theories of 'the State', that gives its peculiar flavour to modern life and modern ideas. It lies at the root of the vestigial political philosophies of Tories, Liberals and Socialists alike. So completely has it come to be taken for granted, that it is only in the last few years that any critical thought has been directed to its nature, and thus to its implications and possible dangers. It is necessary for us now to analyse the transformation and to trace the stages by which it has taken place.

In the Greek city-state the concept of 'society' was by no means unknown, but it was not an integral part of *political* thinking. This made a clear distinction. There was the private realm of the family or household, to whose sphere of 'housekeeping' belonged most of what we now think of as 'economic' activities; and there was the public realm of politics, in which free citizens met together for discussion and for the initiation of political action. The State was the State, and families were families; the idea of 'society', as one large super-family in which the interests of individual families were merged, and which indulged in a kind of super-housekeeping, was a quite foreign notion. Indeed, as Hannah Arendt has pointed out,[1] the term 'political economy' would have been literally a contradiction in terms. Nor was political action a matter of law-making, but rather took place within a *given* framework of law. It was the 'acting together' of men in the political sphere that constituted *power*,* which in itself had nothing to do with force or violence.

Even in Rome, where preoccupation with legislation began to become a feature of politics, the distinction between the public and private spheres remained for a long time sharp and clear; the notion of 'society' in the modern sense had not yet blurred it. The Romans had a peculiar genius for practical government, but they seldom constructed theories. By the time that Justinian commissioned the indefatigable Tribonian to compress and codify the laws of the Empire, Roman law had ceased to run in Western Europe. King Ethelbert of Kent, whose reign overlapped that of Justinian, promulgated the first English laws of which we know; and these, while they owed something to the Christianity he learned from Augustine and something to the Franks into whose royal house he married, owed nothing directly to Rome.

For many centuries the people of this country knew little of the idea that norms of conduct can be prescribed by legislation. Indeed, the idea that new laws could be made at all was of very slow growth. The Frankish feudal system, in part an adaptation of certain land tenure systems and personal relationships of the late Roman Empire, was given a special twist by the Conqueror when he brought it to England, and it developed here in a way different from that of the continent.† Land tenure became completely feudal, but the King

* That is, the potential for action.

† It was some time before anyone noticed this. Maitland observed that the English 'feudal system' was invented by Sir Henry Spelman in the early 17th century and popularised by Blackstone in the 18th.

retained much of the administration of the country under his own control, using some of the old English machinery. Neither taxation nor the administration of criminal justice were wholly centralised. Although England had already been moving towards something like a feudal system before the Conquest, the Normans introduced as an innovation the legal theory that all land is held of the King. The importance of this can hardly be overstressed, since so much grew out of it. As Maitland said, 'the constitution of parliament, of the law courts, of the army, all seems as it were a sort of appendix to the law of real property'.[2] Land and its tenure were not only the basis of feudalism, they set an imprint on the whole of English life and organisation that is still (and to some extent anachronistically) apparent.

Certain other characteristics of life in feudal England are important for our purposes. The first is the dominance of the 'private realm' as opposed to the public. Even before the idea of the nation-state was developed, it was obvious that the kind of political activity possible within the close confines of the city-state was unattainable. Almost the only 'public' activity was that in which people took part together as members of the Church, and for some time 'politics' were primarily concerned with the relationships between Church and State. The Church provided not only a kind of equal citizenship for its members but also a framework of philosophical certainty and moral authority for their lives. Economic activity took place almost entirely in the private domain, which embraced not only family life and the feudal lord's relationships with his household and tenants but the common farming of the peasants and the 'family' of master craftsman with his journeymen and apprentices.

In the early middle ages there could hardly be said to be a 'working class', in the sense of a large body of propertyless men working for wages. The villein was not free, and he owed his lord so many days of working service, but he had his strips of the open fields to cultivate alongside those of free men. The master craftsman might be paying wages to a few journeymen, but they were for the most part temporary employees, each intent on setting up as a master on his own. All these men worked hard for long hours – up to eleven hours a day – but they did it for remarkably few days in the year. In addition to Sundays, public holidays provided the equivalent of at least two months' holiday a year and possibly much more.

Brutally hard and poor as life for the most part was, it gave to each man and family a known status and a measure of protection from above. It seems that the degree of certainty provided by recognised status and an authoritarian religion does satisfy a deep human need, and that the loss of these props has not yet been compensated for by any adequate replacement.

The feudal system, while it imposed fixed duties, also guaranteed certain rights, and it was to the maintenance and restatement of these that nearly all early 'laws' were directed. What Dr. F. A. Hayek calls 'the traditional view that laws are found and not made'[3] endured for a long time.* Important changes in the law, together with the imposition of certain regulations, were made by statute in the reign of Edward I; but for many years even Parliament was primarily a body that validated periodical restatements of what was deemed to be existing law. Only later did the control of the Commons over taxation encourage them to demand 'redress of grievances' as a condition of granting supply, and it was later still that the 'bills' of their grievances became the text of statutes to be passed and promulgated.

Meanwhile the strict feudal system of land tenure was being gradually 'modernised'. The Statute *Quia Emptores* enabled tenancies-in-chief to be bought and sold as freeholds, without creating a fresh tenancy by sub-infeudation. Work service due to the lord of the manor was increasingly commuted to a money rent. By the middle of the 15th century the whole picture had changed. The serfs had been emancipated, but a new class of landless labourers had grown up, in the towns as well as on the fields. As manufacture and commerce grew, a

* Dr. Hayek quotes the parliamentarian Burke as saying in the late 18th century: 'It would be hard to point to any error more truly subversive of all the order and beauty, of all the peace and happiness, of human society, than the position, that any body of men have a right to make what Laws they please . . . all human Laws are, properly speaking, only declaratory; they may alter the mode and application, but have no power over the substance of original justice.'[4]

kind of capitalist system was evolved to finance it. Gradually the capitalists and financiers broke through the barrier of the Church's ban and the usury laws, while the old concept of the 'just price' gave place by degrees to a kind of exchange economy with an open market. Despite the strength of the private control of industry and commerce through the guilds, the Crown and Parliament were induced by the growing national importance of domestic industry and foreign trade to impose more and more regulation upon them, until there developed the full-blown mercantilist system of the 17th and 18th centuries.

However strong the hold of the Catholic religion may have been on the mass of the people – and the evidence suggests that it was very strong indeed except in the east and south-east where Lollardry had taken root – the Church's temporal possessions attracted to it some of the unpopularity that tends always to be attached to landlords. Yet it has been suggested by some historians (though denied by others) that at the time of the Dissolution most monastic houses, however lax or corrupt they might have become, were less rapacious landlords than the majority of secular ones. The extent of their possessions and the lack of justification for them, however, made for much criticism.

The dissolution of the monasteries, for all that the direct and immediate social effects were so small as to indicate how far the houses had declined from their earlier activity and function, nevertheless marked a major turning point in the life of the country. For the expropriation of the religious houses inaugurated an era of much more significant expropriation, coupled with the beginning of a new process and philosophy of the acquisition of *private* landed wealth.

A large proportion of monastic lands fell into the hands of what a modern historian has called 'the most obnoxious class of landlord',[5] and the expropriation of the peasantry developed at a rate that was revolutionary. The new Tudor nobility and gentry (the old nobility having been almost entirely exterminated during the Wars of the Roses) were the beginning of the Acquisitive Society. They seem to have speeded up the process of enclosure of common lands and indulged in rack-renting and evictions on a scale unknown under the old ecclesiastical landlords.* At the same time they intensified the distress caused in the agricultural areas by converting more and more arable land to sheep pasture.

They were the ancestors of the great Whig grandees of later centuries, who brought the manipulation of politics to a fine art. But they, in their own time, marked the beginning of a new political era. In the early days of feudalism the ownership or tenancy of land had implied a fixed and known political status. Now landed *wealth* was to become the basis of political power, which is a very different thing. And once wealth in the form of land had proved a stepping-stone to power, it was only a matter of time before wealth of other kinds began to contend for it. Soon the preservation of private wealth became for its possessors the overriding aim of politics. Indeed, they went further, demanding from the State protection of their right to endless acquisition, which was something that the State had never previously recognised. This was justified by an assertion of something called 'the sanctity of private property', with which it had in reality little to do. For private property, which gives a family its own space in the world and was regarded by the ancients as conferring freedom and political status, is not at all the same thing as private wealth. Nor is the *ownership* of private property of the same nature as the private *acquisition* of wealth; the right to the one does not implicitly confer an open licence for the other. The State may reasonably control acquisition without necessarily trespassing upon the rights of ownership. Indeed, the acquisitive wealthy may be a greater menace to the private property of others, and more careless of its rights, than the State itself.

The break-up of the Catholic Church after the Reformation, together with the dissolution of the feudal hierarchy and the relationships of status, created a philosophical vacuum too vast to be filled by any but a genius. Hooker's *Laws of Ecclesiastical Polity*, although it provided the Elizabethan foundation of the Church of England with a theoretical basis which has enabled it to survive against all the odds of its essential contradictions, was too limited in scope (as well as

* It is possible that the rapid rise in prices, consequent on Henry VIII's debasement of the coinage, left them little alternative.

in appeal to the new political interests) to suffice. Modern political theory begins with Hobbes, the one-time secretary of Francis Bacon and financial factotum of the Cavendish family.

Here, as we come to the beginning of the process that has directed and coloured all our political thinking, it is necessary to pause and consider for a moment the nature and origins of political theories. Even Tories have become so accustomed to the categories of Marxist thought that they have tended to exaggerate the implications of Marx's genuine insights. There are thus few people today to whom it is not a commonplace that, for example, Locke simply 'rationalised' the self-interest of the triumphant Whigs of 1688 (even though it is now believed that he wrote his *Treatises on Civil Government* before the accession of James II). Likewise, it is assumed that the utilitarian economists were concerned primarily to justify the social ruthlessness of the Liberal manufacturers in the late industrial revolution.

What one scholar has called 'the vulgarisation of Marxism that became prevalent everywhere in the years since the First World War'[6] – a vulgarisation for which in this country R. H. Tawney and Harold Laski were largely responsible – has led not only to much bogus historicism but also to a number of theses which the Marxian sources do not seem to justify. Marx's unquestioning conviction of the validity of his theory of history and of the absolute scientific truth of his economics led him to the belief that the ideas of an age are a 'superstructure' derived from, and corresponding to, the material 'substructure' of basic economic facts and class interests. Since it was the latter which 'determined' the course of history, 'ideology' was merely a more or less irrelevant obstacle to the scientific pursuit of absolute truth – a pursuit that would be greatly facilitated in the classless society.

This theory, which has deeply influenced many modern social scientists, is itself of very doubtful validity, not least because it is doubtful whether absolute truth is even a theoretical possibility in politics – or in economics. Yet, even as it stands, it cannot bear the weight of the crude determinism of Karl Mannheim, any more than that of Nietzsche's theory of power-struggle which paradoxically derived from the Marxian insights. The fact is that Marx gave very little attention to the inter-action of ideas and events, since he regarded ideas as of minor importance. Even Engels explicitly noted the omission.[7] The assertion that, from the point of view of the proletariat, certain moral codes and political 'ideologies' had been no more than 'so many bourgeois prejudices, behind which lurk in ambush just as many bourgeois interests'[8] contains a substantial germ of truth; but it is the crude propaganda of youth, never adequately worked out in the maturer writings.

The truth would seem to be – and I do not think even Marx can be interpreted as denying this – that politics cannot for long operate in a philosophical vacuum. Attempts are generally made to hang on to the remnants of a dominant theory long after it has ceased to be relevant to current conditions; but sooner or later it will be necessary to evolve a new theory into which the facts can be convincingly fitted. This does not necessarily imply that the facts, wholly and alone, determine the theory; equally, it does not follow that every political philosopher will design a theory deriving solely from the interests of his own class or of his political patrons. Some will, consciously or unconsciously; but not all thinkers are as deeply conditioned or as venal as this. Again, economic and political interests will naturally tend to adopt the theories – those of Marx, for example! – that seem to provide the most convincing moral justification for what they want to accomplish. But it is an inversion of logic to infer or assume from this that the theory itself can have no intrinsic merit or general validity.

It may, on the contrary, be the only theory into which the currently observable facts can be fitted. At the least (with Marx, for example) it may be the result of a conscientious attempt to explain them. At its best, political theory can also involve an impartial attempt to provide not only a rationale but a set of principles designed to define and achieve ends selected on a basis of ethics. What seems certain is that the political theories that have achieved the greatest and most lasting influence have been those which genuinely attempted to take account of facts, to reconcile their apparent contradictions, and to provide a rational and ethical basis for needed reforms. This is as true of Hobbes and Locke as of Bentham and J. S. Mill, of Montesquieu and Burke as of Rousseau, Hegel and Marx. The fact that they have had no modern successors is the reason why we ourselves are today suspended in a philosophical vacuum almost as complete as that which confronted Hobbes in the 17th century.

Hobbes's objectivity may to some extent be deduced from the degree of irritation provoked by his opinions. Charles II, who appears to have admired and respected his old tutor and certainly awarded him a pension in 1660, yet forbade him to enter his presence after *Leviathan* appeared in 1651. Clarendon, who called Hobbes 'one of the most antient acquaintance I have in the World, and of whom I have alwaies had a great esteem', thought the book might 'produce much mischief in the World' and upbraided its author for his 'extreme malignity to the Nobility, by whose bread he hath bin alwaies sustain'd'. He concluded that Hobbes 'spent too much time in thinking', which is a familiar complaint of politicians against intellectuals.

Thus Hobbes, often thought of as the exponent of the absolute power of the State, was unpopular with monarch and monarchists. But he appealed even less to the Levellers, for what could be more damping to social reforming zeal than the assertion that nothing is unjust except the non-performance of contracts? His sceptical materialism gave no more comfort to the Puritans than to the Laudian high churchmen. Nobody wholly agreed with him, and his thought, though magnificently expressed, was as arid as it was rigorous. Probably no one except Marx has ever been so utterly sure that he was right, and that his speculative conclusions had been scientifically proved. Yet the fact that he had little direct influence and founded no lasting school must not be allowed to obscure his importance.

In the first place Hobbes was confronted with a revolutionary situation – a dissolution of social relationships and a fragmentation of faith, followed by the contention of rival ideas about authority and justice. He perceived the need for a system: one that would reconcile the conflict if possible, and if not would at least resolve it by putting the question of authority beyond doubt or dispute. In this, as in his conviction that reason could supply the answers, he was the prophet of a new age. Again, while he did not invent the contract theory (which was indeed a tenet of the Puritan anti-royalists both here and on the continent), he was the first to attempt the systematic replacement of the dissolved status relationships with a new set of contractual ones. In this he showed the way to Locke and his successors. Perhaps most important of all, he was the first to deal resolutely with the new problem of sovereignty in the nation-state. Sweeping aside the idea that authority is divinely instituted rather than set up by men for their own convenience, and also the whole concept of 'natural' law and rights antecedent to the State, he concentrated attention on the problem of power. In this he was the forerunner of the political scientists of today, who have become so obsessed by the study of power that they have had no time to consider what it would be right for the possessor of power, once identified, to do with it.

Hobbes himself was still too near to the middle ages to be able to reject altogether the importance of custom and of prescriptive rights established after the foundation of the State. He was, however, concerned to identify a sovereign power capable of making and enforcing decisions when there were conflicting interpretations of rights and custom, just as the power of the State must be used to enforce the keeping of contracts. Some 200 years later, his theory of sovereignty was to be restated in legal terms by Austin for the utilitarians. Meanwhile his system adequately covered the philosophical needs of an increasingly acquisitive society and an increasingly mercantilist State. Its ethical content was negligible. Justice consists solely in the performance of contracts, and 'whatsoever is not Unjust is Just'. There was nothing here to hold up the final triumph of the new landlords encroaching on the customary rights of the small peasant proprietors and cottagers.[9]

After this first stepping of political philosophy into the modern world, it took a considerable leap forward under the guidance of John Locke, one time Secretary to the Board of Trade and confidant of the devious Shaftesbury. Here, at first to confront but ultimately to complement the Hobbesian theory of State sovereignty, we find the first major philosophical statement of individualism. With this came naturally a new view of conflict between individual freedom and the law – the classic modern problem of reconciling liberty with order. This had to some extent been implicit in philosophy from the first, but the conditions of the Greek city-state and later the combination of feudalism and the universal Catholic Church greatly limited its scope and importance. The problem had been stated in religious terms (though based on Aristotle) by Aquinas and Hooker; but for Locke, who was a rationalist in religious matters, the terms were inadequate.

At the same time his individualism made it impossible for him to accept the doctrine of absolute sovereignty propounded by Hobbes. We need not concern ourselves with his theory of the 'state of nature' giving place to an 'original contract' by which men bound themselves to live together under common laws. It was no doubt partly allegorical, but in any case it was finally demolished by Hume. What is important is that, unlike Hobbes' contract, Locke's is terminable at the will of the governed. To Hobbes, fresh from the horrors of a civil war and desperately anxious to prevent another one, this would have seemed a recipe for anarchy. To Locke, whose career spanned the origins and results of a bloodless and entirely successful revolution, it was only common sense.

Yet he was driven to resurrect the conception of 'natural' rights and laws, which inevitably involved him in difficulties. Man had brought with him from the state of nature an inalienable right to life, liberty and property; indeed, it was to secure protection for these that he became a social being. At times his argument subsumes life and liberty under the general heading of 'property', and it is the protection of property which is the purpose of government. But the government is not the sovereign power; it derives political power as a 'trust' from the people. The danger of arbitrary power is also to be reduced by dividing political authority between legislature, executive and judiciary – the now familiar concept of the separation of powers, or 'checks and balances'. The importance of this in the development of the modern theory of the democratic nation-state is obvious.

It is of course easy, taking the extreme Marxian view of 'ideology', to represent Locke's theory of property as no more than a venal attempt to justify the interests of his Whig patrons. On the contrary, it seems to me that a careful study of it refutes this view; it arose, as do most influential political theories, from a genuine attempt to understand and explain what was going on around him. We have already seen that no theory had yet come to grips with the phenomenon of the private acquisition and accumulation of wealth, which in a sense began with the expropriation of the monasteries and the emancipation of capitalistic industry and commerce from the restraints of the Catholic Church. After more than a hundred years this had begun to assume the appearance of an endless, and even self-sustaining, process. From this the modern theories of capitalism were to evolve, together with the present-day yearning to believe that even if 'growth' is not, after all, automatic, it ought to be. Somehow Locke had to explain, and produce a philosophical justification for, a process of apparently endless and even automatic acquisition and accumulation of private wealth. The fact that he founded his justification on a principle which, through a process of inversion and exploitation by others, was to become the most damaging weapon used against capitalism and private wealth, seems to me to show that Locke was either an honest seeker after truth or else very stupid indeed. And I do not think Locke was nearly as stupid as he has sometimes been made out to be.

At all events, he founded his theory of property on what has come to be known as the 'labour theory of value'. The institution of property was the fundamental principle of society; but in the 'state of nature' the earth and its fruits and creatures had originally been held by all men in common. Yet reason suggested that when a man had by his own labour changed a thing from its natural state and improved it, he acquired a property right in it. It is no exaggeration to say that this apparently crude proposition was 'the most pregnant suggestion ever offered by any writer'.[10]

From it sprang both the doctrines of the *laisser-faire* economists and the anti-capitalist doctrines of Marx and the socialists. If it appeared to justify the acquisitiveness of the 'improving landlord', it could in the end be turned against the *rentier* and even against the entrepreneur.

Like all pioneers obsessed with a seminal idea, Locke was oversimplifying, and his thought was refined and also amplified by others. But he was conscious of the need to limit the implications of his doctrine, although he was able to do it only in the crudest way. He began by asserting that man had no right to destroy or spoil God's gifts, so that his property rights in the products of his labour were limited to those things which he could use for his life and comfort before they were spoiled. But since the products of 'labouring', as it had been generally understood, were most often things of little durability and designed for consumption, he was at once in difficulties. The answer, of course, was money: this enabled the industrious man 'to enlarge his possessions beyond the use of his family, and a plentiful supply to its consumption'.[11] But this led inevitably to the conclusion that *accumulation is the rational end of the industrious man*, from which belief enormous consequences flowed. Not less important was the complementary implication that the man who was not able to acquire property, and was therefore reduced to day-labouring for a wage, must be less rational and industrious than the property-owner – a social philosophy which, though badly mauled, is still not dead. Locke himself was driven to a position in which his desire as an individualist to regard all men as free and politically equal had to yield to the apparent logic of his argument justifying the accumulation of property. Not only were the propertyless not rational and industrious, but if they were unemployed they were also idle and corrupted. The whole Poor Law philosophy is implicit in this.[12]

While the chief importance of the labour theory of value was as a rationale for 19th century capitalism after Adam Smith had developed it into the proposition that 'labour' is the source of all wealth, it was also to have far-reaching political effects in the hands of Karl Marx. The revolutionary nature of Locke's 'discovery' lies in the fact that, from the time of Plato at least, labour and property had been thought of as not merely unconnected but even as mutually exclusive. Labouring was the unenviable necessity by which the poor and propertyless supported life. The idea that anyone had a 'natural right' of property in the product of his own *labour* was unheard of before Locke. Yet how pregnant was the idea with possibilities! If labour justified the status of the property-owner, why should it not also give anyone who laboured a right to a reasonable share in the product of his labour? From here to the theory of 'surplus value' is but a step.

The political implications were vast. If labour, hitherto a necessary but lowly function, could be thought of as the origin and basis of all wealth and all creative effort, then those who laboured could regain a status – and surely a higher status than the lost feudal one. Thus John Locke, seeking an explanatory justification for the acquisition of wealth, provided the philosophical foundation without which nothing called a 'Labour Movement' could ever have been built up. A Labour Movement is something more than an organisation of labouring men to improve their economic – or even their political – position. It stands foursquare on the status and dignity of Labour itself, claiming, indeed, for labour a predominant role based on the supposedly fundamental importance of its contribution to the creation of wealth.

If anyone still doubts the revolutionary nature and the influence of this idea, let him consider and explain the remarkable way in which many modern radical intellectuals have idealised 'labour' and the 'labouring class', even to the extent of claiming that they offered the only 'real' and worthwhile 'values'. Such an idea would have been inconceivable before Locke: and not just because 'labourers' were a socially inferior and politically non-existent class, but because it had never occurred to anyone that 'labouring' *produced* anything useful and durable at all.

It is particularly significant that the difficulty inherent in this bothered both sets of inheritors of the labour theory of value. Adam Smith was driven to a distinction between 'productive' and 'unproductive' labour which the developments in advanced industrial societies have made more and more unreal. And the same difficulty of reconciling the ephemeral nature of the 'product' of so many kinds of labour with the fundamental notion of labour as the main creator of wealth has generated ingrained prejudices which led a Labour Government in Britain to the extraordinary illogicalities of the Selective Employment Tax.

It may have needed, on the one hand, the industrious cultivation of Adam Smith and the classical economists and, on the other, the genius of Karl Marx to bring to fruition the two harvests that sprang from the seed sown by Locke. But let no one, considering the results of both, ever again imagine that philosophers are not influential – even when they are wrong.

For of course the whole thing was a ridiculous mistake: an honest mistake, but a mistake none the less. *Labour* has no inherent connection with *property* at all, and in a sense Locke's predecessors were right actually to equate it with propertylessness. It may be futile to seek the real 'origin' of property, for any answer to the question involves inventing a myth and pretending it represents reality. It is probably enough to say that property is something that is *acquired*, whether originally by agreed division of a common area or by the forcible private appropriation of parts of the common. It has nothing to do with labouring, which is a continuing process by which the propertyless man deals with the urgent necessity of keeping himself and his family alive. It was no doubt because Locke needed a continuous process to match what had become the equally continuous process of the acquisition of wealth, that he made labour the key to his theory.

It seems to me that Hannah Arendt, in whose book *The Human Condition* these ideas are impressively developed, is right to insist on the distinction – increasingly blurred in the modern age – between *labour* and *work*. If there is no real or significant distinction between the two, why is it that 'every European language, ancient and modern, contains two etymologically unrelated words for what we have come to think of as the same activity, and retains them in the face of their persistent synonymous usage'?[13] Why is it that the *Labour* Movement continually speaks of the rights not of labourers but of the '*workers*'? It is because the essential difference is instinctively recognised, just as it is formally recognised in so many industries which distinguish between labourers and craftsmen. The distinction has its roots deep in the medieval tradition of the guilds, when the craftsman was emphatically not a day-labourer but either a master or a journeyman on his way to becoming a master. It is founded also on an instinctive human belief that the man who *makes something that survives* – who adds something of use or beauty (preferably both) to the stock of objects that provides the environment of human living – is performing a function superior to that of the man who simply labours to support life, even though the labouring may be a necessary adjunct to the work that fashions the product. *Homo faber* is something essentially different from the *animal laborans*.

What has finally obliterated the difference, and led to some of the most worrying social and psychological puzzles confronting modern men, is the growth of continuous factory processes since the industrial revolution. Once manufacture (which still literally means 'making by hand') became a mechanical *process*, the human activity involved in it came to resemble more the continuous process of labouring than the activity of work which distinguishes the craftsman.* Perhaps the most significant index of the very real revolution involved is the marked narrowing of earnings differentials between craftsmen and labourers of recent years. The employer distinguishes between 'skilled' and 'unskilled' men, and the official statistics even recognise a grade referred to as 'semi-skilled'. But they are all 'labour', thought of in the mass, all grist to the same mill. 'The modern division of labour, where tasks formerly assigned to the young and inexperienced were frozen into lifelong occupations'[14] ultimately cast all men in the same mould.

That this has not been accomplished without misgivings can of course be seen in the recriminations, inter-union squabbles and demarcation disputes that have marked the recent history of trade unionism. But the 'solidarity' of the Labour Movement was felt to be too important to be jeopardised by any overt split. It would be politically – and even economically – fatal for 'the workers', for *Labour*, not to stand together. There was, too, some feeling of obligation on

* Even in conveyor-belt workshops there are still, of course, some craftsmen performing skilled tasks with hand tools or simple mechanical ones; but the tendency – and the aim – is to eliminate them.

the part of the higher-paid to help the poorer to a higher wage; in a period of inflation it has been comparatively easy to do this without any serious sacrifice.

There was also another, and perhaps deeper, feeling making for solidarity than those impelling the Labour Movement towards the achievement of political power or the raising of wages. It was the search for lost status. The worker could no longer feel that he possessed an individual status, but 'organised labour' had won a status of its own in which he could consciously share. Was not labour now the sole creator of wealth, exalted by writers for its 'dignity' and 'reality'?

The result was that manual workers became for the first time self-consciously a social class, and were regarded as such by other classes. After Marx the transformation was complete. Just as the individual worker had become submerged in the mass of 'labour', so what mattered was no longer the revolt of particular oppressed or exploited groups but the 'class struggle'. And as the employing classes sought and obtained the protection of government for their right to continue to appropriate, to acquire, to accumulate and to exploit, political action became the aim of labour. Access to the ballot-box was eagerly sought as the key to power and to all that would flow from its possession. So the workers, having been first expropriated, were then emancipated, and enfranchised *en masse*. They still remained labour, in the mass, and the political leadership of labour was soon appropriated by men who either were already, or quickly became, middle-class.

Status – of a sort – had been achieved, at the cost of individual personality. Technological development has intensified the process, so that now we no longer speak much of men's skills but of the 'productivity of labour'. Moreover, men's skills were devoted to a particular productive purpose, even if they were at the same time exploited by a particular employer for his own private profit; but the 'productivity of labour' is valued not for the particular things men make but for its contribution to 'economic growth' and the 'gross national product'.

Depersonalisation can hardly go further. It scarcely matters any more what people make, so long as it can be 'efficiently' produced and people can be persuaded to buy it. Everything is grist to the mill that grinds the flour to bake the 'national cake'. The old idea that everything that was made had its own intrinsic *worth*, which could even be given a 'just price', could not survive in an exchange economy where the money price represented not the object's intrinsic worth but its relative value compared with other objects. Moreover, the continuous process of production requires more and more, if it is to be kept going and contribute to 'growth', that its products should be continuously consumed and replaced rather than endure for use.

Thus we talk of the 'consumer society', and of 'mass society': but how did this concept of 'society' come to assume the dominance it has achieved? To discover this we must return once more to John Locke, the father of modern political philosophy.

The concept of human society was not unknown to Plato. However, whereas the Greeks thought of it in political rather than in familial terms, the Aristotelian view became subtly changed in the medieval Christian interpretation of Aquinas. The idea of the 'organic society' – one important line of development that perhaps reached its ultimate culmination in the thinking of Burke – is already present in the idea of society as the Church, the 'Body of Christ'. But Locke was an individualist; moreover his 'natural man' was born in a state of grace and free from original sin. While driven by the logic of his philosophy to justify great and increasing inequalities of wealth, Locke postulated a natural human equality. Yet it is not the Christian belief that every human being, made in God's image, is an end in himself, although together serving a greater end. Locke's men are themselves individualists, coming together in society as a mere matter of organisational convenience and taking their sovereign decisions by democratic majority vote.* From this view developed the 19th century conflict in which the idea of individual liberty led to

* It is of some importance to recognise that the greatest triumph of Locke's doctrines was to be in the United States, whose early leaders were deeply influenced by them. Locke's theory of property, which had little practical reality in a country where all the land had already been appropriated, made a great deal of sense in the land of the 'open

the desire to define and delimit the functions of the State, with the difficulties of which J. S. Mill dealt at length. For the idea of modern 'society', we have to consider the development of Locke's theories by Adam Smith.

Starting from the basis of Locke's empirical psychology and the elementary propositions of economics he propounded, Adam Smith set out to build up a 'system' based on a science of economics. Here, for the first time, we find the idea of 'society' as an economic universe; it is composed, certainly, of individuals, but it is also a kind of super-family with a kind of super-housekeeping called 'political economy'.

The so-called 'scientific' basis of Adam Smith's system – and indeed most of the classical economics that derived from him – is contemptible. Starting with the individualist thesis, he evolved a theory of 'natural identification' of individual interests. Since every man is supposed to be by nature acquisitive and moved solely by self-interest, the identification can be achieved only by the introduction of an 'invisible hand' which guides the actions of all to a collective end which no single man individually intended. On this anthropomorphic myth, the desperate resort of a man determined to create a science out of unscientific material, the classical economics was founded.* Gunnar Myrdal is quite right to insist that it was not Marx but the liberal economists who were responsible for creating 'an untenable "communistic fiction" about the unity of society'.[16] Their whole theory was based on the doctrine that the operations of a free market tend towards the 'interests of society as a whole', which of course presupposes that there *is* such a thing as the 'interest of

---

frontier'. A post-Reformation community, with no tradition or hang-over of feudalism or established Church, could embrace the individualist thesis and the theory of contract wholeheartedly. Moreover, the founding fathers built into the Constitution Locke's theory of the 'separation of powers'; they took it from Montesquieu, who had assumed from reading Locke that it actually existed in Britain. Since Bagehot, we have known better than to believe this.

* Mr. Enoch Powell, the prophet of the neo-classical economics, has modernised the 'invisible hand', which is now 'the largest and most wonderful computer the world has ever known' and 'tells us all the time . . . what can be produced "economically and competitively" and in what quantity and where'.[15] This is the same myth, but with a modern science-fiction demon in the works.

society as a whole'. But this 'assertion that society must be conceived as a single subject . . . is precisely what cannot be conceived. If we tried, we would be attempting to abstract from the essential fact that social activity is the result of the intentions of several individuals.'[17]

It is a complete error to imagine that the most important factor determining today's concept of 'society' is the 'socialist' slant that Marx gave to the classical economics. It is probable that much the same thing would have happened if Marx had never written as he did. Two themes are implicit in the theories of Adam Smith. One, paradoxical as it may seem, is the whole philosophy of 'planning'. For, once it is accepted that there is such a thing as the 'interest of society as a whole', this becomes an end to be achieved; and it is only reasonable to assume that the processes by which the end is achieved can be analysed and understood. From this it is but a step to the conviction that, if the 'invisible hand' fails to deliver the goods quickly enough or in adequate quantities, it is possible to help it along by a deliberate intervention in the processes. The supreme irony is that the more the high priests of the original dogma (Mr. Enoch Powell, for example) insist that the 'invisible hand' can only do its job properly if it is left to its own devices, the more irresistible is the temptation they offer to 'purposive' intervention. Since the 'invisible hand' is known to be a myth anyway, they can only try to convince us of its efficacy by explaining in detail the processes by which it is assumed to work; and the more comprehensible their analysis makes the processes appear, the simpler it looks to intervene in the processes and improve them.

The second result implicit in the classical theories is even more important. It is that, *with a large enough population, a belief in the reality and importance of 'society as a whole' can be made to come true.* With the development of statistical techniques, economics can be made to look much more like a science. If their universe is large enough, statistics achieve not only validity as a means of summarising the total of individual actions, but also a kind of reality as a portrayal of 'social behaviour'. It is not a genuine reality, but it comes to be thought of as real. The 'behaviour patterns' revealed begin to seem the actual behaviour of an actual entity – 'society'.

This is bad enough, but the next step is even more dangerous. The behaviour patterns, these realised abstractions, inevitably come to be regarded as norms; and the 'normal behaviour' of 'society' acquires an aura of moral correctness, with the implication that it is right to conform to it and wrong ('anti-social') to deviate.

It is no mere linguistic accident that the word 'society', now used to describe the whole population and all the institutions of our nation-state, is the same word that was once used to denote the wealthy and exclusive élite that claimed a monopoly of excellence and the right to dictate standards of taste and morals. The new abstraction has in fact taken over the pretensions and claims of the old.

Yet there is an immense and fundamental difference. The arrogance of the old élite 'society's' claim to enforce a narrow and unimaginative conformism on those who wished to belong to it is obvious enough, and it has evoked rebellion and criticism in a stream of literature from Rousseau to Henry James and L. H. Myers. But the conformism required was, after all, based on rules and conventions of conduct deliberately selected on an ethical basis to form a *moral* code. The conventional morality might be narrow and inadequate, even actually harmful in some of its effects, and productive of much hypocrisy in practice; but it *was* a moral code, and as such it went some way to offer certainty and authority to a circle wider than that of the élite itself.

But the conformism increasingly required by 'society as a whole' has no ethical basis at all. The behaviour enjoined is not a moral code, nor even a set of conventions deliberately chosen to facilitate social living; it is no more than a kind of abstract statistical average of the ways in which people do actually behave already. Once the norms have been determined by the social scientists and statisticians, these abstractions come to be thought of as real, and their 'reality' is established by the media of mass communications. The manufacturers of mass-produced consumption goods and 'consumer durables' have a commercial interest in propagating the conception of the average as the norm: since it is technically more convenient to produce a single standardised product, a mass of advertising is designed to sell the idea that the standard selected by the producer (for technical reasons) is the desirable norm for the consumer. The advertising experts carefully study the statistical record of average 'behaviour', and 'angle' their appeal to the 'normal' individual whose portrait emerges from it. There is thus built up, by a process of interaction, a more and more widely accepted picture not only of 'normal' behaviour but of a 'normal' environment of physical objects.

The repeated presentation and acclamation of the imaginary norm have an inevitable effect. Presented visually in its physical aspects through television advertising and printed displays, and in its other aspects familiarised through the assumptions of popular journalism, the myth of the norm begins to acquire a kind of authority of its own. The patterns of mass behaviour become not only normal but *right*. This feeling is intensified by the reaction to individual deviations. The spectacle of someone behaving 'differently' upsets the illusion of certainty that the authority of the 'social image' is beginning to impose. It arouses uncomfortable doubts. Perhaps, after all, there *is* something better . . .? But there are no longer any accepted standards, other than those of the 'norm', by which one can judge. 'Society' must surely be right; deviation from the norm is anti-social, and therefore wrong ('everyone at school does it!').

The bewildered individual, seeking lost authority, certainty and standards, is reduced to social conformism. It is a kind of 'back to the womb' movement, or at the least a demand not to grow out of the childhood state of security without responsibility. And 'society' is expected to provide the security. Here we have the demand for 'social security', which means that 'society' must increasingly take over the moral and financial responsibilities of individuals and families. But 'society', of course, cannot do this, for it does not exist. The material obligations are undertaken by its formal manifestation – the State – which thus comes to be identified and coterminous with 'society'. However, the State is felt to be a cold and formal abstraction, much too inhuman to suggest either a comfortable womb or a sympathetic fairy godmother. (On the contrary, it suggests politics, of which we have had more than enough. Politics have definitely failed us!) So the myth is developed that 'society' is responsible for everything, like an all-embracing super-family. There is a 'social conscience', which impels society towards something called 'social justice'. We talk of 'social needs' and 'social action'. Individuals and institutions are lectured about their 'duty to society'. 'Society' provides us with our 'social security'.

Now all this is myth, and myth of the most dangerous kind, because it obscures reality and the need for individual action as well as individual responsibility. It is *not* 'society' that provides social security, but State administrators dispensing the taxpayers' money. There is *not* a 'social conscience' – only individuals laboriously seeking to persuade an apathetic (but vaguely benevolent) majority of the need for reforms. There are no 'social needs' – only people in trouble, who need to be thought of and helped as people. The whole conception is a mass flight from reality, in which awkward facts are exorcised by claptrap while a diffuse and sentimental goodwill obscures the obligation to realistic thought and specific action.

In the later stages of this process the philosophers either acquiesced or adopted a defeatist attitude towards the claims of the social sciences, abdicating their responsibilities in favour of what was regarded as a more convincing authority. The optimism of the Enlightenment gradually faded. Faith in the power of reason to prevail in human affairs was fatally eroded by Darwin and Freud – who seemed to have put an end to metaphysics as well. Empiricism dwindled from a system-building philosophic discipline to a mere recording of behaviour patterns which permitted a limited degree of prediction by extrapolation.

In a sense, immensely important and influential as they seemed at the time and have been held to be since, the theories of the utilitarians were philosophically irrelevant. Neither they nor the idealists – and perhaps least of all the scientific humanists – have provided a key to the uncertainty and unease of the modern world. Except in the field of ethics, philosophical progress in this country virtually came to an end in the cautious scepticism of Hume. (There might, perhaps, even be something to be said for going back to him and starting again from there.)

Speculative philosophy gave way first to a concern with realism. Metaphysics was abandoned in the arid desert of logical positivism. Ethics settled down before the second World War to a sterile contemplation of its navel – muttering about the difference between the Right and the Good. More recently linguistic philosophers (notably R. M. Hare and Stephen Toulmin) seem to have been making attempts to achieve a viable synthesis in ethics between the idealists and the rational utilitarians, allotting a place to reason in moral judgements which the pure 'emotivists', from Hume to Westermarck and Russell, had sought to minimise. But others (such as P. H. Nowell-Smith) prefer to leave moral prescription to the psychologists.

Given a total lack of agreement – and later even of interest – in the metaphysical problem of Man's nature and his place in the world, together with only an intermittent concern with ethics, it is scarcely surprising that political philosophy should have failed to develop beyond a certain level of sceptical empiricism. Bentham botched up a kind of philosophical basis for his reforming zeal out of a misunderstanding of Hume, flashes from Priestley and from the *philosophes*, and the main elements of Locke as contorted by the dull and deplorable Helvétius. However, he is significant not as a philosopher, but as the first Fabian reformer. He was essentially concerned, not with what it was right to do or to create, but with how to get rid of what was wrong. His ethical touchstone, the principle of the 'greatest happiness of the greatest number', he borrowed from others and popularised. In addition to throwing rationalist ethics into confusion, it became the basis of egalitarian democracy; but it also stultified political theory.

For political theory, as it has been understood not only by the idealists but also by the empiricists up to and including Hume, requires a basis of ethical theory and certain ethical assumptions if it is to say anything useful to us. But Benthamism was founded on a rejection of ethics. The 'greatest happiness principle' is not a utilitarian ethic, since it has abandoned the idea of *utility* altogether. It has become what

Halévy called 'universalised egoism', which is not an ethical principle at all. The general idea it conveys has been responsible for much harm, while the magic principle itself has proved almost entirely useless as a guide to political action. This was in part because Bentham never succeeded in defining what he meant. He seems finally to have abandoned the idea of the 'greatest number' in favour of 'the greatest happiness of *all*',[18] which even he admitted was to present governments with an impossible task. Just as Adam Smith assumed a 'natural identity of interests' in constructing his 'science' of economics, so Bentham was driven to an 'artificial identification of interests' by government. It does not get us very far.

One is driven to the conclusion that nearly all the political theorising that has gone on in this country during the last 200 years has been beside the point. For a century after 1688 the Whigs lived on Locke and stayed in power (*post hoc*, perhaps, rather than *propter hoc*, since they also owed much to the total disarray of the Tories and the careful arrangements of the first Duke of Newcastle). Bolingbroke made no impression on the supremacy of Lockeian doctrines, and indeed they had compromised the older tradition too deeply for any reaction to it to be viable. Even the genius of Burke, for all its influence on great men, could not prevail against the 'sophists and calculators' of the 19th century. The Liberal manufacturers lived on Ricardo's glosses on Adam Smith, while the radical reformers lived on Bentham. All the arguments about the conflict between liberty and law, which so exercised the Philosophic Radicals (and so many modern Conservatives) have proved irrelevant to our real modern problem. The concern of the neo-Hegelian idealists (such as Bosanquet and T. H. Green) with the State took the arguments of Rousseau no further forward in any relevant direction. More recently the 'political scientists' have become obsessed with power, having apparently exhausted sovereignty. Finally T. D. Weldon[19] has frankly bade us abandon political philosophy altogether.[20]

When it was already too late, the Tories – led by Michael Oakeshott in Britain and Russell Kirk[21] in America – rediscovered Burke. This was, short of the onset of fresh ideas, almost inevitable. Disraeli was palpably no philosopher;

Coleridge, perhaps the most promising of the lot, is unfortunately almost incomprehensible to the modern age;* and Newman, equally unfortunately, was a Papist. What was there left but Burke? But it was too late, because Burke's view of the nature of society had already been implicitly rejected – even by Conservatives. Worse, the society itself had been devoured by 'society'. The 'spiritual partnership' had already been dissolved. The nexus with the past had been severed. Families, neighbourhoods, all the 'little images of the great country in which the heart found something it could fill',[22] had been swallowed up. There was only 'society' left, and what would Burke make of that?

It had been accomplished by stages, but none the less thoroughly for that. First the little social groupings were subsumed under social 'classes'; then the Marxist theory of the inevitable class conflict started the yearning for the 'classless society'; the end-product was the mass society, which is neither classless nor a society in any sense that Burke (or even, perhaps, Marx) would have understood.

The intellectual background to the abdication of philosophy has been described with devastating accuracy by James McAuley, a distinguished Australian poet:

> It is an attitude, an infection, the proper name of which is the English Malady. It is the modern man's residual creed: *that ideas do not matter*, that civilisation can be maintained without intellectual commitment – and incidentally that literature can flourish on talent and sensibility alone. This is a wasting disease.
>
> Two generally remarked characteristics of the English are: lack of theoretical rigour, and the will to retain to a relatively high degree traditional attitudes and institutions. The two things are curiously connected. Only by inconsistency could the children of Cranmer and Locke retain traditional ways and values; but a sound sense and practical wisdom taught them to avoid putting into practice the full consequences lurking in their intellectual treason. Hence arose among the English the conviction that a wise man sets little store by theoretical considerations and is content to live in an intellectual blur. They look askance when the breezes of their sceptical opinions, when unleashed in foreign lands, become unrestrained tornadoes.

* Probably owing to his unhappy addiction to opium.

> But a price has gradually been paid for this admirable desire to have one's 'cake of custom' and eat it too. The traditional heritage of values and institutions has deteriorated because it is only partly desired and is protected only by sentiment and practical conservation, not by theory and doctrine; while all the time the anti-theoretical prejudice acquired by the English mind has continually eroded intellectual culture. A sterilising empiricism has meant that the English have gradually ceased to be important originators in the field of basic ideas. They have made themselves eunuchs – for convenience's sake.[23]

Has no political philosopher anywhere, then, promulgated doctrines that have stood the test of time and kept up with the march of events? Has 'society' no prophet? In fact, by a splendid irony, it has. It is none other than Jean-Jacques Rousseau. Rousseau, the rebel against society, the inspiration of romantic pessimism, has won his victory in the end. For what is 'society' but Rousseau's 'General Will'? At last we can see the full force of Voltaire's bitter complaint, 'It is because Jean-Jacques still has partisans that the true philosophers have enemies'![24] And 'society' is imbued with a pessimism more complete than that of the 19th century Romantics; yet it is a pessismism essentially trivial, for it is rooted neither in thought nor in emotion.

CHAPTER 3

The Sterility of the General Will

If men see no future, they are inadequately equipped to deal even with the present. In such a state people, instead of seeking responsibilities, would decline or avoid them.

Rex Warner, *Pericles the Athenian*

In spite of all the theoretical compromises which were contrived in order to reconcile the European conscience to the harsh realities of its civilisation, the original hebraic vision of an equal, just and bountiful society, which might one day be the happy lot of man, was never altogether lost from view.

J. P. Corbett, *Europe and the Social Order*

Who shall decide, when doctors disagree,
And soundest casuists doubt, like you and me?

Alexander Pope, *Moral Essays*

Many will dispute the proposition that pessimism is an outstanding characteristic of Britain today, asserting that the more urgent menace is rather a kind of Micawberish optimism. But even at its best the refusal to face reality is little more than a hope that 'things will last out our time'; there is little disposition to believe that 'something will turn up', and still less that 'everything will be all right in the end'. This is pessimism. A determination to live for today implies no optimism about tomorrow.

The urge to conformity, too, is pessimistic. It does not spring from a deep conviction that the life of the 'norm' is wholly satisfying and the best imaginable – a conviction which the most optimistic of the Victorians did feel. It is rather an implied admission that life has become too complicated for the individual to have any confidence in his ability to live successfully by standards of his own. The only safety seems to lie in absorption into a group or submersion in a crowd. There is a profound pessimism in the search for security, in the desire to shift responsibility for coping even with the lesser difficulties of life on to a paternalistic Welfare State. There is a fatalistic pessimism in the attribution of every difficulty to 'Them'. The feeling that 'They ought to do something about it' (generally expressed in terms that do not suggest unbounded confidence that 'They' will) implies an absolute conviction that there is nothing the sufferer can do about his troubles for himself. Only too often he is right. The pessimism is not always wholly unjustified.

The educated intelligentsia, including those who were until quite recently proclaiming most loudly their certainty that everything was under control and that progress was proceeding in a thoroughly scientific and emancipated way, are becoming as worried as the next man. Some, indeed, appear to be on the verge of an exaggerated panic. The sociologists are beginning to believe that they have a genuine case in morbid psychology on their hands – although they seem to have little suspicion that they may themselves be in part responsible for the condition.

People of a reactionary cast of mind are naturally less surprised by the trend of events. They were always against progress anyhow, and never expected anything so repulsive as a 'century of the common man' to last the course. They have been waiting with gloomy confidence for the day of judgement:

> And after that this is accomplished, and the brave new
> world begins,
> When all men are paid for existing and no man must pay
> for his sins,
> As surely as Water will wet us, as surely as Fire will
> burn,
> The Gods of the Copybook Headings with terror and
> slaughter return![1]

They have their prescriptions ready: religion . . . discipline . . . unemployment . . . hard work . . . honesty . . . responsibility . . . realistic education . . . and so on. Nor, of course, are they wholly wrong; reactionaries seldom are. In some ways we did get along better when these things could be enforced; it is at least possible that any certainty and any authority are better than none. The trouble is that terror and slaughter are not necessarily the best prescription for relieving pessimism.

And if I am certain of anything, it is that the exorcism of today's sterile pessimism is an essential first step both to improvement and to wisdom.

The error of those who pin their faith exclusively to the Gods of the Copybook Headings lies in their failure to appreciate the nature and extent of the prevailing pessimism. They interpret the post-war lack of economic realism, the belief that the country could go on living in deficit and that wages could go on indefinitely rising, in advance of productivity, as the expression of an irrational optimism which only a salutary jolt will cure. It was not. Certainly there were some who believed that the election of a Labour Government would make all things secure; but the general feeling has long been that neither party had any very clear idea of what it was doing. Most people have thought for some time that we were in a mess; but they had little idea how we got into it, and less of how to get out again. This was definitely a matter for 'Them', although confidence in 'Their' ability was limited. As for rising wages, no one doubted that prices would go on rising, so that there seemed no alternative but to grab what one could while it was there. Irrational this may be, even culpably ignorant: but it has little to do with optimism.

Apart from the 'Good Dose of Unemployment' school and the Capital and Corporal Punishment brigade, reactionary prescriptions have been advanced with a perceptible diminution of conviction in recent years. It is becoming increasingly hard for well-meaning and intelligent people to see what on earth one can possibly react *to*. The old tradition appears to have been so fatally compromised as to have become almost totally irrelevant. Those who still believe themselves to be guided and sustained by it are scarcely living in the real world at all: if it answers all their questions, it is partly because they have given up asking any of the questions that it won't. Even those who are personally sustained by a religious faith, and who are sure that only a return to religion can resolve the problems arising from modern materialism, are without much hope that the churches can bring about a religious revival. Nor is it easy to see what form a revival of '*authority*' could take – in any traditional sense, that is. Certainly there can be no return to the old hierarchical structure of authority, which was part of a system that has long disintegrated and cannot be reconstructed.

This is recognised, although dimly by some. The danger of some kind of near-fascist reaction is, however, proportionately greater. That the mass of people are conscious of the lack of some authority is true enough; but it is the authority of accepted standards and common purpose that they seek, and in default of which they clutch at the protective talisman of the 'norm'. It is quite another thing to have a bunch of people anxious to *impose* authority, particularly when they have no very clear idea what form it ought to take. A generalised belief in the need for 'discipline' has not always led to the happiest results in the past. Fear of the danger of a perverted authoritarian reaction in this country is not new,[2] and it may well still be true that 'it can't happen here'. But the seeds are here, and I seem to detect a perceptible increase in the fertility of the soil. For it is stupid not to recognise that the class war has taken a new lease of life, with the potentially aggressive hostility now concentrated among the 'bourgeois' victims of inflation. Those who are most painfully 'squeezed' most bitterly resent the apparent ability of organised labour to contract out of the effects of inflation at their expense. The resentment was strong between 1945 and 1951, but it was checked by a conviction that the post-war inflation could not last and that in any case the next Conservative government would redress the balance. Thirteen years of Tory rule may have mollified those who held appreciating equity investments, but they did nothing to reassure retired officers or holders of gilt-edged stocks. A return of Labour government has both intensified the squeeze and lessened faith in democratic processes.* The reaction is entirely pessimistic.

What is more remarkable than the reaction of the reactionaries is the disillusionment of the progressives, which goes well beyond mere disappointment with the results of four post-war Labour governments. It is easy – too easy – for the cynic (or the believer in the dogma of original sin) to feel superior to those who have lost a naive faith in the inevitable progress of humanity. If it was a little simple to believe that

* The nature and intensity of some of the support in this country for Mr. Ian Smith was disconcertingly suggestive.

the transfer of industries from private to public ownership would of itself ensure an improvement in the productivity of their workers and the quality of their service to the public, it was surely not wholly unreasonable to believe that the abolition of unemployment and primary poverty would reduce the amount of prostitution and larceny. Conservatives have often accused socialists of encouraging a 'materialistic' attitude among the workers: they might be surprised at the number of socialists (who often possess a strong streak of puritanism) that bitterly deplores a working-class materialism for which Conservatives are held entirely to blame. And indeed it is not easy, in retrospect, to identify the Macmillan administrations with any ideals of a markedly spiritual kind; material comfort and the quick speculative profit seem to have been more characteristic of the social atmosphere they produced.

However, alarm and despondency have spread both wider and deeper than among the disillusioned idealists of Labour. The onset of doubt has been having a shattering effect on many who had been unquestioningly sustained by the dogma of liberal rationalism. It is possible that the loss of a deeply held faith in the ability of human reason and experience to guide mankind along the path of progress towards perfection is even more devastating than a loss of faith in God. For the agnostic can still fall back on reason; the disillusioned humanist has little left but nihilism. Only by way of neurosis is he likely to find an easy path to religion. And current doubts go well beyond the questioning of processes previously believed to be automatic, or disappointment with what may seem the inadequate results of popular education. It may be that progressive intellectuals are beginning to entertain a doubt long felt by simpler folk – a doubt intensified but not initiated by the threat of nuclear catastrophe – whether progress itself is not involving humanity in processes too vast and complex for human reason to control. The question is not simply whether a particular system has proved inadequate to changed circumstances but whether it is any longer possible to rely on any system at all.

Since this is precisely what many Conservatives have been saying for years, there is clearly a strong temptation for them to say, 'We told you so'. Yet there are several reasons why it should be resisted. The first, of course, is that much of the disillusionment is absurdly premature. If the progressives had not, in Bagehot's words, 'inherited from their barbarous forefathers a wild passion for instant action', they would not be so easily disappointed by early setbacks. Life may be short, but the progress of humanity is apt to be a longish business. It is a little soon to write it off as a dead loss before there has even been a chance to make the necessary preliminary adjustments. A second good reason for Tory restraint is that the Conservative Party has lately been showing signs of taking up a new radical theory of progress on its own; but in any case such philosophy as it retains is still so largely compounded of classical utilitarian economic theories as to make some show of fellow-feeling a matter of *noblesse oblige*.

What is more important, it is no laughing matter that one of the great mainsprings of British political thought – perhaps the most important one – is showing signs of running down. It is very doubtful whether we can yet afford to lose it, and there is something to be said for trying to wind it up again until someone can temper a substitute. The danger is that those whom it has hitherto sustained will drift into the nihilism of determinist social psychology – and almost any philosophical theory of progress would be better than that.

There are already signs of this. Many who cling to a belief in the fundamental goodness of human beings have sought an easy escape from the problem posed by the apparent unwillingness of men and women to behave better when they are better educated and freed from the pressure of poverty and unemployment. The answer has to be that 'it is not their own fault'. Whose fault is it, then? It must be either their environment, or unconscious and uncontrollable psychological impulses.

But this will not do. The retreat to determinist psychology is a *volte-face* from optimism to the blackest pessimism, for it implies that the humanist no longer believes that human beings can be fundamentally 'good' in any normal sense of the word. Indeed, it involves the renunciation of the whole conception of good and evil and of all hope of meaningful human progress. The argument for the importance of environment was reasonable in its optimistic 18th century form, since it contained a substantial element of truth and implied the possibility of improving human behaviour by improving the human environment. But in the extreme determinist form of today it involves an irrational pessimism, a retreat from optimism about human nature; for it suggests that human beings cannot be expected to rise above their environment and behave well in difficult circumstances.* This is irrational, because we know quite well that innumerable men and women *have* in fact managed to behave well in spite of an unfavourable environment: are we really to say that they are no 'better', in any meaningful sense, than those of normal intelligence who behave badly? Yet if it be admitted that it is possible to say that some 'behave better' than others, then some blame must attach to those who, without the excuse of sub-normal intelligence, behave worse. In other words, it *is* 'their fault', after all.

The effects of environment must always be borne in mind, but must not be allotted an excessive importance. Intelligent efforts must be made to improve unfavourable human environments, and the effect of environment should be taken into account in assessing the *degree* of culpability of the shiftless or criminal. But the idea that all crime and irresponsibility are to be absolved by the determinism of environment from stigma or censure is to make assumptions about the nature of Man which are not yet susceptible of proof. There is little reason to believe that the pessimism involved in the assumptions is justified.

The dangers involved in an attitude that assumes that crime and irresponsibility among people of normal intelligence are 'not their fault' are surely becoming obvious. Irresponsibility is protected from the need ever to become responsible: the State, rather than the individual, is forced to assume the responsibility. And there is a basic truth in Herbert Spencer's dictum that 'the ultimate result of shielding men from the effects of folly is to fill the world with fools'.[3] The absolution of crime, especially in a social atmosphere of increasing permissiveness, affects much more than just the

* This conviction was very noticeable in intellectuals' comments, both here and in the United States, on the American negro riots of 1966–7.

current attitude towards punishment. There is already a fairly widespread feeling that in some way crime really does not *matter* very much. It is something for 'Them' to deal with, and the contest between 'Them' and the criminals can be watched with complete detachment, as if it were a game. If the criminals get away with a particularly daring and skilful coup – especially if they steal a really large sum of money – they are accorded a kind of connoisseur's appreciation amounting sometimes to open admiration. It is as if they had won a big prize in a football pool. People do not seem to feel in any way that organised crime and violence are a menace to *them*, or a threat to the whole basis of communal living. They are unconscious of any menace to society, because they know only 'society', which remains unaffected by it.

It is, as I have already suggested, an error to believe that these attitudes can be radically altered simply by the 'reactionary' prescriptions alone. Punishing criminals more severely as a deterrent, and toughening the sanctions against irresponsibility, may be desirable and even necessary, but this will not of itself exorcise the essential pessimism that lies at the root of the attitudes we have been considering. If people are unmoved by obvious flaws in the social organisation in which they live, and by threats to its stability, it can only be because they have ceased to take pride in it and have dissociated themselves from any personal concern with it. And this can only mean that the organisation itself has failed. History shows conclusively that people do take a pride in, and feel identified with, a sound and successful social organism, just as they take pride in a successful Army unit or football club. There have been successful societies, which were both the sum total of the families and individuals composing them and yet at the same time something more and greater than that; and their constituent members recognised not only the existence of the societies but their own involvement in, and commitment to them. But 'society' is not like that at all: it is something separate and external which, it is thought, can take over responsibilities while absolving individuals from any share in them.

Unwillingness to accept, or share in, responsibilities is a reflection of pessimism. It implies a lack of confidence in the individual's ability to cope with life; a lack of standards which are felt to be adequate to the demands made on individuals; and a feeling that it is barely worth while trying. It is a renunciation of action, because there seems no point or purpose in action. What is it all *for*?

It is, admittedly, not easy to see what it is that has failed. It is impossible to deny the reality of progress of a kind. The worst poverty has been abolished in Britain, inequalities of wealth have been lessened, and thousands of families enjoy a material standard of life far higher than they ever dreamed of. Yet it is not enough. Those who *are* satisfied with material prosperity, to whom their own comfortable living is the end of all, have in a sense contracted out of society altogether. But for most, prosperity has not seemed to amount to the ideal existence for which they may have hoped. Money brings worries to replace some of those it has taken away. Leisure is less rewarding – and much more expensive – than they expected. And in the end, the two nagging questions remain: 'Will it last?' and 'What's it all in aid of?'

If it does last, the ultimate significance is, paradoxically, perhaps even harder to perceive. 'Is this really all there is to it?' people ask. 'We all die; and if death is the end of everything, what is the point of getting in a sweat about things now? One might as well be comfortable, of course, but it is "Their" business (more specifically, the Government's and the trade unions') to see to that; they can be prodded from time to time and made to get on with it. The next generation, with the same assistance, will probably be able to look after itself. If not, what can we do about it? and why should we do anything about it?

'There are no great causes to excite us. Politics are all a matter of economics and the Welfare State: the first is too difficult, the second a matter of organisation to be looked after by "Them". Foreign affairs have become a matter for the Americans and the Russians to sort out between them – without involving us, of course. After all, what can we do? There doesn't seem to be anything very big and bad and obvious – or indeed anything at all specific – that needs reforming. It's true that this makes politics rather dull, compared with the old days, but it must be an improvement, surely?

'There was a time when the Bomb seemed to be quite a serious matter, but the excitement seems to have died down now. It was always hard to see what good all that marching and sitting down did; after all, it's the Americans and the Russians really, isn't it? Perhaps the world *will* get itself blown up one of these days, though it'll probably last out our time. But what's the point of exhausting ourselves about it? There's nothing we can do, is there? As to building for the future, how do we know there'll *be* a future? The future is something politicians make pompous speeches about. Even if there is a future, what's it to us? We won't be there. All right, suppose we *ought* to try and do something about it, there's nothing we *can* do, is there? It's all too complicated for ordinary people like us. Besides, They got us into this mess, it's up to Them to get us out. Don't forget that. Not that They will, of course. They're only ordinary people like us, after all; can't think what we pay Them for.'

So the circle of futile reasoning goes round. This is scarcely the happy optimism of people living for today without a care for the morrow. There is an almost total lack, not only of faith in the future of humanity, but of simple interest in it. And the paramountcy of the present produces an often exaggerated resentment and touchiness about quite minor grievances and inconveniences in the present. If there happens at any time to be an unusual number of minor grievances, however little related these may be to each other in their nature and causes, then people will vote against the government of the day in protest. Yet they can hardly be said to be voting for the opposition, for they seem to care very little about the content of the policies offered by either government or opposition. No one seems to feel that the accumulation of disorders is in any palpable way symptomatic of a major disequilibrium that can be made the subject of political discussion and action. From time to time a vague feeling wells up that 'something is wrong', that something vital is lacking, perhaps that the political machinery is inadequate to the size and complexity the task that confronts it. But it is all too large to grasp, too difficult to be thought through to the stage of political action. There are, in short, no great causes. 'As the past has ceased to throw its light upon the future, the mind of man wanders in obscurity.' Indeed, it seems to be wandering in ever narrowing circles.

'Once man-made, historical processes have become automatic, they are no less ruinous than the natural life process that drives our organism and which . . . leads . . . from birth to death. The historical sciences know only too well such cases of petrified and hopelessly declining civilisations where doom seems foreordained, like a biological necessity . . .'[4]

But is it really like that? On balance, I do not think it is – or not, at least, with us. It could happen, and we shall see that there is cause for alarm. The reader will, however, be invited to hold fast to the conviction that no trends are truly inevitable in the sense of being inexorably predetermined. This is one field in which it is indeed true that 'there is nothing either good or bad, but thinking makes it so'. Trends persist to their logical ends only because people either want them to or do not care enough to stop them. If people do not care, it is because they have despaired either of the future itself or of their ability to control it. In such circumstances, it is simply not enough to say that if everyone were 'good', or 'honest', or 'worked hard', everything would be all right. It is necessary to enquire why these qualities are no longer considered worth while.

There can be little doubt that this is so today. Apart from the ever present need to 'make a living', for which the mere process of labouring so many hours a week will suffice, all the motives that can make it worth while to undertake conscientiously any 'useful' activity or social obligation have been weakened. Let us consider them in turn.

First there has been a total diminution in the amount of intrinsic satisfaction derived from work itself. This is frequently exaggerated by those who both nurture an idealised vision of a vanished Merrie Englande full of jolly craftsmen and ignore the number of (for example) young men in garages who do quite genuinely enjoy taking motor cars to pieces. But in an increasing number of industrial processes the work of the individual is neither satisfactorily related to the end-product nor interesting in itself. Indeed, it is noticeable that very large numbers of men and women working in factories frankly admit that they prefer the repetitive automatic tasks that make little or no demands on their minds and require very little concentration.

This preference is sometimes represented (generally by those who have an interest in extending the processes) as a splendid justification for the whole business: so far from robbing the worker of satisfaction, they say, we are actually giving him what he likes; and if he likes it, it can't be doing him any harm, can it? This is nonsense. All that the workers' preference means is that they have come to a simple and rational conclusion: since an increasingly high proportion of factory jobs have become thoroughly unsatisfying and boring anyway, it is better to have one that at least minimises the risk of error and leaves the mind free for conversation or day-dreaming. It does not follow at all that any but the most moronic would not prefer a job that seemed to have some point in it and provided some creative satisfaction. The trouble is to find such a job. Meanwhile few psychologists would claim that the repetitive task makes any contribution either to 'self-fulfilment' or to the building of a well-integrated personality. Rather the contrary. For it does not even always make the worker more anxious to enjoy a constructive and creative leisure; despite the undoubted increase in 'do-it-yourself' activities at home, only too often the passive attitude is carried over from work to leisure. Those who tell us that the progress of automation will provide increasing opportunities for 'creative' leisure, and that steps must be taken to encourage this, do not tell us how to deal with the attitudes of mind that mechanisation itself creates.

Two more motives for conscientious work have also been weakened. One is the belief that *good* work (as distinct from *more* work) actually pays better, in cash, than bad. This was once a powerful motive for some people; the trouble now is that it is much less evidently true, even if it is true at all. The other motive is the belief that conscientious work is 'good' in itself, and that it is 'wrong' and 'dishonest' to slack, to skimp, or to fail to 'give value for money'. This is still a powerful motive for some, but I think there can be little doubt that the belief is much less widely held than before, especially among the young. It is a part of the disintegration of the moral code that has led to a very widespread increase in the amount of petty dishonesty, pilfering and 'fiddling', which began during the war and has been attributed by some to the increasing 'depersonalisation' of employers with the growth of employment by public bodies and large corporations; not only are the employing bodies so large that it is felt they will not notice the loss, but since they are not 'people' it is not felt to be unfair to cheat them.

Now this is an attitude which spreads and grows inevitably, especially in a conformist society. Not only is the atmosphere absorbed by new entrants to employment and regarded as normal, but it appears increasingly odd (and therefore 'anti-social') for individuals to resist it and differentiate themselves from the majority ('everyone at work does it').

Yet it is no use simply deploring the 'immorality' of the shirkers and pilferers. For one thing, employers are to a great extent to blame for the situation that has arisen: the fear of losing scarce labour has become so deeply ingrained in a period of overemployment that they have been afraid to impose the discipline necessary to prevent the disease from becoming chronic. But in any case the disintegration of a moral code is too fundamental a development for the apportionment of blame among individuals or classes to constitute an adequate response. The 'Protestant Ethic' has simply lost its force, as it was bound to when its economic sanctions were weakened. Admirably suited as it appeared to be to the social and economic circumstances which brought it to birth, it was never intrinsically attractive to the individual on the receiving end of it. It is not unnatural for an intelligent young person, confronted with an attempt to foist a prefabricated moral judgement on him, to ask 'Why should I?' – or, perhaps more often, 'Why shouldn't I?' And the reply 'Because it's wrong' begs a series of further questions to answer which requires a training in ethics that is no longer common. Certainly one will not get very far with an old-fashioned reference to rewards and penalties in the after-life.

We are left with the two motives for conscientious work and action which are genuinely philanthropic: the desire, dissociated from any notion of reward in this world or the next, to serve one's fellow men to the best of one's ability; and the feeling of 'building for the future' – personal satisfaction in the thought that one is leaving to posterity something a little better than he inherited from the past.

Now it is extremely difficult to generalise safely about the extent to which these motives have been weakened. Without doubt they are still effective for many people, and probably latent in many more. But I do not think many would deny that they are both weaker and less widespread than once they were. There is a more cynical attitude towards the idea of service, and I cannot help feeling that the ideal has been markedly debased by the public relations experts, intent on presenting a quite false philanthropic image of various commercial undertakings ('The International Flue Pipe Corporation is a Public Service for the People of Britain'). More damaging, of course, has been the tendency to shuffle off on to 'society' responsibilities that were once accepted as private concerns, with the resultant incursions of the Welfare State into fields of service that were once privately cultivated. The feeling that 'They ought to do something about it' is not, perhaps, simply a selfish abdication of responsibility; there is also a strong feeling that it is all too complicated for anyone but 'Them' to cope with. There is an increasingly pessimistic tendency to ask, 'What's the use?'

The weakening of the impulse to 'build for the future' is perhaps the most serious development of all, for it is part of the breakdown of those theories of 'progress' that have previously sustained so many people's enthusiasm and so much political action. We have seen how this has been in part due to a premature disillusionment with the results of 'progress'; but there are important economic reasons as well. The emphasis on consumption has pushed into the background the idea of creating things to endure. Moreover the need to make sacrifices for the future seems to have diminished. A prosperous and fully industrialised economy differs substantially from a less developed one. What is now being demanded of the Chinese people, what Stalin demanded of the Russians, differs only in its method of enforcement from what the Industrial Revolution once demanded of the British. Now, not only is a smaller *proportional* amount of capital formation necessary, but adequate capital formation is possible with much less present sacrifice. Yet there is more to it than this.

'All theories of progress offered abundance in the future in return for present sacrifices, and so to that extent at least they were well adapted to an epoch of industrialisation. But if they had offered no more than future abundance they could not have served the wider purpose of reconciling people to the harshness of the present. After all, we do not feel that future generations are so much more important than our own that any amount of sacrifice for their sake is justified. But theories of progress promised more than mere abundance. They promised that total reconciliation of man with man on which the prophets of society have always fixed their gaze, but which society itself has not been able to attain.'[5]

To how many people today does this promise carry conviction?

Is it not clear, in effect, that what is really wrong is that there has been a gradual – but almost total – collapse of confidence in the future? It is often said that the current preoccupation with 'security' arises from bitter memories of an insecure past. This explanation would be more convincing if the search for security were not so disconcertingly obsessive among the young middle-class products of the public and grammar schools. It is beginning to look much more like a widespread fear of an uncertain future; and this does appear puzzling in a generation that not only has no direct knowledge of pre-war conditions but has lived all its life in conditions of full employment that have never seriously looked like being threatened. Surely what is present here is no mere apprehension of intermittent short-term economic fluctuations, but a fundamental collapse of confidence and enthusiasm about the whole future of the country – and even of humanity at large? The essence of the pessimism we have been discussing is to be found in one frightening thing – a loss of confidence in life itself.

The process has been unerringly described by the novelist Rex Warner, in what is clearly intended to be a tract for the present times. The philosopher Anaxagoras describes the 'magnificent self-confidence' of Periclean Athens, predicting that if 'this superb confidence in life were to be lost' the whole fabric of its civilisation would collapse.

'For, if men see no future, they are inadequately equipped to deal even with the present. In such a state people, instead of

> seeking responsibilities, would decline or avoid them. They would either delegate or surrender power to others and in so doing would cripple their own natures. . . . The functions of government would be performed either autocratically by a monarch or invisibly by a small minority of experts. For good men, if any such remained, there would be no public use. . . . Superstition, of course, would be rife, since without hope there is no incentive to discover the reason of things. Those who acquiesced in an imposed convention would be most happy and the most honoured would be the rich and those who, by the exercise of some talent or other, were able to entertain the masses with some substitute for pleasure.'[6]

This seems to me an entirely accurate analysis, not only of the symptoms reflecting the condition of 'society' but of the nature of its pessimistic malaise. That this is something new and real, not just another figment of the imagination of the perennial *laudator temporis acti*, can surely be seen by comparison with the optimism habitually expressed until quite recently by those who were supposed to be the most 'modern' interpreters of the social scene. When H. G. Wells praised the developments that had made it possible to pose meaningfully the question, 'Yes, you earn a living, you support a family, you love and hate, but – *what do you do*?', he can scarcely have foreseen a time when almost anyone would answer, 'What *is* there to do? and why?' For him it was an accepted certainty that there *were* things to do, and things that made sense beyond the immediate present. There was an almost infinite scope for *action*. Who envisages the possibility of acting now? Of course there are plenty of 'calls for action', the newspapers are full of them; but they are calls for action by 'Them' – generally by the government.

Mr. Warner's diagnosis is essentially the same as Dr. Hannah Arendt's. To her, politics are becoming more and more a mere matter of administration, of bureaucracy – of 'government by nobody'. We are becoming a society of 'jobholders', alienated from the idea of construction.

> 'Within this society, which is egalitarian because this is labour's way of making men live together, there is no class left, no aristocracy of either a political or spiritual nature from which a restoration of the other capacities of man could start anew. Even presidents, kings, and prime ministers think of their offices in terms of a job necessary for the life of

> society, and among the intellectuals, only solitary individuals are left who consider what they are doing in terms of work and not in terms of making a living.'[7]

And again:

> 'It is quite conceivable that the modern age – which began with such an unprecedented and promising outburst of human activity – may end in the deadliest, most sterile passivity history has ever known.'[8]

When, however, Dr. Arendt – and she was writing in 1958 – warned of the danger 'that such a society, dazzled by the abundance of its growing fertility and caught in the smooth functioning of a never-ending process, would no longer be able to recognise its own futility',[9] she was possibly being *too* pessimistic. There are increasingly significant signs that, in Britain at least, a recognition of futility is beginning to grow. And, while this dawning awareness can only result at present in a deepening of the prevailing pessimism about the future, it can be taken also as a sign, if not yet of grace, then at least that there may be a hope of ultimate regeneration. We have so far been spared the ultimate degradation of a general and total self-satisfaction with our condition.

Now it can scarcely be doubted that men who are wholly pessimistic in their outlook very seldom accomplish anything constructive on a significant scale. Individuals may produce impressive literary works, as some of the 19th century Romantics did, but pessimism is never the hallmark of a great age of literature. It may be true, as Alfred Cobban has suggested,[10] that constructive practical action can flourish in a society whose prevailing intellectual atmosphere is pessimistic, since the practical men may be living on the intellectual optimism of the preceding generation. This was no doubt the case in the 19th century. But the intellectual heritage of Western Europe today is one of almost unrelieved pessimism going back to the time of Rousseau and reaching its culmination at the *fin de siècle,* thereafter rapidly running down into nihilism. Despite a limited flicker of enthusiasm among a few dedicated people confronted with the post-war challenge, and another attempt to kindle a spark at the beginning of what was hailed as a 'new Elizabethan age', there has been in Britain no disposition to optimism among practical men (except in wartime) since 1914. I am aware that some of the enthusiasms of technologists may appear to contradict this; but these are the dedications of specialists, not reflections of a prevailing spirit.

It is of course true that a limited pessimism – the kind of empirical scepticism that has no exaggerated ideas of the nobility of human nature, for example – does not necessarily inhibit effort; indeed, by imposing a realistic conception of the difficulties of the tasks ahead, it may actually stimulate it. Its effect is by no means always stultifying. The sceptic may be as free of ideals as of illusions, but he is not necessarily without hope or convinced of the futility of action. But action is bound to be almost completely inhibited by a pessimism that goes so deep as to amount to a total lack of confidence in the future; for this is a loss of confidence in life itself, a denial of the meaning of human existence. Not only action, but effort, is inhibited; it is as though the human spirit had simply lost the will to live.

This process seems to have gone farther and deeper in the northern countries of the Western world than in the rest, and it has attracted most attention and comment in Britain. Diagnosis of the 'English sickness' has almost become a disease in itself. Half-hearted attempts have been made to deny the existence of the malaise, and even to assert a virility supposed to be indicated by the pathetic flickers of neurotic 'swinging'. Almost no one seems to have found the attempts convincing; the general consensus appears to be that our civilisation is decadent. This, however, is a pretty meaningless proposition, since it implies a continuity of process which is very doubtful. Ours is patently not the same civilisation as the pre-industrial one, and not even the same kind of civilisation; it seems much more reasonable to suppose that it is a transitional phase, in which case the notion of decadence is irrelevant, or at least premature. It is tempting to describe the present transition as a preparation for something new; but this would imply an optimism as yet unjustified, since there is no evidence of conscious preparation for anything.

That the symptoms of a morbid *Zeitgeist* have been intensified in this country by causes peculiar to Britain is certain. One of these causes, of course, has been a slowness – and indeed unwillingness – to recognise the nature and extent of the changes taking place in the outside world, and consequently in the international status of Britain as a world power. This reaction is neither unnatural nor unprecedented; it is, however, irrational. At all events, the change has been widely interpreted as a 'decline', a concept that carries with it important psychological overtones. It is possible for a nation to react constructively and with spirit to a diminution of its international influence and relative military power; once the diminution is thought of as a 'decline', however, it is viewed as an inevitably *continuing process*. A 'decline', since Gibbon (or at least since Evelyn Waugh), is inexorably followed by a 'fall'. And a fall is final. The present may be bleak, but the future is bound to be worse: hence the emigration statistics.

Britain has been suffering, too, from an exceptionally acute attack of disillusionment with progress. The symptoms have already been discussed, but a word may perhaps be added to explain why this country should have reacted more sharply than others. The explanation is to be found entirely in the unique experiences of Britain during and immediately after the second World War.

First, Britain was the only major industrial country to conduct the war for six years on a basis of free democratic institutions. This basis was not removed by the temporary suspension of many individual freedoms during the war, including the right to strike and to choose one's own job; it remained true that the whole direction of the war effort rested on the basis of the agreement of a constitutionally elected Parliament, which could at any time have voted the Government out or even demanded a negotiated peace. In the same way the efficiency of the war effort depended on the largely voluntary co-operation of millions of civilians through six exhausting and uncomfortable years.

No doubt also influenced by his Labour Party colleagues in the Coalition Cabinet, Winston Churchill adopted a technique with which Lloyd George had made him familiar in the first war. Large promises and preparations were made during the war for economic improvement and sweeping social reforms to be introduced as soon as the war was over. The idea caught on, and was widely and eagerly discussed. The famous Beveridge Report on Social Insurance became a best-seller. Organised lectures and discussion groups in units of the armed forces spread the idea wider. Certainly it served its wartime purpose: the conviction grew, not only that Britain after the war would be a much better country to live in that it had ever been, but that the achievement of this better Britain was the country's real war aim. It stimulated enthusiasm and effort – but it also implanted a belief that the end of the war would automatically bring fulfilment of the promises in the form of immediate material improvement. It cannot be said that the 1945 election campaign, which ended in the return of a Labour government with a large majority, did much to damp down a general optimism which had been heightened by the widespread illusion that Britain had won the war.

Unfortunately, Britain ended the war in very bad shape even for the limited business of supporting life, let alone building a heaven on earth. She had, as a reward for showing an unparalleled example to the civilised world, achieved the worst of every world for herself.* She had neither the American benefit of an immensely stimulated and expanded economy, nor the technological advantage available to those continental countries whose industries had been so plundered or destroyed that they could be replanned from scratch. With her foreign assets decimated and her export trades in disorder, she had neither the hope of quick recovery nor the challenge posed by ruin. For six more wretched, souring years her people endured the frustrations of rationing and the gradual dilution of Utopia. The promised reforms were duly put in train, but in an inevitably emasculated form. Shortage of resources, combined with an unwillingness to appear to dishonour the universal promise by concentrating on priorities and postponing even the pretence of some reforms, spread the

* The chief cause of the débâcle was adherence to the fatuous modern heresy, which no civilised statesman embraced before 1914, of carrying on war to 'unconditional surrender'.

benefits more thinly over the wide field of the social services than had been expected. Full employment was maintained, but at the cost of an inflation which eroded the value of cash benefits from the start. This was the beginning of the peculiar British disillusionment with progress. It had simply failed to match up to the promises – and not only the wartime promises, but the promises implicit in years of Labour Party propaganda about the benefits to be derived from socialism and a planned economy. The planned economy dissolved in the economic crisis of 1951, and faith in the promises with it.

Back in 1919, at the end of an earlier war, Winston Churchill had said, 'The true measure of nations is what they can do when they are tired'. But by 1945 the people of Britain had been told so often that things would be done for them that they had begun to believe it. When, after 1947, the Labour Government began a desperate propaganda campaign to persuade the public that governments can do no more than the people are prepared to earn, the reaction conspicuously lacked enthusiasm; it might, people felt, have been better to say this frankly in the first place. The result has been an enduring scepticism about politics and governments, together with a marked disinclination on the part of individuals to interest themselves personally in national recovery.

If this, the peculiarly British reaction to peculiarly British circumstances, were all, the right prescriptions for the malady would not appear too difficult to devise. We shall, indeed, be considering some of them later. But they have been superimposed on an already existing Western *Weltschmerz*, which the indicated British political prescriptions can hardly eradicate; and indeed, until it is eradicated, the political prescriptions would fail even of their own limited purpose. Apart from a few scientists who are dedicated to inventing and creating a new kind of man, or to controlling and speeding up the process of evolution by genetic mutation; apart from a few technologists and cyberneticians who believe that humanity can ultimately be 'conditioned' to be entirely happy in a world subordinated to the necessities of an efficient technology; apart from a few sociologists, who also feel that somehow they hold the key to human happiness in their scientific hands; apart, that is to say, from the paranoiacs, the Western world has begun to despair of its civilisation. Finding that the civilisation is less than wholly satisfying, men are also unable to imagine a future that is not much the same only more so. Man seems to have reached the limit of his ability to cope constructively with the increasingly complex problems he has created for himself – or so Man himself seems to believe. Hence the pessimism, the loss of confidence, the sense of futility, the 'opting out'.

Yet the diagnosis cannot possibly be right. It contains an entirely unwarranted assumption that evolution has come to an end, and that we are stuck for ever with Man as he now is. It is also caused by an inability, or a refusal, to come to terms with what the scientists have been up to. Only the depressing implications of scientific discoveries seem to have seeped through, without any notion that they may contain some seeds of hope.

Any viable political philosophy must be based on some kind of assumptions in metaphysics and ethics, and admittedly this is now very difficult. The philosophers have handed metaphysics over to the scientists, who hardly know what to do with it and are unable to come to terms with the Churches. Since we have got to come to some provisional conclusions about the nature and status of Man if Man is to be prevented from going into a psychological decline, it might be worth looking again – with the eye of hope – at what the scientists have to say. It seems not wholly unreasonable to accept the scientists' view of the nature of the universe (until they change it again), while reserving the conviction that nothing in it is in the least inconsistent with a rational belief in the existence of God. It seems to me that the scientists have – whether they meant to or not – given us back our future.

CHAPTER 4

Mankind in Perspective

I have of late – but wherefore I know not – lost all my mirth, forgone all custom of exercises; and indeed it goes so heavily with my disposition that this goodly frame, the earth, seems to me a sterile promontory; this most excellent canopy, the air, look you, this brave o'erhanging firmament, this majestical roof fretted with golden fire, why, it appears no other thing to me than a foul and pestilent congregation of vapours. What a piece of work is a man! how noble in reason! how infinite in faculty! in form and moving how express and admirable! in action how like an angel! in apprehension how like a god! the beauty of the world! the paragon of animals! And yet, to me, what is this quintessence of dust? man delights not me; no, nor woman neither.

William Shakespeare, *Hamlet*

I doubt whether there is a more decisive moment for a thinking being than when the scales fall from his eyes and he discovers that he is not an isolated unit lost in the cosmic solitudes, and realises that a universal will to live converges . . . in him.

In such a vision man is seen not as a static centre of the world – as he for long believed himself to be – but as the axis and leading shoot of evolution, which is something much finer.

Pierre Teilhard de Chardin, *The Phenomenon of Man*

Now, for the first time, the history of mankind reaches back into an infinite past to which we can add at will and into which we can inquire further as it stretches ahead into an infinite future. This twofold infinity of past and future eliminates all notions of beginning and end, establishing mankind in a potential earthly immortality.

Hannah Arendt, *Between Past and Future*

It seems to be very hard for men and women to realise themselves in the new perspectives of time and space, to accept a new locus and the implications of a new status in the universe. The progressive conquest of the technical problems of space travel has made but little difference. Man-made satellites, even actual photographs of men walking about in space, are mere science fiction, without subjective reality. It is true that to some – and not only to scientists and cosmonauts – the whole enterprise is immensely exciting. It is the modern equivalent of the lost adventure of exploration, of the expansion of the frontiers of the world, which allows even those unable to take a personal part in the undertaking to share vicariously in the excitement of it.

To some the prospect of space travel seems to bring a sense of impending relief which has remarkable psychological implications. It is as though the world had become a prison from which they need the assurance of the prospect of ultimate release. Yet this seems to represent no virile enthusiasm to challenge and conquer the unknown – only a hopeless feeling that the problems of the world have become so oppressive that any escape from them, even (or perhaps especially) into the sterile emptiness of space, would be preferable to remaining here to grapple with them. To carry the *Weltschmerz* into the infinite may seem a strange ambition of despair, but its very futility is symptomatic.

The conception of infinite space, however dimly felt, is to some people an exalting and inspiring experience. To many more, however, it is either terrifying or depressing. It is an affront to their humanity, for it seems to dwarf with a crushing finality not merely the individual but the whole achievement of mankind. The concept of almost infinite *time* is less generally and less significantly apprehended, but the immediate reaction tends also to be one of depression. If even the whole sweep of our recorded history is but a moment of time, then what is the significance of a man's life on earth? If a human being is only a tiny particle in space, and the span of his life no more than the flicker of an insect's wing, can the actions of individuals have any conceivable significance at all? How can it matter what, if anything, comes after us? Even the idea of the immortality of mankind seems, however paradoxically, to shrivel away from grandeur to nothing in the context of infinity.

The common reaction is to shut the whole business away from the level of conscious thought. Infinity – or the fear of it – is there, a dark shape seen dimly out of the corner of the mind's eye; but it is still too new, too strange and terrifying, to be faced steadily and brought into perspective. It is too much of an effort to rearrange the categories of thought to deal with it. 'Without hope there is no incentive to discover the reason of things.'

So we stand still, in something of a no-man's land between past and future, unwilling to leave even the illusory remnants of cover provided by a traditional concept of man's relation to the universe. For this, the continuing inability of scientists and churchmen to come to any kind of metaphysical accommodation is in part responsible. Although the physical scientists have almost nothing to the point to say about the inwardness of man, while intelligent Christian theologians no longer pretend to be dogmatic about the organisation or behaviour of matter, the memory of old conflicts seems to inhibit anything more constructive than a kind of armed truce between them. There are, of course, dogmatic scientists who simply do not admit that there can be any compatability between the new scientific theory of the universe and a devout Christian faith with wide supernatural implications. Yet to go to the lengths of *denying* the existence of God, simply because the current physical theory of the universe does not seem to *need* God to hold it together, is surely as irrational as to deny the existence of the sun at night. An unpretentious agnosticism would perhaps be more seemly, for the defiant atheism of many scientists can be highly provocative to churchmen; the two sides seem sometimes to be deadlocked in a mutual antipathy of unreason, each denying to the other the very right to ask questions that it claims so vehemently for itself.

All this is not merely unhelpful to the non-scientific layman, but actually encourages him to leave the scientific theories unexamined and their implications unexplored. And this unawareness, whether it is due to wilful ignorance or to a timid refusal to face the issues, condemns him to a hopeless and frustrating confinement within a body of knowledge and tradition that has ceased to be adequate to the circumstances and problems of his life. Worse, it deprives its victims even of the hope of release or improvement for posterity. A narrowly bounded vision of time forces people to see Man as he is *now*, with his present mental capacity and categories of thought, as the *ultimate* culmination of evolution – as something static, incapable of any further development as a thinking being.

Now if this were true, it would follow inexorably that

civilised Man is doomed. The accelerating tempo of technical innovation would make it certain that sooner or later the scale and complexity of social and institutional problems would become too great for Man, equipped as he is at present, to cope with them. This is, in fact, precisely what very many people do now fear, whether they see the outcome as a gradual seizing-up or a catastrophic dissolution. Moreover, there are already enough failures and inadequacies to appear to justify the fear. Yet the truth is that the hypothesis on which the fear is grounded is false. For Man has only just this moment begun.

Our sun, around which revolve the earth and our familiar planetary system, is only one of the stars in a galaxy that contains perhaps 125,000 million other stars. Yet this inconceivably vast congregation is, in its turn, only one of *billions* of galaxies sprawled throughout a universe which may still be expanding.

It is worth while making an effort to imagine, if not to comprehend, these fantastic figures. Alarming as they may seem, there is no security in recoil from them; it is necessary to take a deep breath and advance. If the first individual reaction to the prospect is one of horror, of resentment at the apparent futility of being dwarfed into such minute insignificance, some comfort may be derived from going on to contemplate the other part of the picture. For the mathematical series from man to the infinite magnitude of the universe is only half of a total series which extends also to an infinity of smallness. The truth seems to be, if only we can comprehend it, that the monstrous complexity of the galactic universe is no more remarkable, no more exquisitely ordered, than the molecular structure of a single human chromosome. In short, an individual man is a mighty universe in himself.

This re-focusing of apprehension has much more significant results when we turn from the infinities of space to consider the relativities of time. The discovery of these is comparatively so new that it is easy to see why adjustment to them is still incomplete. It took about 150 years for the revolutionary ideas of Copernicus to gain anything like general acceptance even among the learned. It should not surprise us, then, that the implications of the discovery of prehistory are imperfectly appreciated by the majority after only a century.

In 1636 Archbishop Ussher, in his memorable synthesis of Biblical chronology, demonstrated that the world was created in the year 4004 BC. This precision, remarkable in an Irishman, characterised the whole of his work, which placed Noah's flood in exactly 2501 BC. The same precision may well have had a daunting effect on anyone feeling an urge to question his conclusions. However that may be, no one did successfully challenge his chronology for more than 150 years; and then it took another half-century for an accumulating corpus of archaeological evidence to overcome the inertia of learned scepticism and religious dogmatism. Not until 1859 was the antiquity of Man formally acknowledged by the learned world. Thereafter, the theological fundamentalists continued a stonewalling rearguard action.

Now the significant thing is not that there were still, only 100 years ago, learned men who believed that the world had been created less than 6,000 years before them; it is that they still believed that Man was coeval with the earth. It is the persistence of *this* myth – or rather, perhaps, the fact that the implications of its destruction have still not been widely appreciated – that is important. For, once that formidable barrier of time was breached, the effect was fully comparable with that of the first astronomical use of the telescope. The frontiers of time, like those of space, were rapidly pushed back to infinity; and by a simple paradox Man, while achieving a much greater absolute age as a created being, began to look relatively much younger than before. He was seen to be, in fact, quite a newcomer to the world even of living creatures: younger, less finished than he had seemed, and therefore possibly with scope for further development. When the astronomers and physicists completed the series by postulating a future as nearly interminable as the past, the picture looked entirely different from anything our ancestors could imagine. It may be helpful for us to take a look at this picture – recognising that, while nearly all the figures are still wildly approximate and highly debatable, the relative orders of magnitude involved simply have to be accepted. And they are what matter for our purpose.

The earth condensed from solar gases to its solid form something like 4,500 million years ago. If the astrophysicists are right (and if I understand them aright), the earth will probably go on existing for at least as many years more. How long Man will be able to survive in its changing physical conditions is quite uncertain, but the period appears to be a matter of millions rather than thousands of years.

We can be reasonably certain, it seems, that some sort of organic life has existed on earth for 1,500 million years and it may have existed for as much as 3,000 million. During the last 1,000 million years the process of evolution began to speed up a little, after the establishment of chlorophyll vegetation provided free oxygen for lunged creatures to breathe on land. Mammals became recognisable around 150 million years ago, and they emerged clearly above the reptiles only within the last 100 million years. Then, very recently indeed, came the last critical break-through – to a creature possessing the unique faculty of Man.

Somewhere between 500,000 and two million years ago, something that had been developing in the brains of certain anthropoids seems to have reached a critical stage and exploded into thought. This new characteristic was more than the ability to *know* things; in so far as metaphysicians allow that the power to know exists at all, then many animals possess it. But this development was a conscious turning in of the mind upon itself in a process of reflection, which is 'no longer merely to know, but to know that one knows'.[1] Man had arrived.

The date of his arrival has now been pushed back from a mere 6,000 years ago to perhaps a round million or so. But at the same time the creation of the world has been pushed back from 6,000 years ago to a matter of 4,500 million. We thus come to the staggering conclusion that thinking Man – not even *homo sapiens*, but the much more simian creature who first used fire and handled rough tools – has existed for only one-fiftieth of 1 per cent of the world's history, and certainly for no more than one-fifteenth of 1 per cent of the history of organic life on earth.

One-fiftieth of 1 per cent of the world's past! These are the terms in which it is possible to assert that Man has only just happened. So far from being near the end of his road, burdened with problems of his own making for which he is incapable of finding a solution – why, he has scarcely taken his first faltering steps along the road! He has scarcely had time to do more than rub his eyes in bewilderment at the dawn of consciousness. He is probably still cluttered up with the emotional disturbances brought down with him from the tree-tops!

To the reader who has borne with this apparent digression, but has so far failed to derive much present encouragement from it, I can only counsel patience and hope that he will consent to pursue the matter a little farther. There is more to it than this. Even so, it would appear to be more encouraging to see Man as stumbling on the threshold of his history than as being at, or near, the culmination of his development. For if what we are now is the best that we can hope to be, what a strangely imperfect end this would be to such an exquisitely complex process of evolution! But let us bring forward to the present day the time series we have so far considered only up to the birth of Man.

Our most primitive human ancestors, then, appeared no more than two million years ago, and possibly much more recently than that. To get the relative periods of time more clearly in perspective, we now have to remember that it was not until at most 15,000 and possibly only 7,000 years ago that there was any fundamental revolution in our ancestors' way of life. They were, and remained for all those thousands of centuries, hunters of wild animals and fish, and grubbers of roots and berries. Between 15,000 and 5,000 BC, somewhere in the Middle East, the practice originated of herding animals and sowing and gathering crops. From the birth of agriculture, although there had certainly been small settlements and communities before, we can roughly date the beginning of static social Man. It was, in fact, the dawn of civilisation.

Human beings, then, have existed on earth for only a small fraction of 1 per cent of the duration of organic life; and even the rudiments of civilisation have existed for between 1 and 3 per cent of the history of Man.

We come finally to the second of the great transforming revolutions affecting humanity, a revolution through which we are still living. The industrial revolution, which has involved the transformation, through the development and application of new forms of energy, of a way of life based on the land and its products, is to all intents and purposes only 200 years old. Modern, mechanised Man has thus existed for between 1 and 3 per cent of the history of static, social, civilised Man. This may seem to represent a pretty steady rate of evolution: but industrialised Man is still very, very young.

He is still young enough, at any rate, to be seriously worried about the large and manifold problems that confront him. Anxiety, however, is inseparable from the process of reflection; it is thus as old as Man himself. Its antidote, the one thing that can consistently overcome it and remove its inhibitions, is confidence. And the essential element of confidence is the taking of a long view – the certainty that *in the end* troubles can be surmounted and problems resolved, despite temporary setbacks and the apparent slowness of progress. It is this confidence that is lacking today, and its flagging is largely due to a distortion of the perspectives of time.

Because the pace of technical innovation and change has so enormously accelerated of late – and perhaps also because the political complexion of the world and its international groupings have altered with so revolutionary a speed since the war – an exaggerated disappointment is felt when desired objectives are not attained with the same rapidity. It is recognised that rates of progress in different fields have moved out of phase, and this is thought to imply a widening time-lag of social and institutional response which must ultimately prove fatal. The problems, because they have not been solved yet, begin first to look as though they cannot be solved now and then begin to appear inherently insoluble. This, of course, strikes at the very heart of confidence in the future.

Now the whole point of the evolutionary exegesis of this chapter is to demonstrate, by setting the present period in the context of time and history, the utter absurdity of the short-term conclusions now being reached by so many people. Let us look at one or two obvious examples. It is perhaps not surprising that 'reactionaries' should conclude that the failure of newly independent nations in Asia and Africa to achieve political and emotional stability in ten or twenty years proves something that they are instinctively inclined to believe. What is more remarkable is that even some 'progressives' are becoming disillusioned with the results of a mere fifteen years of mass prosperity and two decades of very experimental compulsory secondary education in Britain. The fact that after this minutely short period of transition and experiment men and women are behaving no more (and possibly even less) morally and intelligently than before, can hardly be held either to prove the doctrine of Original Sin or to deny the essential rationality of human beings. It is scarcely an adequate experimental basis either for total political reaction or for the rejection of the whole optimistic thesis of the Enlightenment.

Of course it can be immediately objected that the experimental results equally fail to prove that the optimism *is* justified and that the experiments are not doomed to fail. This is obviously true, but it is beside the point. One has got to make *some* assumptions, even in order to set up an experiment, and to abandon the assumptions before they are invalidated is to invite chaos. Certainly there are those who have never accepted the assumptions and would like to substitute others; but there may be something to be said for waiting until the assumptions on which we have actually been working are clearly disproved.

I am naturally aware that this argument, if it were universally applied, would almost inhibit political change of any kind; it could be used to prevent a new government from reversing any of the policies of its predecessors in a quinquennial parliament. But in politics one must have a sense of proportion, and always be prepared to oppose common sense to the strictest *minutiae* of logic. When one is considering assumptions underlying the details of policy; when a majority of people qualified to judge are utterly convinced that the assumptions are wrong; and when the experience gained seems to indicate that the results of continuing to act on the assumptions will be swiftly disastrous; then it is clearly not unreasonable to discard them. But there are certain assumptions which are fundamental to the undertaking of any human endeavour; these are entitled to be treated with rather more respect, and to be given rather longer to show their worth or worthlessness.

For example: is it rational to assume that men and women will in the end behave more rationally if their innate intelligence is carefully cultivated, if they are taught to exercise the faculty of judgement, and if they are given both the data necessary for informed choice and the opportunity to make choices for constructive purposes? Or is it more rational to assume that human beings will always act irrationally, and that it is a waste of effort to try to prove the contrary?

It may in the short run be *safer* to assume the latter hypothesis, and to make some provision against the consequences of irrationality. But in the long run the first assumption, in addition to being essential to the maintenance of democracy, is essential to civilisation and even to humanity itself. One *must* work on it, or abandon not only politics but hope. And once again the point is that it cannot conceivably be said that time has yet invalidated it. Man is still very young.

None of this, of course, justifies failure to watch the current progress of each experiment very carefully and to be prepared to modify the experimental methods and machinery accordingly. It does not tie one indefinitely, for example, to a particular educational curriculum or type of educational institution. But it does make it ridiculous to assert, on the basis of a very short period of experiment taken out of the whole context of history, that 'popular education has failed'.

Of course it is true that the problems and worries of modern Man are different in kind, as well as in degree, from those of his ancestors. They are not, as is sometimes suggested, simply the latest results of the eternal folly and cussedness of humanity. Consider the proliferation of invention. The more men do, the more they know, the more processes they initiate, the more every individual needs to learn and the more he has to worry about. The faster the rate of innovation becomes, the harder it is to keep up with things; the development of human organisation and institutions tends always to be slower than the rate of innovation and complication.

Yet it does not follow, because the gap has been widening, that it will continue to become wider and wider until chaos ensues. It is, however, the belief that it will which is at the root of much modern pessimism. The fatalistic belief that these 'man-made historical processes have become automatic', so that 'doom seems foreordained',[2] can take two forms. The first sees the onset of chaos as swift and dramatic, an imminent danger to the present generation. The second concedes that things 'will probably last out our time', but makes the prognosis for posterity one of gloom and dissolution. Neither takes at all seriously the possibility that men might somehow learn to cope, to assert a measure of control over the 'inevitable' processes. The reasoning behind the conviction also takes two forms: either that in the nature of things men *cannot* succeed; or that in the nature of men they *will* not succeed, being unwilling to deploy enough wisdom, foresight and effort. 'Men are unwise, and curiously planned.'

Pessimism about the remoter future can, I believe, be perceptibly mitigated by reflection on the perspectives of time. But it has to be admitted that there is nothing certain about success in the short run. It is perfectly possible that things might get a great deal worse before they begin to get better. We shall consider in later chapters how this deterioration can best be prevented, demonstrating (I hope) that there is nothing inevitable about it. But it is necessary to pause here for a moment to consider a fear that is inherent in much of the pessimism concerning both the near and the remote future. That is the fear of total destruction by nuclear war.

This is not the place to discuss what the wisdom and organisation of men can do to prevent a nuclear war from starting, or the difficult military question of limiting nuclear warfare, but my own conclusions are fairly optimistic. I happen to believe that nuclear proliferation will be halted, that the balance of nuclear force among the great powers will be maintained in deadlock, and that the chances of a nuclear war being started by miscalculation or 'accident' are small. But what we are considering now is the risk of an all-consuming nuclear holocaust, the kind of débâcle that so many science-fiction stories assume as their *point de départ.* There is nothing so inhibiting to confidence in the future as the question, 'How do we know that Man will not destroy himself in a nuclear catastrophe?' For the answer must be, of course, that we don't know that this will not happen. We do not even know it in the sense that we 'know' the sun will rise tomorrow morning. Yet I believe the fear can be exorcised by logic and common sense, requiring neither a religious faith in God's providence nor an exaggerated faith in human nature.

How do we know that the world will not be destroyed in its prime by a collision with a giant comet? Or that life will not be destroyed in some science-fiction way – by an unforeseen change in the balance or metabolism of living organisms, or by the ravages of some hitherto unknown (or at any rate hitherto limited and controllable) disease of animals or plants? Again the answer is that we don't know, although the scientists can no doubt assure us that these things are extremely unlikely.

Yet surely a sober consideration of the processes of evolution should convince any but the most neurotic that a sudden ending of humanity by nuclear destruction is, equally, quite monstrously unlikely? It took thousands of millions of years to evolve organic life, and then hundreds of millions more years to evolve Man: moreover the process has taken but half of the probable total of earth's existence. Since thinking Man is self-evidently the highest achievement of evolution, yet equally evidently capable of greater intellectual, psychic and social development, is it really likely that the process of evolution would just stop? Stop in the air, so to speak, either for ever or in order to start all over again? Looking at the whole process in perspective, is it reasonable to suppose that the 'axis and leading shoot of evolution' will be blasted after a mere million years or so of life?

The odds against it seem fantastically large. It would not only be 'against nature'; it would make no kind of sense at all. To those who believe that nothing makes any sense anyway, catastrophe may appear as likely as anything else. But the whole point is that evolution – and therefore its continuation – *does* make sense. A living cell *is* a higher and more remarkable achievement than a molecule of inert matter; the vertebrates *are* enormously superior to unicellular micro-organisms; thinking Man *is* an altogether finer achievement than the unreflecting mammals. Every one of these progressive achievements of evolution took hundreds of millions of years – but they happened, and the process went on. It continued over so long a period, and with a multiplicity of numbers so vast, that even the processes of chance achieved a kind of infallibility. They culminated in Man; and Man has only just begun, his potentialities as yet almost undeveloped. From the point of view of evolution, Man is irreplaceable. The mathematical probabilities seem to deny his sudden dissolution.

It can indeed be said that Man is to all intents immortal, whatever we may believe happens to the individual's psyche after death. We are assured of an almost infinite posterity, in which we and our achievements can both survive and be transcended. There *is* something worth while to work and construct for, after all. Moreover, it seems wholly unreasonable to suppose that the process of evolution will cease. There are well recognised theoretical limits to physical growth, but who knows what are the limits of evolving mind?

It is no answer to this question to object that the limits are set by the physical size of the brain-box, and that there has been no perceptible increase in this for some hundreds of centuries. This is merely an extension of the familiar complaint that in more than 2,000 years humanity has produced no minds superior to those of Plato and Aristotle, and that it ought to have done so if evolutionary progress is real. Even granting the premise, which may well not be true, the answer is still inadequate, for it ignores the time scale of evolution. A mere 2,000 years, or even 40,000, are of no great significance in the hundreds of millions of years of life. But there is another aspect of the matter. The evolution of thinking Man is no longer simply a function of the development of the cerebral capacity of the individual.

There is first the rapid development of technical aids to thought. A mathematician or a physicist who has at his disposal an 'electronic brain' capable of performing decades of calculation in a few minutes has, in a sense, evolved into a new dimension of thought. Again, the thinker of today and of tomorrow, starting from a steadily increasing foundation of existing knowledge, is by that much farther ahead in the progress towards whatever ultimate truth there may be. Most important of all, thought is no longer bound by the limits of the *individual* mind. Thinking is, in a sense, becoming a communal activity. Modern communications have brought the best minds of the world together, so that they stimulate each other. Research is becoming communal, and seminal ideas can be elaborated with unprecedented speed, then criticised or taken up and developed at a dozen points all over the world. It does not seem too fanciful to see in this more than just a matter of increasing speed, to see it as a new dimension of thinking, even perhaps the beginning of a new kind of thought.

The late Père Teilhard de Chardin, a learned palaeontologist and a devout and dutiful Jesuit priest, whose writings so seriously disturbed his Superior that they could not be published until after his death, developed this idea well beyond the plane of the practical in *The Phenomenon of Man*. The result is a kind of mystical metaphysics in deeply convoluted and neologistic language, containing a central theme that is certainly stimulating and not without emotional attraction. One need not, however, commit oneself to Père Teilhard's evolutionary pantheism (the theology of which may well be suspect, for all I know), to recognise realistic possibilities in the idea of future mental evolution as a 'psycho-social' process leading to new dimensions of mind and thought. And while this further lengthening of the perspectives opens up possibilities of some grandeur for the distant future of our posterity, it is not without its limited encouragement in the present.

At all events, a recognition of the relativities of time involved in Man's progress to the present day should help us to avoid becoming depressed by irrelevant symptoms and to refrain from prescribing irrelevant remedies for the wrong ills. Of course we are living in a 'period of transition' (what period is not?), and the transition is exceptionally rapid. The question is what is it a period of transition to? To this the most helpful answer is almost certainly 'nothing'. This is likely to be a very long – possibly even permanent – transition. It may well be true that from now on 'permanence is entrusted to a flowing process, as distinguished from a stable structure',[3] in which case all our categories of thought, as well as our institutional responses, will need to be changed. Otherwise we shall never be at rest, in the modern world or in our minds.

One notion that we should do well to reject at once is the frequently heard complaint that our civilisation is 'decadent', generally made by people who simply don't like it, and accompanied by ominous comparisons with the fates of ancient Greece and Rome. Nothing could be more dangerously misleading and more productive of irrelevant prescriptions. Whatever similarities historians may purport to perceive between the courses of pre-industrial civilisations – and a sufficiently ingenious historian with a 'theory' can discern in history any pattern he happens to be looking for – there are few valid comparisons to be made between pre-industrial history and the present age. It must be obvious, when one comes to assess the differences of pace, of scale, of techniques and of communications, that what we have to deal with now are *new* problems. It is easy enough to dislike many features of our present culture, but it is necessary to assert that 'immorality' is not synonymous with decadence. To attribute 'decadence' to our civilisation – like bewailing the 'decline' of Britain – is to suggest a continuing and irreversible process of deterioration, when all that has happened is a sudden change.

Once again, we are not predetermined by 'inevitable trends' to ultimate disaster – unless we allow ourselves to believe that we are, or acquiesce in a process of 'conditioning' that will leave us without hope and even without humanity. There are hideous dangers, none the less, but without danger there is no progress and little satisfaction.

There is the danger of the scientists. They may have given us back our future, but they must not be allowed to take control of it. Godlike as their miracles may be when they begin to 'act into nature', the control of their activities will become as politically important as the control of the Delphic Oracle became to the city-states of ancient Greece. Here again one must distinguish the essential from the inessential and the practical from the impossible. It is futile to denounce the scientists' activities as 'unnatural' or 'wrong'. They are not unnatural: they are, in a sense, a facet of evolution. It simply has to be accepted that, so long as there are things unknown, men will aspire to know them. Nothing will stop them asking the questions; and to ask is ultimately to find (or believe that they have found) the answer; and to find the answer is to seek to act on it. Scientists will never be content to 'leave nature alone', and their ability to interfere with her is likely to become more, rather than less, alarming.

It is sobering to reflect that Man, in what is regarded as his most terrifying and awe-inspiring achievement – the fusion of hydrogen atoms into helium – has done no more than imitate the very first, infinitely distant, act of the evolutionary process. He is thus some thousands of millions of years behind nature, and madly anxious to catch up. 'Men are unwise, and curiously planned', indeed; but then so, it can be argued, are the processes of nature. Taking a long view, it might be said that the contestants are fairly evenly matched, but nature has been at the game very much longer – and may have some surprises for us yet.

The scientists will not be content with comparatively simple victories – over climate and weather, for example. They are going to create life, perhaps even men of a sort, and some of them can hardly wait to 'improve' *homo sapiens* and his breeding. Science is, of course, 'ethically indifferent'; but this will not stop some scientists saying that it is 'all for our own good'.

The trouble is that when a scientist is possessed by an exciting idea he may become, quite unconsciously, dangerously unscientific. He may commit himself to positive assurances and reassurances which his experimental data cannot possibly justify. The physicists advising the British government were grossly over-optimistic, for example, about the 'acceptable' levels of fall-out from atmospheric nuclear tests, and had to back-pedal in a hurry. There have had to be second thoughts about a number of drugs, sprays and chemical additives. Above all, some scientists are extraordinarily careless about secondary effects, and apt to be rather cross when they happen – as if it were all nature's fault (which in a sense it is). No, the practical application of their discoveries will have to be increasingly carefully controlled. Who is to do it? Most certainly not the scientists, in any shape or form; and it is very doubtful whether it will even be safe to leave it to governments, which are only too apt to have scientific advisers. It looks as if it will have to be the people, which may lead to some ugly scenes.

There is another character on whom a very wary eye must be turned – the technologist, who is already in control of 'society' and regrouping his forces for further advance. But the question of how to control him requires a later chapter to itself.

Chapter 5

Back to Political Philosophy

Philosophy triumphs easily over past, and over future evils, but present evils triumph over philosophy.

François, Duc de la Rochefoucauld

The implications of the scientific approach confirm an attitude which is public and egalitarian rather than esoteric and hierarchic; for facts are publicly inspectable and open to revision in a way in which *a priori* moral postulates are not. Hence, moral philosophers have avoided the deduction of abstract schemes of human betterment from axioms within a postulational system, and the bolstering up of existing systems by similar means. They too, then, have played their part in the gradual dissolution of authority and certainty.

G. H. Bantock, *The Pelican Guide to English Literature* (*Vol. 7*)

Sure, he that made us with such large discourse,
Looking before and after, gave us not
That capability and god-like reason
To fust in us unused.

William Shakespeare, *Hamlet*

This unfashionable insistence on the importance of a philosophy will no doubt seem strange to many people, and it may well be assailed from two different angles. There are first those who are temperamentally antipathetic to ideas and theories of all kinds, and who believe that everything that is wrong with this country could be put right by a few practical men tackling the problems empirically as they come, with a determination to make things work 'efficiently'. It is theories and philosophies (by which they generally mean 'ideologies') which have, they believe, been responsible for most of our troubles. That plenty of men who claimed to be practical, and boasted that there was no nonsense about them, have already tried to solve our problems and failed, does not seem to be apparent to these objectors; nor, probably, would it seem conclusive if it were. Yet even 'practical' men, dealing with immediate problems, must have some implicit idea of their ultimate objectives. This, whether they know it or not, is likely to involve at least a philosophic attitude; and what is so often the matter with practical men is not that they have no philosophy, but that they are motivated by a philosophy that is out-of-date and irrelevant to the situation in which they are operating.

A more dangerous attack on the relevance of philosophy – since it is one in which even some modern philosophers have joined – is that which asserts that our human problems and social needs can be best (or, indeed, only) understood and dealt with through the techniques of psychology and the other social disciplines. This appears to be the attitude adopted, for example, by moral philosophers such as P. H. Nowell-Smith and by political theorists such as T. D. Weldon.

What seems to be unsatisfactory about this position is that it avoids a clear definition of the nature and scope of the 'social sciences' themselves. The question is whether they are indeed *sciences* or not, and the failure to answer this question convincingly is responsible for much that is wrong both with our sociology and with our politics.

If they *are* sciences, then they are concerned with the pursuit of knowledge – with the accumulation of facts, which are then more or less capable of being systematised and subsumed under general laws. Any hypothesis or theory put forward must remain subject to experimental verification. Yet it is clear that many 'social scientists' are not prepared to accept this discipline, which would indeed seriously limit the claims they have been disposed to make.

There is another, equally important, limiting factor implicit in the acceptance of a true scientific discipline. Science, being concerned with knowledge, cannot in itself be concerned with *ends*, except in so far as it can predict consequences. The physical sciences are, and of course must be, 'ethically indifferent'. If the social studies are to be classed as sciences, then they must not purport to do more than provide a factual background for the ethical choices involved in the determination of ultimate ends. This is in no way to depreciate their usefulness in helping to plan means and in predicting the consequences of action. But, if we are to have ethically indifferent social sciences, then we need moral and political philosophers as well. As Jeans said, 'wherever science leaves off – and in many places its boundary is ill-defined – there philosophy begins.'[1] If one day the social scientists were able to prove that human behaviour is wholly determined and wholly predictable, then philosophy might be deemed to have become superfluous. But we are a long way from that day, if indeed it ever dawns; and if it does, it will be partly the social scientists' own influence on society that will have conditioned social behaviour to this point.

If, on the other hand, the 'social scientists' are simply research students at large, they can legitimately concern themselves with the ethical implications of human behaviour and social organisation. To the extent that they do this, however, they will be dabbling in philosophy, in which case they must conform to the disciplines of philosophy. They cannot have it both ways, nor can they operate effectively in a state of suspension between both. This is, of course, by no means to say that they are wrong to work in accordance with some kind of 'scientific method', as most of them claim to do. Probably all that is meant is that they ought to do their best to verify their data, test their hypotheses, and reason honestly by logical intellectual processes.

The social and political scientists are at their most suspect when they advance determinist theories, often little more than analogues of those once promulgated by the physical scientists in whose image they believe themselves to have been created. It is scarcely necessary to fight one's way through the philosophical jungle of a discussion on 'free will' to be sceptical of excessive claims for the relevance of determinist theories to politics. One may accept the psychiatrist's assertion that a man's behaviour is affected by unconscious and sub-rational impulses, without being convinced that these conform to any definable natural law. One may even accept, with reservations, that man in the mass (or 'society', if the term is thought to be meaningful) is subject to some analogous urges. But the therapeutic purpose of the psychiatrist is to enable the patient himself to identify in his unconscious the nature and cause of his sickness and thereafter cut himself loose from it. There is no predetermined inevitability about the persistence of the illness, and only a charlatan psychiatrist would try to convince his patient that there was.

Yet sociologists and other social scientists, who can at their best perform an invaluable service through the study of communities and institutions – in some respects analogous to the psychiatrist's service to the individual – frequently go beyond measurement and extrapolation to allege the existence of 'inevitable trends'. Sometimes, it is true, these seem to amount to little more than a statement of the trends which the particular writer would welcome; but often the proposition is based on a supposedly scientific prediction of how men in the mass will behave. Now it is one thing to say that X has happened before and that therefore – other things being equal – it may well happen again. It is quite another to assert that men *will always* behave in a certain way because of their psychic and social conditioning.

One can accept – again with some reservations – that what a man is has been determined in large measure by his heredity and by the environment in which he has grown up. This theory has, however, only a very limited application to a social community. The attempt to apply it, which is at the root of the increasing modern preoccupation with 'inevitable' trends, is exceedingly dangerous. First, under the guise of providing data and guidance for politicians, it ultimately involves the stultification and even renunciation of political action. Secondly, there is the hideous danger that false prophecies may become self-fulfilling.

The tendency to reduce a human community to a system of statistics not only paralyses political thought but makes its own contribution to the build-up of a 'mass' psychology. Individual men can *act*; mass society can only *behave*. The more this 'behaviour' is analysed, documented and – above all – predicted, the more likely it is to become the norm. The social scientists did not create the mass society, but they have contributed abundantly to the passive acceptance of its encroachments on the lives and responsibilities of individuals and families.

Those who think in terms of 'society as a whole', and

purport to perceive system and inevitability in social processes, may propagate their theories so convincingly that the processes actually begin to acquire a kind of permanence, suggesting inevitability. The menace of behaviourism lies less in the unsoundness of the theory than in the possibility that it can be made to come true. If men lose the capacity to act, then there is nothing left to them but social behavour, and this behaviour will be on its way to being totally conditioned. What is even worse, the conditioning will in the end be done by those who have a vested interest in particular patterns of behaviour – whether it is the financial interest of the purveyors of a materialistic 'way of life' or the convenience of a tidy-minded administrator.

We should beware, then, of the modern heresy of accepting social or economic processes and trends as 'inevitable'. The term is encountered in discussions of anything from equality, culture and higher education to inflation, automation and factory farming. Some of the trends discussed may be desirable, others deplorable; some are likely to continue, others are less likely; some can be quicky and easily reversed, others altered only with great difficulty and by a supreme effort of men's will. None is irrevocably predetermined.

It is, of course, necessary to be alert if one is to distinguish between the different senses in which the concept of inevitability is presented, and between the different motives of those who advance it. There are those who call a trend 'inevitable' simply because they like it, and want to persuade others that it ought to continue. Others are in effect saying, '*We* don't see how this trend can be arrested, therefore presumably it can't'. Others again have been genuinely misled by the apparent logic of determinist theories, because they are unable to appraise objectively the validity of the data and techniques of the social scientists; they are akin to the man who has swallowed a 'theory of history'. Some are simply suffering from a surfeit of half-comprehended and ill-digested Marx: to them it is legitimate to point out that it is precisely in those areas where Marx predicated inevitability that his theories have been shown by events to be obviously wrong.

The worst menace of all is the man who shakes his head sadly and says, 'This trend is no doubt deplorable, but of course it's inevitable.' The danger lies in the fact that this is a kind of perversion of a legitimate proposition. It is one thing to say (as did all the best Old Testament prophets), 'If we go on doing X, then the inevitable consequence will be Y'; it may be possible to justify this contention. But the man who alleges that a 'deplorable' trend is nevertheless 'inevitable' is nearly always saying in effect, 'Y, which is deplorable, is the inevitable consequence of continuing to do X: I am not prepared to stop X, therefore Y is inevitable.'

It is remarkable how often today this fallacious syllogism can be discerned as implicit in the elliptical statement that something is 'inevitable'. Hideous, soulless, standardised housing estates are inevitable – i.e. cheaper and less trouble to design and build, and who cares anyway? Increasing centralisation of control and administration is inevitable – i.e. only too often, I am at the centre.

The French philosopher Jacques Ellul, whose book *The Technological Society* appears at first sight to comprise the most rigorously deterministic thesis, puts the matter admirably in perspective at the outset.

> I have tried to perform a work of sociological reflection, involving analysis of large groups of people and of major trends, but not of individual actions. I do not deny the existence of individual action or of some inner sphere of freedom. I merely hold that these are not discernible at the most general level of analysis, and that the individual's acts or ideas do not *here and now* exert any influence on social, political, or economic mechanisms. By making this statement I explicitly take a partisan position in a dispute between schools of sociology. To me the sociological does not consist of the addition and combination of individual actions. I believe that there is a collective sociological reality, which is independent of the individual. As I see it, individual decisions are always made within the framework of this sociological reality, itself pre-existent and more or less determinative. . . . We are dealing with collective mechanisms, with relationships among collective movements, and with modifications of political or economic structures. . . . It is not possible for me to treat the individual sphere. But I do not deny that it exists.[2]

This is then precisely qualified:

> If we may not speak of laws, we may, at any rate, speak of repetitions. If we may not speak of mechanisms in the strict sense of the word, we may speak of interdependencies. There is a certain logic (though not a formal logic) in economic phenomena which makes certain forecasts possible. This is true of sociology and, to a lesser degree, of politics. . . . An extrapolation is perfectly proper and scientific when it is made with care. . . . But it never represents more than a probability, and may be proved false by events.[3]

Finally, the crucial point is made beautifully clear:

> The reader may be inclined to say that, if everything happens as stated in the book, man is entirely helpless – helpless either to preserve his personal freedom or to change the course of events. . . . I would reverse the terms and say: if man – if each one of us – abdicates his responsibilities with regard to values; if each of us limits himself to leading a trivial existence in a technological civilisation, with greater adaptation and increasing success as his sole objectives; if we do not even consider the possibility of making a stand against these determinants, then everything *will* happen as I have described it, and the determinants *will* be transformed into inevitabilities.[4]

And again:

> If an increasing number of people become fully aware of the threat the technological world poses to man's personal and spiritual life, and if they determine to assert their freedom by upsetting the course of this evolution, my forecast will be invalidated.[5]

This seems to me to get as near the truth of the matter as it is possible to get. Men's actions and behaviour are very largely influenced, but not wholly determined, by the social framework within which they live. The determinants are *not* 'inevitabilities', however likely it may now seem that a particular trend will continue. A trend can be upset by the resolute action of a sufficient number of people. (But they must first, of course, be convinced that the trend they are opposing is not 'inevitable'.)

What would be the motives behind such a revolt? Is it not clear, in the particular hypothetical case postulated by Ellul, that they would be entirely philosophical? In order to make this stand, people would be explicitly grounding themselves on certain philosophical assumptions. Ellul is thus not merely asserting the continuing relevance of philosophy, but placing it in opposition to the sociological determinants. Indeed, he is saying that *action*, grounded on a philosophy, may be the only hope of avoiding the logical consequences of dangerous social trends.

This is surely right. In the last resort, what is there that can withstand the pressures of the social determinants, and even provide a substitute for them, except the will of a sufficient number of individual men and women? To maintain that this is impossible, on the ground that men's wills are themselves wholly determined, is to deny not only the relevance of philosophy and politics but the very possibility of their existence. Even if this were not manifestly absurd, a contradiction of nearly all the wisdom of the ages, it would still be necessary to reject it out of hand. To deny the possibility of effective political action towards ends chosen on ethical grounds is to deny the human spirit. It means abandoning not only politics but hope.

Political philosophy is not precisely an alternative to sociology, any more than it has been effectively supplanted by it. It is a necessary counterpoise, for it represents the denial of the universality and sufficiency of sociology. It stands for the insistence that there are ethical ends in politics, with which no science can be concerned, and that rational Man is neither wholly determined nor incapable of moral choices. To this conviction we must return and hold fast.

We have seen that it is now not unreasonable to say that Man, while still very young, is to all intents and purposes immortal. He has survived, and will survive, civilisations and societies. The determinant social pressures on men and women today are not the same as those that impinged on men and women in previous social communities, yet Man today is still essentially the same being that he was before the 'society' of today evolved. There is something of him and in him that survives and persists undetermined and unconditioned.

The other persistent factor that survives civilisations and

societies, not unchanged but essentially the same over long periods of time, is Man's natural environment. This is subject to alteration by more or less predictable long-term climatic changes, and it can also be substantially affected – even corrupted – by Man himself. But if we are looking for the elusive certainty we have lost, we have here at least two enduring permanencies. On these, then, we might do worse than try to ground a philosophical attitude.

We have to make some assumptions about the nature of Man if we are to deal in politics at all. We cannot set out to discover and influence the nature of human communities without some assumptions about the nature and motives of men and women. This seems obvious and trite enough when the proposition is posed in those terms; yet when precisely the same proposition is phrased in another way, asserting that political action must be based on a philosophy which is itself grounded on some assumptions of metaphysics and ethics, it is not nearly so readily accepted. Yet the two propositions are to all intents and purposes identical.

Every political philosopher who had anything useful to say has had to make some metaphysical and ethical assumptions; indeed, most of them found it necessary to construct their own systems before they could venture into political philosophy at all. Moreover, what they had to say about political philosophy was seldom intended to represent a mere abstract theoretical exercise; they set out to provide a guide to political action, and some of them powerfully influenced practical politicians over several generations. Thus political action had a metaphysical and ethical basis, even if sometimes this basis represented little more than an attempt to understand and explain in systematic terms the facts of life as they presented themselves to an observer at the time.

The difference between this process and the determinist system-building of social scientists today is concerned with the making of ethical choices about ends. If the behaviour of men and women is wholly conditioned by their heredity, upbringing and social environment, then the social scientists should ultimately be able to predict their behaviour fairly precisely. Their behaviour in the mass should be predictable with certainty, while the behaviour of individuals and small groups will be predictable in certain circumstances. Now obviously, given the assumptions, it follows that the behaviour can be deliberately influenced and changed in the future by altering the determinant conditions now. Nor will this be only a matter of changes deliberately made in social organisation and in the human environment; the time is coming when it will be possible to influence the determinants of heredity as well. The question is who will decide on the changes to be made, and on what factors they will base their decisions.

Let us be clear as to what kind of decisions these will be. They will be decisions about how people shall be conditioned to behave. No doubt they will purport to be based on information which itself purports to show what the majority of people (or the 'average' person) *wants* to do. But the action taken to change the conditions determining future behaviour will not be taken (except in very exceptional circumstances) as a result of a conscious and deliberate decision made explicit by a majority of people. It will not be in any real sense a political act, and certainly not a democratic action. It will no doubt be taken by people who are convinced that the change will be for the good of the majority and that it will in the long run make them 'happier'; it will in any case involve a conditioning process designed to make them *feel* happier.

Since it will be the social scientists who have established the causal link between determinant conditions and behaviour and made the predictions, they will be the experts who pronounce what changes must be made to ensure a particular pattern of future behaviour. As to what the 'desired' behaviour pattern shall be that is selected for them to produce, a number of interests will seek to influence the decision. These interests will fall roughly into three groups. There will be the economic interests, anxious to influence the behaviour of people as consumers and as workers, and to influence it in the direction of behaviour that is convenient to the productive techniques of industry and predictably conducive to steady economic growth. There will be the administrators, equally anxious to eliminate variations and unpredictability, and equally anxious to secure behaviour convenient to the requirements and limitations of their own techniques. Finally, there will no doubt still be a (probably diminishing) body of ideologues, dedicated to the fruitless task – fruitless because the ruling determinist ideology will have rejected their assumptions – of seeking to bring about an 'ideal' pattern of behaviour which takes no account of the 'necessities' of the other two groups of interests.

It may be that the men who finally decide, after being subjected to the pressures of these interests, that certain changes shall be made in social organisation to produce a selected pattern of behaviour among the mass of the people, will still be men who could be reasonably described as 'politicians' and would in some sort be recognised by us as conforming to what we now mean by the word. But their politics will be of a very restricted kind. It will be hard for them to think of the people whom they govern as in any meaningful sense individual human beings. Their metaphysics will be limited to the conviction that Man is a conditioned being whose determinant conditions they themselves can manipulate – a conviction which probably no man could entertain and remain uncorrupted. And if it be argued that they will be making genuinely ethical choices in deciding, under conflicting pressures from different interests, what future behaviour patterns shall be preferred and imposed, it must be retorted that these choices would be ethical only in an impossibly restricted utilitarian sense.

To anyone who believes that ethics must be concerned, *inter alia*, with the moral principles by which conduct is regulated, it must be apparent that the relevance of ethics to the whole situation is minimal. For the people whose conduct is ultimately in question are deemed to be incapable of making any moral choices of their own, with or without reference to principles. Their conduct is to be, by and large, determined by the manipulators of their social environment and organisation. If both ethical motivation and political action are to be, by definition, the monopoly of the manipulating élite, then not only moral and political philosophy but politics themselves can have little meaning. Moreover, *quis custodiet ipsos custodes*? By what forces will *they* have been conditioned? and if they are conditioned, can they be capable of making ethical choices?

It may be objected by some that, so far from discussing a

hypothetical dilemma of the future, I am simply describing in somewhat exaggerated terms the situation that exists today. This is not so. Political decisions are not at present of the kind I have been discussing, and to imagine that they are is to take altogether too mechanistic a view of life – or too pessimistic, according to the viewpoint. Even if sociological techniques were good enough to permit the accuracy of analysis and forecasting required – which at present they are not – it would still be necessary to accept the theory of the relationships involved. And, while it is still possible that this could one day turn out to be a 'self-fulfilling prophecy', it seems to me impossible to accept this deterministic relationship in its entirety at the present time.

If this is so, then it is necessary to find another set of relationships; and these must be based, as we have noted before, on certain assumptions concerning the nature of Man. Man is the product and the 'leading shoot' of a process of evolution, and what marks him off from the other animals is the gift of conscious reflection which at some stage developed in him. Man is a rational being, capable of working things out by a process of reasoning. This remains true, despite frequent examples of 'irrational' behaviour by individual men and women. To maintain that all behaviour is determined by the individual's previous conditioning – whether the behaviour appears 'rational' or 'irrational' – is to reduce the faculty of reasoning to nothing. Apparently irrational behaviour may be the result of subnormal intelligence or mental illness, so that the reasoning faculty is either undeveloped or impaired; but it may also be preceded by rational calculation. What cannot be accepted is that reasoning is no more than a mechanical process which automatically converts previous conditioning into current and future behaviour. We can easily allow that heredity, environment and upbringing can cause the reasoning faculty to be more highly developed and refined in some individuals than in others; that they can lead different individuals to use the process in different ways; that they can cause some people to come to apparently more 'sensible' conclusions than others; and that they can have a marked effect on the propensity of the individual to *act* in accordance with, or in opposition to, the reasoned conclusions he has come to. If a man uses his reasoning process to work out what seems to him a sensible course of action and then – as most of us do at some time or another – does something quite different, which is it that is conditioned and determined? his reason, or his actions? Surely they cannot both be determined by the same factors?

The most sensible summary seems to me to be that of a contemporary philosopher who concludes that 'human beings, in addition to having natural propensities, inclinations, instincts, or desires and in addition to behaving in ways which result from the conditioning of these, can also act *after and in accordance with deliberation*'. He adds that 'human beings inherit a system of working out what is the best course of action open to them and also the ability to follow the results so obtained (the will), even when this means acting contrary to the strongest felt desire'.[6]

In other words, Man is a rational being, capable of making and acting upon rational decisions. If we accept this, we may be able to get somewhere; if we do not, then there is little point in anything and no point at all in politics. It is impossible even to evolve a social or economic policy without an assumption as to whether men and women are capable of making rational decisions and choices; but if we decide to assume that they are, then it is possible to follow certain lines of policy that would be meaningless on the contrary assumption. Indeed, it is more than possible: it is almost inescapable.

Similarly, it is hard to see how we can plan policies for maintaining law and order, or for organising education, without some firm assumptions about men's moral responsibility and capabilities. Here again it is not a question of arriving at conclusions which we can absolutely prove to be correct, but of finding the most reasonable assumptions on which to base political action. We can, if we choose, reject the whole concept not only of the spiritual element in Man but of any rational or moral element in his nature. That this rejection seems to me repugnant to instinct, reason and common sense is not to deny that it is intellectually possible. What I do maintain is that the deterministic behaviourism which this assumption implies is incompatible with politics, which involve deliberate action taken to achieve ends which have been consciously chosen in accordance with ethical considerations. If, therefore, we believe that men and women are essentially rational beings rather than conditioned automata, we must believe that the political process defined above is more likely to meet their essential needs than a system that relies on determining their behaviour by allowing sociologists to manipulate their environment and social institutions.

Let us then follow those modern philosophers who have begun to take a fresh interest in ethics, and assume as a working hypothesis that if Man is a rational being he is also a moral one. Let us accept the reasonable proposition that men and women are capable of making moral choices on grounds that are at least partly rational, and neither wholly emotional nor wholly conditioned.[7] If this assumption be made, it seems only reasonable to answer in the affirmative an important series of questions we posed in Chapter 4. We can now, therefore, phrase them in the form of statements.

If men and women are capable of rational judgements, they will be likely to be more responsible, and to behave more sensibly, if their innate intelligence has been carefully cultivated and if they have been taught to exercise the faculty of judgement in a logical way. This at least gives us the beginnings of a rationale of education; but the next stage in the argument is even more suggestive. It must surely follow, if we have men and women capable of making informed choices, that we ought to go to some trouble to give them access to the data necessary to make informed choices. Moreover, there is at least a case for saying that we should give them as many opportunities as possible to make effective choices for constructive purposes.

Now this may not seem a very original theme on which to base a political philosophy, and indeed it is not. Nevertheless, it is one that has never been wholly accepted, and certainly one that has never been consistently followed through in practice. Conservatives, having acquired a rather muddled modicum of *laisser-faire* theory with the Liberals who joined them in the 19th and 20th centuries, frequently talk about freedom of choice and the importance of the individual. Yet

Tory philosophers, suspicious of the taint of Liberal rationalism, have tended to mutter uneasily about Original Sin. Being convinced that fallen Man is not capable of attaining perfection, they have been afraid of the logical consequences of admitting that he can be encouraged and assisted to achieve significant improvement. The Liberal individualists themselves, once committed to a system of economic *laisser-faire* which required a 'communistic fiction' to make it hang together even in theory, inevitably ended with 'society as a whole', in which the individual was sunk without trace. In any case, the working of the *laisser-faire* economic system in practice gave the vast mass of the people very little freedom of choice about anything – a fact which Marx was not the first to note. Those rationalist Liberals who finally evolved and adhered to a theory of socialism rejected the idea of free individual choices affecting the nature and pattern of society, preferring the concept of a fabricated ideal society designed to create ideal living conditions for the individual. Finally, of course, there was no place for creative individual choice in the theories and systems of the Marxists and other determinists.

It does not seem to me to be either necessary or helpful at present to become involved in discussions about theories of sovereignty. If we are concerned with the freedom of choice of individual men and women, and determined to give them every possible opportunity to exercise choice effectively and constructively, then we shall want a system of government which leaves them as free as possible to plan their own lives. At the same time, where communal and corporate activities are necessary to provide services which the individual cannot provide for himself, we shall tend to prefer the smaller organisation or agency to the larger, and try to keep the decision-making body as close as possible to the individuals in whose interests the decisions are being made. Since direct democratic government is seldom, if ever, possible in a populous country, we accept the principle of representative government at every level. In the last resort, it does not matter very much whether we say that the Queen in Parliament is sovereign or that the people is sovereign. In fact, each has a limited sovereignty of a different kind. Parliament can make laws which the people must obey; but in the last resort the people can change the Government and insist on the laws being altered.

We have seen in earlier chapters that a system of political philosophy, to be useful, must take account of existing relationships and be capable of explaining what is already happening, rather than simply setting forth an ideal to be aimed at. We have also seen that much of what is happening is the result of changes in relationships deliberately brought about or unconsciously acquiesced in under the influence of deterministic theories which are in a sense a denial of political philosophy. Unlike theories that have been influential in the past, some of these appear to be capable of being self-fulfilling. Once 'society' comes to be seen as a self-regarding entity on its own, with an increasingly powerful State as its agency, the pressures making for the diminution of individual choice and responsibility are bound to become steadily greater unless the trend is reversed and the myth destroyed. Not only does the cult of 'society as a whole' destroy the importance and autonomy of the little local groups and communities through which men and women were able both to express their individuality and to exercise some control over their immediate environment; the whole process is intensified by the fact that new generations are brought up and educated to become conformist members of a society which is itself the determining factor of their lives, rather than something to be critically assessed and shaped to the ends of its component members.

Once we begin to look at community life from the opposite viewpoint – that is to say, with the object of creating conditions in which individual men and women can enjoy the maximum independence and exercise the maximum of personal choice – then it becomes clear that many of the economic and social trends that have become accepted are in reality incompatible with our objectives. A number of things begin to fall into place. The progressive encroachments of industrial and administrative technique can be seen for what they are and for what they are becoming. As Jacques Ellul says in *The Technological Society*, 'at the present, neither economic nor political evolution conditions technical progress.

. . . The converse is actually the case . . . . Technique elicits and conditions social, political and economic change. It is the prime mover of all the rest, in spite of any appearance to the contrary and in spite of human pride, which pretends that man's philosophical theories are still determining influences and man's political regimes decisive factors in technical evolution. . . . Technique has become a reality in itself, self-sufficient, with its special laws and its own determinations'.[8]

From the point of view of technique, as Ellul says, 'the individual is a brake on progress'. Man 'is a source of error . . . ceaselessly tempted to make unpredictable choices'. There is therefore continual pressure to eliminate, as far as possible, not only the risk of human error but the element of unpredictability involved in individual choice. Essentially the same impulse is behind the automation of industrial processes, the 'planning' of the economy, the management of consumer demand and the socialisation of what were traditionally the responsibilities of individuals and families. Exactly the same intention lies behind the pressure to enlarge the size of administrative units, since this is intended to eliminate the variety and unpredictability involved in the existence of a large number of smaller units enjoying some measure of autonomy.

In each case the motive alleged is the achievement of greater 'efficiency', and the planners hold out the promise that the results will be more satisfactory to the individual. Automation cuts out hard and unpleasant work; socialisation of welfare services provides greater security and better health services, etc., for the people; larger local government units can provide more and better services of all kinds. It is even alleged that the result of all this is to give *greater* freedom of choice to the individual. But the process involves conditioning people to make the choices convenient to the planners, and a considerable degree of persuasion to convince them that they are happy.

If we believe, however, that men and women are rational beings, capable of rational and moral choices, it makes little sense to suppose that this unique and potentially satisfying faculty evolved in Man in order to be artificially suppressed. To argue that the 'socialisation' of men's decisions is actually a natural stage in evolution is specious and misleading. This is not the same as the possibility, mentioned in Chapter 4, of a development involving the evolution of some psychic blending of men's minds and wills, so that a genuinely 'common will' was at work in the ordering of men's affairs. What we are here discussing is something very different. The decisions which affect not only men's environments but an increasing proportion of the details of their lives are being made by fewer and fewer people, and these increasingly remote from the individuals and communities affected by the decisions. The exercise of choice is being increasingly limited; and the faculties of decision and choice can actually begin to atrophy if they are left too long to 'fust in us unused'.

If these faculties are an essential, and indeed unique, attribute of Man, then it must at least be a matter of concern if their use is being deliberately suppressed. Indeed, what is happening is the suppression – almost the attempted abolition – of an essential part of Man's humanity. Man would in fact be less than human if he became what the determinists believe he is and what the apostles of technique intend he should become. It should, then, be a part of our therapeutic philosophy to insist that it must be considered an end in itself to restore and encourage, wherever possible, the opportunities for freedom of choice. Since it seems logical to suppose that men and women will use their reason more constructively if they are given the opportunities to use it for constructive purposes, they will actually become more complete – and in a sense 'better' – human beings if the opportunities and encouragement are provided. In practice, then, we should always tend to lean towards the systems and methods which provide and encourage the maximum of individual and local decision and freedom of choice. And this will be particularly important when what is at stake is the control and development of the environment in which men and women live. If it be objected – as it always is – that this will reduce 'efficiency' and actually militate against the 'welfare' of the individual, it must be answered that 'efficiency' can be bought at too high a price, and that freedom and independence are essential constituents of human welfare. They are essential to confidence, which is vital.

We are of course still very far from having established anything like a complete philosophical basis for future political action. All we have done is to suggest a yardstick by which the merits of certain alternative courses of action may be measured. The position we have reached is not that of the abstract individualist, despite our rejection of the current notion of 'society'. What we have rejected is not the belief that human communities and societies are 'natural' institutions and essential to the fulfilment of the individual's life and personality, but the abstract concept of 'society' as an end in itself. In particular, we are forced to reject the idea of 'society' as a sociological concept purporting to represent common behaviour patterns and to be capable of automatous action.

The vast and intricate complex of interconnected and interacting ideas, relationships and institutions which can be called our 'society', but should perhaps rather be called our civilisation or culture, is something very different from the abstract construct of the statisticians. We cannot deny that it does, and must, to a considerable extent condition and determine the beliefs and actions of individual men and women; for it provides not only the framework within which their reason is exercised, but the corpus of tradition and experience which includes most of the data upon which rational decision will be based. To the extent that we recognise, as in large measure we must, that this civilisation is built up on the slow deposit of centuries of social evolution, so that each generation accepts and builds on much that it has not itself willed or planned (and of which it may not even be consciously aware), we take up a position nearer to that of the British school of empirical philosophers than to that of the pure rationalists. In particular, we must recognise that something so complex, intricate and slowly evolved that no individual or group of individuals could ever have devised and planned it at any given time as an abstract exercise of reason, cannot successfully be radically re-planned and reorganised as a whole by any group of individuals at a particular moment.

At the same time we must be alert to perceive the dangers implicit in the empirical approach. While it preserves us from the unreality of radical utopianism and the collectivist authoritarianism of ideologues, it offers great temptations to determinist social scientists to erect more solid structures than the philosophical foundation can bear. The empirical approach holds out the promise that the structure of society and the complex of civilisation can be analysed and 'understood' through appropriate methods and techniques. It would, of course, be absurd to deny that this is to some extent true, or that much that is useful may emerge from the study of institutions and of human behaviour. Nevertheless, just as it is true that 'the result of the experimentation of many generations may embody more experience than any one man possesses',[9] it is easy for the enthusiastic analyst to imagine that he has fully comprehended something when in fact he has not. Existing techniques are not necessarily either appropriate or sufficiently refined to permit accurate analysis of very complex relationships, nor are techniques generally adequate substitutes for the perception of genius. Just as the physical scientists have shown themselves apt to deliver confident verdicts which were subsequently proved to have involved a total inability to foresee the secondary effects of primary reactions, so the social scientists are not yet equipped to comprehend the most complex relationships or to predict the far-reaching secondary effects of particular social changes.

Dangerous as it is for rationalist radicals to imagine that they can improve the quality of our lives by replanning our institutions and relationships in accordance with an abstract ideal system, it can be almost equally dangerous for empirical students of 'society' to claim to be able to guide the development of institutions and other determinants of social life in accordance with the results of an analysis which may be either superficial or actually inaccurate. But this is not to say that there will never be occasions when deliberate and positive action of this kind may be possible and beneficial. That would be to restrict the field of political choice and action too drastically. It would be as futile to reject the benefits of the limited discoveries and insights of political and social science as to rely too confidently on their infallibility.

Reasonable men, with a proper ration of humility, recognise that the millennium is still quite a long way off; this makes them sceptical about the possibility of taking short cuts to it. It is as well to distrust – or at the least to keep a very wary eye on – people who purport to know the answers to questions which reason and experience tell us may be more complex than the answers seem to suggest. This applies not only to utopian radicals and determinist planners, but to scientists and technologists as well – in fact especially to them, since they can do more harm to Man and to his environment.

There are clearly dangers in too doctrinaire an approach to political philosophy, from whatever angle the approach is made. We have considered the dangers of radical rationalism and also of building too much on an empirical foundation. There are dangers also in the 'evolutionary' approach. It is true that the civilisation and culture which provide the framework for our social living have evolved gradually and in a sense spontaneously; certainly they have not been imposed by any deliberate decision or plan. It is tempting to conclude, as many liberals do, that we need only refrain from meddling and allow the process of social evolution to continue, in the conviction that it will adapt itself to changing needs more closely and smoothly than could be achieved by any deliberate intervention in the process. It is probably true, too, that the results would be preferable to those brought about by massive intervention of the kinds proposed by enthusiastic ideologues. The objection is simply that it is impossible in practice. Even the liberals who believed most passionately in the theory very soon found themselves involved in contradictions and compromises. Even if you decide to set no positive ends for political action, it is impossible under a democratic system of government to abstain from all intervention to remove or mitigate social evils and grievances. Once the process is begun, there can be no theoretical limits to it; at any rate, the original theory of non-intervention is soon discarded.

Nor is it possible to sustain a purely 'conservative' attitude. However wise it may be to regard the wisdom and experience of the ages with respect, and to deprecate the casual destruction of standards, habits and institutions evolved through long experimental trial and error, it is hard to find any theoretical answer to the question: what must we conserve, and what must we allow to change? To be afraid of all change is to deny the fact of evolution and to face the inevitable consequences of stagnation. To attempt only to slow down and moderate change may be to get the worst of all worlds. Just as the liberal is at the mercy of change, liable to be swept on by any passing fashion or ephemeral trend, so the moderate conservative is apt to be dragged along protesting behind it. His foot may be on the brake, but his hand is not on the steering wheel.

It is easier then, to see what we should not accept than what we should; but this is commonly the way with politics, and at least it is better than total agnosticism. Blind and exclusive adherence to any one of the philosophical theories advocated in the last 400 years would be excessively dangerous: each of them, if persisted in to its logical extremity without regard for what is valid in the others, could do us more harm than good. Yet each of them contains some valid insights, and each offers some useful suggestions for policy and action.

Rational Man, capable of intelligent decision and moral choice, has a potential which is superior to that allowed to the 'Organisation Man', the conditioned Social Science Man, or the manipulated puppet Man dreamed of by the apostles of technique. It follows, however, if he is to develop this potential and avoid the degradation of his reason, that he cannot afford to be a complete Rationalist in politics. For politics are not a technique, nor can technique prescribe rules for political action. 'Rationalist politics', observes Michael Oakeshott, 'are the politics of the felt need, the felt need not qualified by a genuine, concrete knowledge of the permanent interests and direction of movement of a society, but interpreted by "reason" and satisfied according to the technique of an ideology.'[10] Most political problems do not admit of 'solutions', in the accepted sense of the word at all. The mischief of the modern all-pervasive influence of Rationalism in politics is that it has frozen political thought in the naive categories of the schoolroom. If something – whether it be the balance of payments or the prevalence of crime – is described by the newspapers as a 'problem', then it is assumed that there must be a 'solution' to it which can be inscribed by authority on the blackboard and remain uniquely correct.

The real danger of this is not that it gives the Marxists, or the political opportunists and charlatans, an electoral advantage, but that it tends to stultify genuine political debate and encourage ill-considered action. There is a correct solution to an algebraic problem; not only will it remain correct, but the consequences of adopting it can be accurately predicted. Political 'problems' demand, in addition to adequate information and careful analysis, a clear definition of the end to be achieved (which will be prescribed by ethical as well as material considerations) and a balanced judgement between alternative means.

Moreover, again contrary to rationalist conviction, no political decision – no 'felt need' – can be isolated and dealt with on its own by the pure light of reason brought to bear like a spotlight uniquely on this one problem. It has to be dealt with in its context, which is to say in all its immensely complex relationships with everything else, in the past, the present and the future. It is this 'context', which involves an awareness of history and tradition as well as of the whole feeling and texture of the contemporary situation, which the rationalist tends contemptuously to ignore, if not deliberately to reject as a positive hindrance to action.* However, even if the decision is approached with all these factors in mind, the immediate and secondary effects of the action to be taken can generally be predicted only on a basis of probability; in few cases will there come a time when it can be said with certainty that the action taken was 'right'. To know this is the essential beginning of political wisdom. The art of politics, then, can be usefully practised only within the framework of a tradition, and it requires instincts and insights which can be acquired only by experience; for the rest, it is a matter of knowledge, morality and disciplined intellectual judgement.

Now one of the crucial difficulties of the present time, and one that is desperately dangerous for politics, is that the tradition within which politics have worked has been seriously weakened and compromised. Two things seem to have been primarily responsible for this. The first is that the pace and

* 'Only those who hold the past in complete contempt,' said Dr. Edmund Leach in his 1967 Reith Lectures, 'are ever likely to see visions of the New Jerusalem.'[11]

volume of innovation have created a discontinuity which makes it extraordinarily hard to discern what Michael Oakeshott calls 'the permanent interests and direction of movement of a society'. The second is that rationalism has bitten so deep into the thinking and attitudes of all the political parties that the manipulation of technique and the deliberate reshaping of institutions to achieve a desired end have come to seem the normal (if not the sole) mode of politics. This is quite incompatible with either an evolutionary theory of political change or the valid conservative recognition that 'the greater part of what we have is not a burden to be carried or an incubus to be thrown off, but an inheritance to be enjoyed'.[12] A rationalist approach to politics is itself part of our political tradition (and indeed, as I have argued in Chapter 3, a very important part); but it is far from constituting the whole of it. As Samuel Butler said, 'reason, uncorrected by instinct, is as bad as instinct uncorrected by reason'.[13] He might have added that even both together can be dangerous unless they are backed by a corpus of available relevant knowledge and the wisdom and humility to use it. All these things, acting together within an institutional framework slowly evolved throughout a long history, are a part of our political tradition.

It is right that the rationalist should be heard in politics, for it is necessary that there should be someone to assert that the human reason, sometimes transcending its biological and social determinants, must be allowed to question both the assumptions and institutions of tradition and the determinist assumptions of historians and sociologists. Yet he must not be left unchallenged, for the rationalist is apt to try to impose his own perceptions (which he considers to be uniquely valid) on others, who may be perfectly open to persuasion by rational argument but still be moved by a sound instinct that too rapid and radical change may have secondary effects which are dangerously disturbing over wider fields than the rationalist has imagined.

It is right that the empirical social scientist should be heard in politics, for it is necessary that someone should study how and why institutions have developed and question whether they are still adequately fulfilling a useful function. Yet his conclusions must always be open to question, no less than are the reasoned conclusions of the rationalist. It does not always follow, because an institution has gradually evolved to meet a particular need which has now given place to a new need, that it will be immediately possible for the 'scientific' student of institutions to design a 'ready-made' new institution that will adequately take the place of the old one in the new circumstances. We have already noted, too, the danger of pronouncing trends to be 'inevitable'; and this is dangerous even if the determinists are not, as the followers of Marx were, guilty of the 'uneasy slip from saying, "This is what will be," into saying, "This is what ought to be." '[14]

Because the pronouncements of these schools of thought have of late tended to become too presumptuous and have been too little questioned, it is easy for conservatives to attack them as foreign to, and forming no part of, our political tradition. This is a mistake, for they have been an integral part of our political tradition for a very long time. That they have not hitherto done the damage of which, left to themselves and unrestrained, they would be capable, is due precisely to the fact that they have been operating within the confines of this tradition. It is because the tradition has become weakened and compromised that they have recently been able to break loose from it and to threaten to establish an unhealthy dominance.

To recognise what is happening, to perceive the dangers, is only in part to understand what needs to be done. One or two things, however, are clear. If we accept that it is an essential element in Man's humanity to be capable of making rational choices and decisions that sometimes transcend his determinant conditions, then we should be chary of encouraging any tendency to narrow the range of these choices and decisions and to extend the range and potency of the determinants. This tendency is clearly visible today, and two things are mainly responsible for it. The artificial concept of 'society' is one. The increasing range and subtlety of the mass media of communication, which are capable of being used as a new form of 'conditioning', constitute the other. It is one thing to acknowledge, as a fact of life, that men and women are conditioned in large measure by their heredity, upbringing and environment: it is quite another thing to allow them to be deliberately conditioned by the conscious manipulation of a minority for ends selected by the manipulators themselves. If this is not something specifically new, at least the scale and success of the operation are unprecedented. And it is necessary to insist that this is something quite different from political persuasion; it is a technique different in kind, as well as in degree, from anything that has been hitherto known.

It is one thing to be in part conditioned by a culture and a social framework which have evolved through a long process of historical change and development. These are the result of the interaction and synthesis of many influences and of the thought and action of many thousands of people. They have emerged through the heat of many conflicts and embody the product of many compromises. The result has been accepted, sometimes consciously, sometimes implicitly, by the people operating within it. Above all, it embodies certain explicit or implicit assumptions about the ends of political action – and indeed, certain ethical assumptions about the ends of life. Nor is the danger only that the new 'conditioners' have selected their own ends for their own purposes; it is rather that some of them have dispensed with ends altogether, so that the means have become all-important. Some of them would no doubt claim that they were acting in the interests of the Benthamite principle of the 'greatest happiness of the greatest number'; as often as not, however, they have simply assumed that material prosperity and the possession of material things are equivalent to human happiness, and then sought to condition the mass of the people to believe this in their turn.

An imposed conformity, based on a conditioned acquiescence, is a poor substitute for the confidence that springs from the free acceptance of commonly agreed ends involving the possibility of constructive action. It would of course be absurd to pretend that this kind of confidence, or even the possibility of action, has ever been enjoyed by everyone in the community. Indeed, it could be argued that for many acquiescence in an imposed condition has been the common lot. Yet there *is* a difference between this and what is happening now. In the past there have always been *enough* people who were sustained by confidence and believed that what they did had some general significance. This is no longer the case.

It is necessary, then, to assert that the provision of higher material standards of living cannot be an ethical end of politics if the process involves a diminution of the status, freedom of choice and decision, or independence of action of the individual. For the preservation of the attributes which constitute the essential humanity of Man, and give him his unique status in the world, must be a higher political end than the acquisition and consumption of material things. Nor are we thinking here of the establishment of that basic minimum standard of life, the absence of which may itself prejudice the individual's humanity. As I argue in Chapter 14, the current political consensus goes far beyond this; for it assumes, not only that an adequate material standard of living is essential to the good life, but that the continual upward projection of material standards will of itself continue to make the good life even better. And this is an assertion which cannot be accepted without substantial qualification.

That the acceptance of economic growth as an end in itself is dangerous will, I hope, emerge from the argument in Chapters 10 and 11. This is not simply because it involves a confusion between ends and means, but because the pursuit of growth for its own sake inevitably involves increasing pressure on the individual – both as consumer and as worker – to conform to a pattern prescribed by the necessities of technique rather than by the conscious choice of the people themselves. It involves a conditioning process, the insidious plausibility of which is apparent in the arguments which are widely used to support the original thesis.

We are told that there is nothing essentially wrong with a system which depends for its motive power on the continuous artificial stimulation of consumption and the deliberate creation of more and more previously unfelt wants. Yet is it unreasonable to ask what age or civilisation was ever remembered with admiration and respect for the amount that its members managed to *consume*? A great age is surely one which leaves to posterity a lasting heritage of beautiful and useful things, of significant creative ideas and inspirations, while using its own people with intelligence and humanity and passing on to posterity a physical environment improved rather than damaged. And this requires that the people of that age should be inspired by a vision which goes well beyond the material things of the present.

We are told also that adoption of the material calculus of economics will enable men and women to fulfil and enrich themselves on a higher plane than the purely material. There will be more widely available art, music, foreign travel and access to the beauties of the countryside. This is perhaps the most dangerously misleading argument of all. It is not simply that 'a short visit to the U.S. is enough to convince one that wealth, competition, and free institutions provide no safeguards against the prevalence of appalling standards not only of environment in city and suburb but also in journalism and broadcasting entertainment'.[15] It is that this whole complex of inducements is offered as part of the 'package deal' of the conditioning process of technique. These things are to be *provided*, and largely on a commercial basis. The beginning of this process has already begun to pose a dangerous threat to the preservation of the countryside. It may even end by devaluing the very things it purports to exalt above the material calculus, because they come to be thought of in the same material terms.

Nor is it a valid argument that only economic growth can provide needed improvements in the welfare services. Of course a sound economic base is essential for the communal provision of these services, but a preoccupation with increasing private consumption is more likely to distort priorities so that public provision lags behind private affluence, as the United States and Australia demonstrate. We ourselves could have better hospitals now, if we wanted them enough.

It is, to put it no higher, unlikely that the malaise and the loss of self-confidence from which the British people are suffering will be relieved by an intensification of the process which has hitherto coincided with them. It is more likely that what is needed is a political philosophy which is aimed not at conditioning the individual into conformity with a prescribed pattern of behaviour, but at enlarging his independence, his choice and his scope for action. Whatever diminishes, stifles or corrupts these diminishes, stifles and corrupts the society in which he lives.

This philosophy must recognise the importance of the institution of private property, and justify it by the principle just enunciated. We should not seek to justify private property by justifying the right to unlimited private acquisition and accumulation. It may or may not be true that those who are strong enough, or clever enough – or even just rich enough – to get their hands on more and more property are likely to use it more effectively than those who were too weak or simple or poor to hang on to it. As Keynes said, 'The world is *not* so governed from above that private and social interest always coincide,'[16] and the case for private property does not rest only (or even primarily) on the useful employment of wealth. If you believe that people are important as individuals, and that their essential humanity is diminished if they are made mere ciphers in a mass society, then it is necessary to go on to enquire what are the essentials for a free, full and meaningful life. And the ancient Greeks were surely right in their conviction that full and complete citizenship is impossible without the possession of some personal property. It is the only thing which gives the individual and his family a special private space in the world, confers the necessary degree of independence and a recognisable status, and *also* brings them into a meaningful relationship with their environment and with their neighbours.

As was argued in Chapter 3, we must also accept the consequences of the belief that Man is a rational and potentially moral being. In other words, while recognising the importance of environment and upbringing in assessing degrees of culpability in wrongdoing, we reject the assertion that the criminal and irresponsible – if they are of normal intelligence – are wholly determined and free from moral guilt. If it is right to give individuals more responsibility and more scope for free choice, in the belief that this will in the long run make them more responsible and able to choose more wisely, then they must be held responsible for those actions which damage the freedom and integrity of others.

We shall wish to use the educational system much more

fully to develop the intelligence and logical faculties of judgement, to encourage individuality and critical independence, and to inculcate a recognition of the social convenience of respecting the rights and welfare of others.

We shall certainly look very carefully at the dogmatic pronouncements of the apostles of 'social justice', to see whether their claims are objectively or philosophically valid. This is discussed in Chapters 7 and 8, where the case for 'equality' is critically examined.

We shall wish to examine the underlying assumptions of our economic system with new eyes, to see whether its purported objectives make sense and whether the employment of workers conforms to the philosophical principles we have laid down.

Finally we shall consider the implications of all this in terms of party politics and their future development.

CHAPTER 6

Education for What?

But if despondency and violence are both of them forbidden to the believer in culture, yet neither, on the other hand, is public life and direct political action much permitted to him. For it is his business, as we have seen, to get the present believers in action, and lovers of political talking and doing, to make a return upon their own minds, scrutinise their stock notions and habits much more, value their present talking and doing much less; in order that, by learning to think more clearly, they may come at last to act less confusedly.

Matthew Arnold, *Culture and Anarchy*

The education of the child . . . is not directed toward some merely abstract social end. . . . One of the most important factors in the child's education . . . is social adaptation. This means that – despite all the pretentious talk about the aims of education – it is not the child in and for himself who is being educated, but the child in and for society. And the society, moreover, is not an ideal one, with full justice and truth, but society as it is. . . . And there is the danger. It makes men happy in a milieu which normally would have made them unhappy. . . . The intelligentsia will no longer be a model, a conscience, or an animating intellectual spirit for the group, even in the sense of performing a critical function.

Jacques Ellul, *The Technological Society*

Vagueness is bound to prevail when the aim of the school is no longer instruction in subjects, but education in attitudes to meet the needs of life. From the premise that life demands other qualities than learning, which is true and important, we have come to the conclusion that in a school scholastic ability and scholastic subjects are indecent and ought to be disguised.

Jacques Barzun, *The House of Intellect*

Vagueness, alas, prevails whenever anyone begins to discuss the purpose and content of education. This is possibly why politicians, who at the national and local levels of government are responsible for most of the country's schools, never do discuss it. When they are not discussing the amount of money to be devoted to education, they argue interminably about how schools should be organised. One may wonder how it is possible to decide upon an ideal organisation before making up one's mind about what is to be taught in the schools, and how, and to whom; but this presents no difficulty to politicians. In particular, it presents no difficulty to egalitarian left-wing politicians, for the simple truth is that most of them do not care a button what is taught in schools; if they did, they could not possibly attach so much importance to the *social* implications of the types of school available.

'Today,' wrote Jacques Barzun in 1959, 'the Western world . . . is headed towards mass schooling, the European half of that world making the attempt some sixty years after the United States. Our current discussion of education in America is thus of peculiar interest, because we, dissatisfied with our handiwork, are seeking to change just at the time when England, France and Germany are courageously starting to repeat our mistakes.'[1]

It is, of course, well known that the United States evolved its own version of the comprehensive, mixed-ability High School as an instrument for welding the diverse racial and social elements of an immigrant people into a single society, and that the experiment largely justified itself in the critical years. A deliberate decision was taken to sacrifice, for social purposes, certain educational requirements. Now, when the social purposes have been achieved, the educational sacrifices are felt to be too heavy, especially as they have been intensified by the egalitarian and anti-academic pedagogic theories against which Barzun inveighed so tellingly in *The House of Intellect*. For some years there has been a movement in favour of more selection, particularly in the interests of the more gifted pupils. It had not escaped the notice of educationists that even the more intelligent High School graduates in the United States tended to leave school with academic achievements anything up to two years behind those of a comparable grammar school sixth-former in England, with the result that what we should call advanced sixth-form work had to be done in the early years at university.

It was during this period, as Barzun has noted, when Americans were beginning to react against comprehensive, non-selective schooling, that pressure to abandon selection began to build up in Britain. As had been the case in the United States two generations before, the pressure was social rather than educational in its origins. There was, however, an important difference. Whereas in America there had been an obvious practical need to weld a wide variety of racial groups into a single people and nation, the pressure in Britain to abandon educational selection came from the proponents of an egalitarian ideology. Naturally enough, it has not proved easy for them to make the kind of case on grounds of practical necessity that could formerly be made in the United States. The case has been largely theoretical, and attempts to impose the theory without adequate material resources have led to serious practical inconvenience. What is much more serious, however, is that the resulting controversy has distracted attention from the content of the education itself.

We shall never be able to think straight about education, or get the practical details of organisation right, unless we have a much clearer idea of what it is that we are trying to do. This means going back to first principles and asking what we are actually trying *to do to the individual child.* Unless we are clear about this, theories about the institutional organisation of schools are worthless. It is not even enough to say that we are aiming at 'equality of opportunity'. Equality of opportunity to do what, to learn what, to *be* what?

Most answers to the question 'What is education for?' are either too vague or too narrow. It is not really very helpful to be told that the sole aim of education is to enable the child to 'fulfil himself'. And it is certainly not enough to aim at enabling him to 'earn a living'. There are people who would have us reorganise our educational system for no other reason than that our schools and colleges are turning out a smaller proportion of scientists and technologists than are those of the United States and Soviet Russia. Others talk of 'education for citizenship', or of 'character' and 'qualities of leadership'. None of these provides an adequate definition or a sufficient aim, any more than would an obsession with the passing of examinations.

American education has suffered from an excessive preoccupation with the problems of 'social living', and there is a danger that we in this country could become hypnotised by this potentially deadly illusion. The menace is far from apparent to many people, and it is worth thinking about. The nub of the problem is to be found in the quotation from Jacques Ellul's *The Technological Society* at the head of this chapter. The danger, to which American education long ago succumbed and from which it is now belatedly trying to rescue itself, is that children will be deliberately brought up to conform to the 'norms' or 'behaviour patterns' of an imperfect society, instead of being encouraged to question them and try to improve society itself. Thus the originally reasonable aim of trying to minimise the tensions of society and of the individual in society ends in the paralysis of social improvement and the alienation of society's best and most intelligent members. Hence much of the current student 'protest'.

Of course it is necessary to preserve a reasonable balance. People do have to live in some kind of social relationship with their neighbours and conform to some essential requirements of civilised living. But it is more important to build a society which will be good for the individuals in it than to mould individuals to fit into a preconceived order of society. What the individuals need is to grasp the essentials of social morality, which should be based on a conception of the rights and freedoms of others and of one's own personal responsibility to respect them. This the 'protesters' have still to learn.

Indeed, it seems to me that there are today three fundamental things that a good education must provide: a sense of individual independence; a sense of responsibility towards others; and an appreciation of quality in people, things and behaviour. To achieve this, education must concentrate *primarily* on 'the child in and for himself', and only secondarily on 'the child in and for society'.

Clearly it is of no use to turn out young people with a will to be independent unless they are provided with the equipment to secure and retain independence. This requires an education that will enable the boy or girl to earn a living, of course, but it requires something more than that. If the individual's working life is to be at all satisfying, he must be able to use his innate talents in it to the best advantage, which means that these talents must have been identified and adequately developed during the course of his education.

Our educational system makes a reasonable job of turning out boys and girls equipped to earn a living. It is, of course, far from perfect even in this respect, but its standards have been rising and may continue to do so. It is obvious that this is the first demand that will always be made on any system of education, whether publicly or privately provided, by those who pay for it. Indeed, it is probable – however earnest may be the wish to achieve the ideal of a balanced and humane education – that this preoccupation will always tend to 'distort' the curriculum. It is perfectly natural, and it would be foolish to blame unduly those who are responsible for the distortion. Time and resources are scarce, and the number of things which can be taught to intelligent children is almost limitless: there will always be a substantial number of parents, to say nothing of taxpayers and ratepayers, who believe that almost all knowledge that is not directly related to the business of earning a living is useless. Moreover, quite a lot of the rates and taxes are paid by employers, who know (or think they know) the kind of education they want their employees to have.

Indeed, it is scarcely too much to say that the requirements of employers are the most important factor in determining the school curriculum for the majority of boys and girls. (That they determine the curricula of further education almost completely is obvious.) What is taught to the academic minority in independent and grammar schools is to a much smaller extent determined by the demands of employers – or at least the influence is not direct. The determining factor here is the requirements of the universities, as expressed through the syllabuses for their entrance examinations and for the General Certificates of Education.

It is not at all easy to decide just how good or bad, on balance, is the content of the education meted out to our boys and girls – if only because there is so little agreement on what ought to be required of it. There is also the difficulty of striking any sort of an average from among schools which vary so enormously in quality and achievement. It is not easy to be sure whether the total failures are wholly, or even mostly, the fault of the schools. Where no vital spark is struck at all, is it always because the teaching is uninspired or based on the wrong principles? What impression can even a good teacher make, if in a particular school a majority of children from one social environment come to school with such a prejudice against learning more than the essential minimum required to live that they present a blank wall of boredom and incomprehension to whatever is put before them?

Yet one has seen high schools and secondary modern schools in which quality and enthusiasm are at once apparent even to the visitor. They manage to keep a good proportion of their pupils beyond the statutory leaving age, to run sizable sixth forms, and to provide successful G.C.E. courses while widening and developing the interests of the less academic children. Two things are generally apparent in each of these outstanding schools: one is the influence of an outstanding headmaster, and the other is that the school has been modelled pretty closely on grammar school lines without the rigidity which might have proved fatal for the non-academic children.

It does not follow from this that every outstandingly good county school has to be like a traditional grammar school, although in fact most of them are. Nor does it follow that the traditional grammar school is perfect, or even that it necessarily represents an ideal to be aimed at. Many of them, lacking the blessing of an inspired headmaster or headmistress possessed of both imagination and confidence, tend to be rigid and restrictive and to intensify the tensions to which their less gifted pupils are inevitably prone. Moreover, many grammar schools seem to be held too inflexibly in the grip of the examination syllabus, so that interest, imagination and breadth of thought are limited.

Despite the popular myth that English public schools are unimaginative and stuffily conventional, the best of them manage to loosen up and liberate the imagination and instinct of inquiry in boys and girls rather better than do the grammar schools. This ability is shared by those older direct grant grammar schools which are almost indistinguishable from public schools. The difference can be seen quite clearly in the questions and discussions provoked by lectures on subjects outside the academic curriculum. Those who have addressed sixth-formers in several types of school can hardly fail to notice the difference in reactions. Grammar school pupils do tend to be more costive in discussion, and less imaginative and penetrating in their questions, than those from good public schools or the larger direct grant schools. To some extent this may be due to the differences in family background, and undoubtedly the larger size of classes in the maintained grammar schools has something to do with it. But I suspect that the most important cause is the more obsessive preoccupation with the limited G.C.E. curricula, with a corresponding inability to develop the faculties of speculation and imaginative thought. Whatever the causes, the result is a deficiency of certain qualities which it should be an aim of good schooling to encourage: independence and individuality of outlook; a spirit of enquiry; freedom in self-expression; a developed critical judgement; and an awakened imagination.

It is not easy to find practical methods of dealing with these deficiencies. Undoubtedly smaller classes would mean better education, and ultimately classes will have to be made smaller; but it will be a very expensive process. Certainly we should not be satisfied with the present restrictions on curricula imposed by concentration on G.C.E. 'A' and 'O' level examinations. But it is easy to forget that the G.C.E. and its predecessors have undoubtedly been responsible for a substantial raising of average academic standards in schools. Those who talk most earnestly of the need to develop the qualities enumerated in the last paragraph are often those who are most anxious to decry the importance of academic standards – and indeed of learning itself.

There is a real dilemma here. It is easy enough to complain of the dangers of excessive competitiveness in education – and indeed in our society as a whole. It is perfectly true that competition for places in schools and universities, and for certain kinds of job, produces stresses and concentrations which are incompatible with the highest aims of education. Yet some element of competition is inevitable – and, within limits, healthy – wherever young people are being educated together. It is easy to remove an important incentive to endeavour and to acquiesce in a deliberate lowering of the standards of learning; an obsession with the psychological effects of competition can be as dangerous to education as an excessive preoccupation with competitive examinations. It is too easy to equate competition with striving, and to eliminate all incentive to strive. The temptation to make everything easy, and to lower all the heights of endeavour to the level of the uninspired, is one that simply has to be resisted.

Ideally, of course, the pupil's competition should be with *himself* rather than with others. The true measure of successful endeavour is not the accomplishments of others but one's own capacity. This is well known to all good teachers; but it is virtually impossible to eliminate all the stresses of external competition in class teaching. Moreover, individual accomplishment must be measured occasionally by some tests, or the incentive to accomplishment is weakened. There are teachers who proudly announce that they never publish examination marks, but communicate individual results privately to each pupil; they must be remarkably naive if they imagine that the pupils do not compare the results among themselves. Competition is not so easily eliminated.

One thing that is perfectly clear is that the comprehensive school is not *in itself* a solution. It removes one form of competition, but introduces fresh problems of its own. In particular, it is quite impossible to expect that individuality and independence of outlook will be properly developed in a school of anything up to 2,000 pupils.

The egalitarian purports to want only that every child should have an equal chance of a good education. In reality, his emotions do not permit him to stop there. He instinctively dislikes anything which enables some children to emerge markedly ahead of the rest. Not only does he dislike competitive tests, he also dislikes the thought of any test which some children will fail. He has a prejudice against the disciplines of academic subjects, and much prefers 'education for social living' to real learning, since it is impossible for any recognisable élite to emerge from anything so fuzzy and unmeasurable. Under the guise of a concern for the psychological effects of 'stress', he seeks to remove from the process of education anything which stretches the efforts of children and incites them to excel. In short, he wants everything made as easy for them as possible.

Of course there is no hope for any educational process based on so absurd a set of emotional prejudices. It provides no useful preparation for life as it actually is. The only possible result is to induce disappointments, frustrations and resentments when the adolescent finally has to face the realities of life. Nor is it any use pretending that a change to such an educational system will ultimately result in life being changed to fit the pattern. Even if it were possible to remove the difficulties and challenges from life, the only result could be that life would no longer be worth living.

The real problem is to make learning – real learning – interesting without making it superficial. The answer does not lie in trying to make it too easy. The first step is to convince the child that there is a real and worthwhile purpose, for *him*, in learning; only thus will most children develop a genuine eagerness to learn. To make the learning itself interesting is the second step. The chief obstacle to this is the excessive size of classes in most schools, the rigidity of the curriculum where it is determined by examination syllabuses, and the lack of inspiring teachers. There is a great deal of talk about new theories and techniques in education, but most of them tend in the same direction. Generally the idea is to get away from the inculcation of facts, and to help the children to find as much as possible out for themselves; at the same time they are encouraged to work co-operatively in groups rather than competitively. Now this theory is not without its merits, provided that its limitations are also recognised. Only too often, however, they are not; the most eager devotees seem to be convinced that they have evolved a process which will solve all the problems of education and will work equally well with all kinds of children and all academic subjects.

The new techniques have some uses, but they are far from perfect. In any case, their success will depend to a great extent on how they are used. The new language laboratory systems can show striking results in some cases; very often, however, they produce results in no way commensurate with the very heavy capital expenditure involved. The exploratory group techniques can often provide the opportunity for a genuine 'breakthrough', winning the interest and co-operation of pupils at a critical stage. But they are not necessarily the right way to get the best out of all children, nor does it follow that they can take the cleverest children far enough. The advocates of the system are, however, very often committed egalitarians, who are perfectly prepared to hold back the full development of some children's talents in order to avoid 'discouraging' the rest.

The truth is that no system of education that relies on treating all children in the same way can possibly work. Either it will fail to bring out the best in the cleverer children, or it will end by discouraging those who are less gifted. It sounds splendid to talk about 'giving every child an equal chance', but this is very far from being the same as giving every child the *best possible* chance to make the most of his talents. This is what we ought to be trying to do.

Unless this is really what we are trying to do, compulsory secondary education after the age of 14 makes no sense at all. There is everything to be said for keeping the majority of children at school until they are 16, provided that they are still willingly learning and that they are continuing to broaden their outlook and use their imagination. There are, however, some children who not only derive no benefit from remaining at school for an extra year but actually do harm, both to themselves and to the other pupils. In present circumstances, this minority of children would probably in the long run be better off if they left school and went to work at 14 or 15; not only would they probably develop into more satisfactory citizens, but they might even learn more. There would, of course, be nothing to prevent them from continuing with some kind of part-time further education.

Ideally, then, when we talk of raising the minimum school-leaving age to 16, we should be thinking in terms of raising it for perhaps 90 per cent of the school population. Most school-teachers could point to a small minority of their secondary school pupils and say with some certainty that, as things are now, not only these children but the whole school will suffer if they are retained against their will for a final year. The traditional argument against any form of exception to the rule of a universal compulsory minimum leaving age has been that there will be some ignorant, irresponsible or grasping parents who will insist on removing bright children from school to the detriment of their future prospects. This is in fact much less likely now than it used to be. Since the harsh pressure of primary poverty has been removed from most normal families, the great majority of parents are much more anxious to assure a better education to their children. In any case, there is no suggestion that the child who is capable of benefiting from an extra year at school should be made to forego it. The question is whether to force an extra year on those who will *not* benefit from it – and will probably disrupt a whole class by staying. Ideally, all boys and girls would benefit from an additional year at school: but our schools are not ideal, and it is folly to pretend that they are.

This selective release of a few bored children from a profitless bondage would be violently opposed on two quite incompatible egalitarian grounds. First it would be said that the boys and girls released were securing an unfair advantage by getting a year's start at work. Then it would be said that they were being discriminated against, and that their future prospects were being jeopardised by denying them the educational opportunities of their fellows. In fact, the two arguments cancel each other out. We might as well admit that there are some children who should be kept at school after the age of 15 only on one of two conditions. Either they should be segregated and given special treatment; or someone must somehow devise a method of capturing their interest and actually teaching them something.

Jacques Barzun quotes with approval an American professor who said simply, 'Our concern as a profession is with the liquidation of ignorance.'[2] This is of course true, although it could be argued that there is something more to it than that. There is a pretty wide area of ignorance to be liquidated, and when all the educators have done their best, a great many people will still remain ignorant about a great many things. It seems to me that there are two other tasks of equal importance which the educators must carry out. One is to make quite sure that their pupils, having learned as much as possible, are aware of the remaining areas of their ignorance.

It is much less dangerous to be ignorant and know it than to be ignorant and not know it. The other thing is to make sure that their pupils regard their own ignorance as something regrettable rather than satisfactory. People who take a smug pride in their ignorance are even more dangerous than those who are unaware of it.

The appreciation of quality, in learning, in people and in the physical environment, is bound up with this, for the appreciation of quality demands a proper humility in the observer. If the educational process is to inculcate a respect for quality, then those who are responsible for education must have a proper respect for quality in education. This means firmly disavowing the modern egalitarian pretence that all kinds of education are of equal worth and importance and that all kinds of educational institution are of equal status. A technical college, however large and however dignified by fancy names, is *not* the same as a university; and a course of further education which is designed to provide a ticket for a job is *not* of the same worth as a liberal education designed to widen the mental horizon and deepen perception. This is not, of course, to say that a thorough and well-grounded course in pure science or technology may not be of more educational value than a superficial smattering of a variety of 'liberal arts' or 'social sciences'. Depth is important.

Quality cannot be achieved by making things easy. One must strive, and strive hard, to achieve it. One must be prepared to learn, and to work, without the luxury of short cuts. But when that quality *has* been achieved, it should be recognised for what it is and respected.

The pendulum has of course swung too far. It is one thing to oppose pretentious intellectualism, but quite another thing to pretend that intellect and its cultivation do not matter. The pursuit of quality will mean that some will excel, and it is no use trying to pretend either that this will not happen or that it is wrong. Any attempt to prevent the emergence of an élite will simply mean the gradual decline of quality – in people and in thought. In the name of 'fairness', sentimentality (masquerading as 'compassion', or even as 'social justice') has gone altogether too far in softening the essential element of toughness, in education and in our society.

It is possible to overdo the insistence on toughness, and in certain ages it has been overdone. There is no real virtue in suffering for suffering's sake. But there are certain things of lasting value that cannot be achieved except by rigorous and applied effort; and there are certain standards of quality which civilisation itself requires should be maintained. The utmost toughness is required to insist that they should be maintained. In particular, it is necessary to be very tough with the egalitarians, who would abolish or lower the standards out of 'sympathy' with those who fail to measure up to them. They must simply be told that their ideals of 'social justice' are prescriptions for mediocrity or anarchy, and they must be prevented from having any control at all over the education of the young.

A society which abandons all toughness in its educational system will in the end become soft itself. What is worse, fewer and fewer people in it will have been taught to take the trouble to do anything properly or to think any problem through, with rigour, to its essence. We are some way towards this situation now. It is time to reverse the trend – to reject the theory of equality – and to proclaim, with passion, the ideal of quality.

CHAPTER 7

Social Justice and Inequality

We hold these truths to be self-evident: that all men are created equal; that they are endowed by their Creator with inalienable rights; that among these are life, liberty, and the pursuit of happiness.

Thomas Jefferson, *Declaration by the Representatives of the United States of America*

Deformed persons and eunuchs, and old men and bastards, are envious; for he that cannot possibly mend his own case, will do what he can to impair another's.

Francis Bacon, *Of Envy*

Social justice . . . is not a simple and a single ideal of society, but is an essential part of a great complex of social change for which some things may have to be sacrificed at times and which itself, in turn, may need at other times to be sacrificed for greater goods.

Kenneth E. Boulding, *Social Justice*

Social justice can be a noble ideal or a neurotic obsession. The pursuit of it may lead to great improvements in the lot of the poor and oppressed, or it may poison the whole atmosphere of a society, destroying unity and frustrating constructive energy.

It is frequently said that a society cannot function efficiently 'except on a basis of social justice'. But it is equally true (though less frequently remarked) that no society can function efficiently if its members are obsessed with a preoccupation about social justice to the exclusion of other equally important objectives. To some people, it is true, there *are* no equally important objectives; but this is the argument which, carried to its logical conclusion, would rather that all should starve in equal misery than that all should prosper though in unequal degrees.

The difficulty, of course, is that it is almost impossible to define social justice objectively. To those who are satisfied with things as they are, then things as they are are socially just. To those who are not, social justice represents something different from the existing state of affairs. But how far different? In most societies, it is possible at any given time to point out features which nearly everyone would agree are undesirable and should be changed. It is easier to recommend reforms than to describe the ideal society. It is easy to inveigh against 'gross inequalities of wealth'; but when a definition of 'gross' is sought, the only answer is that the inequalities ought to be less than they are now.

It is not to be doubted that the best society is one that is humane and reasonably (though not excessively) tolerant. But a society that is obsessed with social justice is not a healthy one, especially if there is no general agreement about what actually constitutes social justice. Apart from the fact that an excessive preoccupation with the distribution of wealth can sometimes inhibit its creation, it can produce a climate of querulous envy which is divisive and unconstructive. Moreover, the belief that 'society' ought to ensure distributive justice can lead to an increasing conviction that it is to 'society' that one should look for any improvements in one's own lot, rather than to one's own efforts.

The British people are at present in a very woolly mental state about social justice. They combine an edgy desire to assert their own 'rights' with a vague and diffuse benevolence towards their fellow men. They have neither clearly defined criteria of justice nor the slightest interest in thinking clearly about relative priorities. This is a deplorable state to be in, and it is the politicians who must bear the blame for having allowed it to develop. The desire to outbid political opponents in social welfare benefits, and an unwillingness to go beyond vague general talk about 'priorities' to the point of actually confronting the electorate with stark choices between alternatives, have caused the politicians to abandon constructive leadership in this field. It is time they resumed their proper responsibilities – for it is hard to see who else can undertake them.

Discussion about the scope and definition of social justice has for many years been largely polemical rather than objective. To the left-wing progressives R. H. Tawney's *Equality* has been a political testament for thirty-five years, and its theme has been subsequently reworked by equally partisan sociologists like T. H. Marshall and Morris Ginsberg. But Tawney's book, impressive as it may be to those who are impressed by that particular mixture of messianic moral authority and pseudo-Shavian sarcasm, is a political tract rather than a work of philosophical scholarship. As a tract for the 1930s, it had its uses. It has less that is useful to say to us today.

In an epilogue written for the 1952 edition of the book, which had been first published in 1931, Tawney quoted with approval a passage from a recent work of T. H. Marshall:

> The unified civilisation which makes social inequalities acceptable, and threatens to make them economically functionless is achieved by a progressive divorce between real and money incomes. This is, of course, explicit in the major social services, such as health and education, which give benefits in kind without any *ad hoc* payment. In scholarships and legal aid, prices scaled to money incomes keeps real income relatively constant, in so far as it is affected by these particular needs. Rent restriction, combined with security of tenure, achieves a similar result by different means. So, in varying degrees, do rationing, food subsidies, utility goods and price controls. The advantages obtained by having a larger money income do not disappear, but they are confined to a limited area of consumption.

Tawney adds, 'The consequent "enrichment of the concrete substance of civilised life" is a matter, not of opinion, but of historical fact.' It seems only too probable that rationing, food subsidies and utility goods did appear to Tawney to be an 'enrichment of civilised life'; what is remarkable is that it should not have appeared to him to be a matter on which there might be two opinions.

Let us now try to see whether we can arrive at any sensible conclusions about the nature and limitations of the concept of social justice. And perhaps the first question we ought to ask – if only because so few of those who discuss this subject ever *do* ask it – is why anyone should ever have thought it to be a meaningful concept at all.

To those who have become familiar with social justice as a fruitful subject of controversy over a whole generation, this question may sound startling or absurd. Yet it is not as silly as it sounds: and in any case, as Denis de Rougemont observed, 'it is only "silly" questions that can enlighten us; for behind whatever seems obvious lurks something that is not'.[1] What does the term mean? Does it mean a society or social order that is just, and if so how and to whom? Or does it mean a special kind of justice, to be distinguished from legal or political justice? If so, is 'justice' the right word, and why should it be 'social'? If 'social justice' is indeed a special kind of justice, what are the justiciable issues covered by it, and what justiciary is responsible for it? Is it a code that society itself is supposed to enforce? If so, what is this 'society' that is supposed to be capable of enforcing it? Is it the State? If so, why is the justice 'social', rather than legal or political?

None of these questions is particularly easy to answer immediately, and indeed it is clear that not all of those who confidently discuss social justice would answer them in the same way. Social justice means different things to different people. And in that case, is there any point in discussing it at all? Ought we simply to say that the concept is a purely subjective one, and therefore objectively meaningless? That when advocates of particular political, social or economic changes adduce the argument of social justice in aid of their claims, they are doing no more than state what they believe to be right?

This may indeed be a reasonable conclusion to come to, and it would certainly be supported by a study of the speeches and writings of some of the most passionate social reformers. Yet it would not really be very satisfactory to leave it at that. If 'social justice' is in fact no more than a meaningless cant phrase, then we ought to expose it convincingly for what it is and banish it with contempt and ridicule from the vocabulary of political controversy. This would clear the air considerably; and besides, it would not be right to allow simple people to continue to be taken in by it. If, on the other hand, there is a sense in which the concept might have some useful meaning, then we ought to try to discover what it is and seek to persuade people to limit their use of the term to this meaning. This, too, would clear the air of a great deal of irrelevant claptrap.

First, then, what do we mean by 'justice'? On this, at least, we ought to be able to reach some measure of agreement, or the whole process is futile.

In fact, it is pretty clear that by 'justice' we can mean either of two different things; in one of these senses an agreed definition is comparatively easy, in the other much more difficult and even, perhaps, impossible. In the first sense, justice is a purely formal concept; this has sometimes been called the 'regulative' aspect of justice. It assumes the existence of certain accepted rules, and is concerned only with the way in which these are applied. Thus Morris Ginsberg says, 'Justice in the broadest sense consists in the ordering of human relations in accordance with general principles impartially applied';[2] and according to Alan Gewirth, 'it involves the idea of something deserved because of conformity or correspondence to certain rules or principles'.[3]

This is pretty straightforward; and in this sense 'social' justice is hardly a meaningful concept at all. 'Society' does not lay down rules or principles and enforce them formally; this is the concern of the law. It might perhaps be said that some societies adopt an accepted moral code, and that if they do so then social 'justice' requires that they apply their sanctions of approval or odium impartially – not hounding or ostracising one individual for a breach of the code while extenuating or condoning a like breach by another. But this is clearly not what is normally meant by social justice in ordinary discussion.

The other sense of the word 'justice' has been called the 'advocative' sense. Here we are concerned not with the fair, impartial and equal application of known rules and principles, but with the content of the rules themselves. We are accustomed to the idea that justice requires that the law should be impartially applied, that all men and women should be considered equal before the law, and that no man shall act as judge in his own cause. It is perhaps possible to argue that this is all there is to justice, properly defined, and that when we go beyond this we are really dealing with notions of what is 'right' or 'fair' rather than of what is 'just'. However, this may be thought to be carrying linguistic precision too far. We do, in fact, commonly talk of laws and principles – irrespective of whether they are equally and impartially applied – as being intrinsically 'just' or 'unjust'. This is the 'advocative' sense: when we say that a law, or a social system, is 'just', we are expressing an opinion in its favour; we are in fact saying that we believe it to be right and fair. We are making a moral judgement, based on certain norms which we ourselves accept but with which others may well disagree.

There is, then, something of importance here which is more than a linguistic quibble. Our democratic society has accepted certain norms of 'regulative' justice which are no longer seriously challenged; they can be taken as established and can be referred to with confidence. They have an objective validity. But the norms of 'advocative' justice are subjective, and have no such universal validity. We ought, therefore, to be much more careful both in making and in accepting claims about 'social justice'. When someone says that 'social justice demands' a certain change, we should by no means accord the assertion the respect that would be due to an assertion of the claims of 'regulative' justice. Unless we are confident that there are certain norms of social justice which are so generally accepted as to have attained a status of objective validity, then we should treat the claim that 'social justice demands something' as no more than a personal statement of opinion about what is fair and right.

Now one has only to read the writings of philosophers from Aristotle to Aquinas and on to those of the present day to see at once that there is very considerable disagreement about the content and norms of social justice – so much disagreement, in fact, that they cannot be said to have achieved any objective validity at all. Whereas it would be very hard to find anyone in Britain or the United States who would seriously question the validity of the principle of the equal treatment of individuals by the law, there is wide disagreement about what constitutes a 'just society' and widely divergent views about equality.

In so far, then, as social justice can be said to exist at all, it is no more than a general state of mind. It could be defined either as those few basic principles on which *everyone* in a particular society could agree at a given time, or as those principles to which a *majority* can be persuaded to agree. The first definition would reduce the content of social justice to a bare minimum, but it would imply a certain objective validity; the second would allow a larger content, but it would vary with shifts of opinion and political persuasion, possessing very little objective validity at all. Social justice, as defined in the second of these two sets of terms, will always be a subject of political controversy, since there will always be egalitarian socialists and other radicals striving to widen the content of what is generally accepted as social justice and seeking to extend both the scope of communal action for social ends and the degree of equality within society. It cannot, therefore, possibly be thought of as anything in the nature of an absolute standard of justice, or indeed as having much to do with 'justice' in the strict sense, at all.

Unless the concept of social justice is to remain in its present degraded state, and to be no more than a left-wing political cry, it is necessary to see whether we can rescue anything that is worth using and making respectable as a criterion and guide to action. And if it is to have any real meaning, it must at least aspire to achieve some measure of objective validity.

This means, I believe, that we must at once reject any use of the term which implies specific relationships or *ad hoc* benefits. What we are looking for are principles of universal validity, which are, so to speak, the hallmarks of a just society.

We should not consider any form of national organisation to be just, unless it provides equal and impartial legal justice and those institutions which we consider necessary to provide political justice: that is to say, the equality of political rights which is part of the Western democratic tradition, including such things as equal voting rights, non-discrimination on grounds of colour or religion, freedom of speech and assembly, and so on. But social justice goes beyond the formal rules of legal and political justice, embracing the more informal relationships of society and its members.

It is necessary, however, always to remember that we are discussing *justice*, not benevolence, which is something quite different. I agree entirely with William K. Frankena when he says, 'Social justice is not the only feature of an ideal society.

Societies can be loving, efficient, prosperous, or good, as well as just, but they may well be just without being notably benevolent, efficient, prosperous, or good. Our problem is to define the concept of a just society, not that of an ideal society.'[4]

Plato and Aristotle maintained that justice consisted in treating equals equally and unequals unequally, the question being how to define equality and how (if at all) to limit inequality of treatment. Adequate as this proposition might have been in the conditions of the Greek city-state, it is hardly adequate to the complexity of a modern industrial society and the modern nation-state. Even as developed by Aquinas, the Aristotelian concepts of 'commutative' and 'distributive' justice do not take us far enough. What we are looking for is a set of basic principles that will tell us something about how wealth should be distributed, how merit and/or virtue should be rewarded, and what opportunities should be open to all individuals, in a just society.

We can surely start from the purely formal proposition that all men and women are equal, and should be treated equally, in one respect – their humanity. Since they are all, equally, human beings, their humanity and human dignity must be equally respected. No one should be treated as if he or she were less than human; and it is just as important to treat no one as if he were *more* than human. Again, we can surely all agree that men and women are not born equal in respect of innate intelligence at least; and it is probable that they are unequal in respect of some other innate characteristics or abilities, although there is room for dispute as to how far these differences are really innate and permanent and how far they can be reduced by education and training.

From this it would seem to follow that justice requires that all shall have a chance to follow the natural human instinct to make for themselves a reasonably happy and satisfactory life. But, to quote Professor Frankena, 'The equal concern for the good lives of its members also requires society to treat them differently, for no matter how much one believes in a common human nature, individual needs and capacities differ, and what constitutes the good life for one individual may not do so for another. It is the society's very concern for the good lives of its members that determines which differences and which similarities it must respect (and which are relevant to justice).'[5]

Professor Frankena goes on to make the important point – never more important than it is today – that 'none of this implies that society may impose or presuppose any fixed conception of the good life', and he quotes William James's insistence that 'the pretension to dogmatise about [this] is the root of most human injustices and cruelties'. This is something which many radical reformers would do well to ponder.

We are now coming in sight of the real difficulties. It is tempting to go on to say at once that social justice requires that everyone must be 'given' the fullest opportunity to make for himself the best life of which he is capable. This is in fact what a great many people do say; but it is an assertion that is capable of being interpreted too widely to fit within a strict definition of justice. Moreover, it does not take full account of the interactions of each individual's efforts on the opportunities of others, nor of the extent to which social justice may require that merit and social usefulness should be rewarded and criminal or 'anti-social' activities punished or curbed. The 'giving' of opportunities seems to be more a function of beneficence than of justice. It would be more appropriate, perhaps, to think in terms of the removal of arbitrary barriers to equal opportunity, although even here (as we shall see) there are difficulties of interpretation, and even worse difficulties when it comes to translating the principle into action.

What seems to me the source of most of the confusion in discussion of these questions is the failure of most of those who discuss it (including many of the social philosophers) to distinguish clearly between the requirements of social *justice* and those of social *expediency* (i.e. the self-interest of society as a whole). This is really the nub of the whole problem. If we can restrict the content of 'social justice' to that – and only that – which strictly partakes of the nature of justice, we shall find that it is very much easier to solve the practical problems that arise for action by applying the criteria of society's *interest.* Most of the argument that rages today about social justice is hopelessly confused: claims that purport to be based on social 'justice' are supported or opposed on grounds of social *expediency*, with the result that no sensible conclusion is possible. It is hard enough to strike a practical balance of social interests, without unnecessarily confusing the issue by mixing the categories.

It is possible now to start clearing the decks of some of the lumber. For example, it is, as Professor Frankena says, 'difficult to deny that the recognition of differences in desert, merit, and service, in the form of reward and punishment and unequal apportionment, is one of the principles of social justice'.[6] But it does not in the least follow that *how* they are rewarded, or *how* unequal apportionment ought to be, is something that can be determined (except in the very broadest terms) by any criterion of *justice*. Indeed, it is almost certain that it cannot. This is a matter of social expediency, or – if you like – utility. The question can now be discussed in practical terms, without the emotion engendered by talk of social justice.

Professor Frankena asserts that social justice 'does not involve direct action on the part of society to promote the good life of its members, whether this be conceived of as pleasure, happiness, self-realisation, or some indefinable quality. Such direct action is beneficence, not justice'.[7] He is, however, moving on to more difficult ground when he continues: 'It seems reasonable to assign to the just society a more positive interest (though one which falls short of beneficence) by saying that it must, so far as possible, provide equally the conditions under which its members can by their own efforts (alone or in voluntary associations) achieve the best lives of which they are capable. This means that the society must at least maintain some minimum standard of living, education, amd security for all its members.'

In point of fact, it could be argued that the two parts of this proposition are contradictory. If only *minimum* standards are to be maintained, then it is hard to see in what sense society is providing 'equally' the conditions required to enable *all* its members to achieve the best life of which they are capable. This may be a mere matter of semantics, but I think there is a genuine confusion here, arising from the fact that Professor Frankena has framed his argument in order to arrive at a conclusion previously foreseen and desired. He goes on to say that his 'theory of social justice lies between those of the classical liberals and those of the more extreme welfare theorists', and it is hard to believe that it was not precisely this middle ground that he had all along wished to arrive at. He points out, quite rightly, that the welfare theorists unduly extend the range of '*justicised* social action'; that, whatever may be thought of the merits of their conclusions 'about what society and the state may or should do . . . they cannot plausibly defend them all as requirements of justice'.

It seems to me very doubtful whether Professor Frankena can plausibly defend his 'minimum standards' as 'requirements of justice', either. They look to me much more like the requirements of *humanity*, which is something quite else again. With the best will in the world, I cannot see how *justice* requires that society should 'maintain' a minimum standard of living for someone who makes no attempt to achieve it by his own efforts, who makes no useful contribution to the welfare of society as a whole and may indeed be actually damaging it.

On the other hand we can easily agree that a *humane* society would refuse to allow any of its members, however undeserving, to starve, to be without a roof over his head, or to exist in a state of subhuman squalor. It is quite likely, too, that humanity would impel people to see that no child was allowed to grow up without the opportunity of an education designed to develop his talents and enable him to live a reasonably civilised life; and this would equally be a requirement of social utility or expediency, since society itself may be presumed to be better off if the useful talents of its members are developed.

It seems not unreasonable, then, to suggest that the maintenance of minimum standards is a requirement of humanity rather than of justice. It is formally established by the State, as a result of political decisions, and the level at which the minimum is fixed will always be a matter of political controversy. But the minimum will not be allowed to fall below whatever level majority opinion in the country feels to be humane. It is probable that majority opinion will favour the raising of the minimum standard roughly in proportion to any increase in the general level of national prosperity; but this, too, will be prompted by feelings of humanity rather than of justice. Once a basic minimum has been established which ensures a decent life for all, it is difficult to show that *justice* requires that its ratio to the general level of prosperity shall remain constant. There will, however, probably always be a general feeling that the gap should not widen too much, and a benevolent desire to do what is possible. While it cannot be said that justice requires that all old-age pensioners should be able to afford television sets as well as enough food and fuel, there will always be plenty of people who feel that 'it would be nice' if they could.

At the same time, the level at which the minimum is fixed, over and above the point below which humanity will not allow it to fall, will be largely determined by considerations of *expediency*. First, there will be a realisation that the level must not fall so low as to produce 'alienation' from society among those on the minimum; serious discontent and resentment lower the efficiency of the community. Secondly, there will be the difficult question of what levels of minimum wages and social service benefits the community can 'afford', if it is not to damage the general level of prosperity and the efficiency of the economy. Expediency requires a level somewhere between that at which efficiency is impaired by discontent and that at which it is impaired by too high a financial cost to the economy.

We shall be considering some of the practical implications of this later, when we come to discuss the social services and education in detail; but there are three issues on which most of the recent controversy about social justice has hinged, and it may be as well to try to clarify certain points of principle about them now. The three issues are inequalities of wealth and income; the existence and transmission of inherited wealth; and provision for education, particularly the existence of a private system of education for fee-paying pupils. All these things have been held to 'offend against social justice'; demands have been made, in the name of social justice, for the reduction of inequalities of wealth and income, and for the abolition of privately provided education and of the transmission of private wealth to subsequent generations.

I had probably better say at once that I have never yet seen, in all that I have read about these controversial subjects, any case made out which would justify these radical changes on grounds of *justice*. The nearest anyone seems to have come to it is to assert that the changes ought to be made because a large (though unspecified) number of people *feel* that the present situation is 'unjust'. But, as Professor Gregory Vlastos pointed out in his beautifully logical study of social justice and equality,[8] 'the fact that envious people are made unhappy by an institution is no evidence of its injustice'.

If, however, the unhappiness is a matter not merely of envy but of a very widespread frustration and conviction that the institution is unfair and wrong, then there may of course be a reason – not of justice but of utility or expediency – for doing something about it. It is a question of trying to weigh the possible gain from the 'disalienation' of a large section of the population against the possible loss which might result from the change.

There are two difficulties about trying to estimate the seriousness of popular resentment against inheritance, private education and large inequalities of wealth, together with the advantages to be gained from radical change. One is the nature of the evidence for the resentment. Since the volume and depth of the resentment are nearly always emphasised by those who adduce it as proof of the 'injustice' of the institutions and the need to change them, it is natural to look at the evidence with some suspicion. It is remarkable how many of these advocates start by declaring, without any attempt to prove its validity, their own conviction that these institutions are 'unjust', proceeding thence to the assumption that everyone else naturally shares their conviction.

Thus R. H. Tawney proclaimed in the 1951 'Epilogue' to *Equality* (and the italics are mine): 'The two most massive pillars of *indefensible* disparities of income and opportunity consist, as before the war, of inherited wealth and the educational system.' And again (once more the italics are mine): 'The *fact remains* that the transmission of more than a minimum of wealth from generation to generation has, in the conditions of today, little more to commend it than would have a right to travel in perpetuity in first-class coaches . . .' The calm interposition of these two subjective and unsubstantiated assertions into what purports to be a reasoned argument is positively breathtaking. Then there is Professor Morris Ginsberg, who interpolates the following in what is certainly a rather more scholarly and closely reasoned book than Tawney's: 'To bring about a state of affairs in which a scale based on equity would tend to coincide with the results of supply and demand, the following conditions would seem to be necessary, though they may not be sufficient. Firstly, there must be a narrowing of the range of differentials to avoid great disparities in earned income. This, together with the erosion of property-derived income, would tend to reduce differences in the standard of living . . .'[9] At no point in Professor Ginsberg's argument, either before or after this passage, is any attempt made to show why 'distributive justice' requires that present differences in the standard of living should be reduced, nor to discuss the justice or otherwise of arbitrarily 'eroding' incomes derived from property. It is calmly asserted that these changes 'would seem to be necessary' in order to secure 'equity'. Professor Ginsberg happens to be a socialist (there is an equally startling 'proof' of the inescapable need for public control of industry on the following page), and this is his idea of equity: therefore this is what equity requires.

One is left wondering whether there is really a deeply felt popular conviction of the injustice of the institutions complained of – or whether it is simply that the socialist professors (and the politicians influenced by them) have been proclaiming their own conviction of injustice for so long that people are beginning to believe that all these clever fellows must be right.

There is yet another difficulty. Even if the extreme radicals *are* right, there is no certainty that the changes they advocate would abolish the resentment they postulate or produce the greater social cohesion which they claim the inequalities prevent. The influential egalitarians do not demand absolute or mathematical equality, indeed nearly all of them specifically disclaim it as an end. They simply say that present differences are too wide and should be reduced by an unspecified proportion. But de Tocqueville put his finger 130 years ago on the weak spot in the argument: he asserted that, in a society moving in the direction of greater equality, the narrowing of differentials causes the inequalities that remain to be *more* resented rather than less. And the irony of the thing is that the egalitarian professors themselves are neutralising in advance the possible effectiveness of their own prescriptions. The more persuasive they are, the greater will grow the volume of demand for the reduction of inequalities and the more likely it will become that a further reduction will be enforced. But because the professors will not – or cannot – say now how far the process ought to go, there is not the slightest chance that they will be able at any stage in the process – even if they were able to recognise the appropriate moment – to persuade people that the time has come to call a halt. They are the sorcerer's apprentices of politics. Their crime is not that they know too little about politics – though that is true enough – but that they have allowed their (no doubt wholly philanthropic) emotions to get the better of their scholarly discipline. It is they who are responsible for the political degradation of the concept of social justice. As Bagehot said, 'This burden might almost all have been spared us if philanthropists . . . had not inherited from their barbarous forefathers a wild passion for instant action.'[10]

How great, how deep and widespread, *is* the resentment against the institutions we are discussing? I have no more certain knowledge about this than have the egalitarian polemicists, and they tell us nothing to the point; they appear to do no more than assume its existence because they feel it ought to exist. I can do no more than give a personal impression: but this personal impression is based on an amount of intensive political canvassing and discussion – on doorsteps generally chosen precisely because they did *not* belong to known Conservatives – which probably exceeds that carried out by a whole college of professors. It is based also on a pretty long and wide experience of the kind of questions asked at political meetings both at and between elections. And I say without hesitation that if there were anything like the feeling in the country which the egalitarians allege, it is inconceivable that I should not have become aware of it. Moreover, I believe an impression based on this kind of experience in depth to be a great deal more reliable than a summary of what people might say on the spur of the moment to a public opinion poll interviewer.

Here, then, are my impressions. The amount of feeling against the existence of privately provided education is negligible, and what there is of it is almost exclusively expressed by intellectuals and on theoretical grounds. There is a great deal of disquiet and doubt about the system of selection for maintained secondary schools; but British 'public' and 'preparatory' schools are not an issue of social justice to more than a tiny minority of the people. Most people appear to be almost totally uninterested.

Much the same can be said of the transmission of wealth by inheritance. This seems to strike nearly everyone as a perfectly normal and natural process, with no injustice about it at all. Most people are aware that the State takes a sizable cut from large estates, and there is no discernible eagerness to have the cut made substantially larger, on grounds of social justice, envy or anything else.

Finally, there is the question of inequalities of wealth and income, which is certainly more difficult to assess. For what it is worth, however, my impression is that there is an almost surprisingly small amount of conscious feeling about wide disparities of wealth and income in general. There is often considerable concern – especially during a period of acute inflation – about the *absolute* level of income of lower-paid workers and pensioners, but this is a matter of falling real income causing personal hardship. There is no tendency for even this to provoke resentment against the wealthy in general, for it does not seem to be felt that impoverishing the rich would in any way benefit the poor. I have encountered, on the other hand, quite bitter working-class feeling – very much more intense than anything felt about the wealthy – against what were regarded as the excessively high earnings of Birmingham motor-car workers and even, occasionally, young building labourers. There is no doubt in my mind – and it is remarkable that the professors seem to have had no inkling of this – that the narrower differentials of working-class earnings are far more productive of discussion and resentment than the wider differentials of wealth. However, I confess it does not seem to me at all surprising.

I can recall only one period at which the existence or activities of the wealthy have in recent years been seriously called in question or openly resented. This was during the land and building development boom of the early 1960s. At every political meeting from 1963 to 1965 there were innumerable expressions of concern about the large 'windfall' profits made in speculative property deals and about the profits made from betterment of land values through grants of planning permission for development. The name of Mr. Charles Clore resounded in every village hall and was bandied on every doorstep. And this seems to me extraordinarily significant, because it is the exception that proves the rule I have been describing.

Here was a case where the accumulation of wealth by others was actually felt to be having an adverse effect on the interests of the people themselves. It put the price of houses up. And this was felt to be unjust because the complainants could not see that the beneficiaries had done anything particularly useful in return for their large gains. But the interesting point is that it was only when the price of building land really began to boom that people seemed to get at all excited about it: in other words, only when the results of the accumulation of wealth in a particularly spectacular way began to show themselves in effects that were personally and consciously felt. Surely the fact that interest and resentment did become markedly noticeable on that issue at the time points up the very marked contrast with the total lack of interest or resentment about wealth or profit-making in other fields and at other times. When people feel that something is unjust, or that the wealth and activities of other people are injuring them, they *do* express their feelings clearly, and no politician can remain unaware of them. What, then, is one to make of their total lack of expressed interest or resentment about wide disparities of wealth and income in general? Why, if they felt so strongly about Mr. Clore, are they so utterly uninterested in the wealth or activities of – say – Sir John Ellerman or the Marquess of Salisbury?

Surely the conclusion is obvious. And it makes a total

nonsense of the argument which many egalitarians apparently consider to be central to their case.

This is precisely the conclusion arrived at by Mr. C. A. R. Crosland in *The Future of Socialism*, which is by far the most moderate and closely reasoned discussion of equality and social justice yet produced from the left. 'Contrasts in wealth, taken in isolation,' says Mr. Crosland, 'do not now seem to cause widespread resentment.'[11]

Mr. Crosland purports, however, to identify certain 'group' resentments and hostilities which he believes stem from present inequalities. Such measures of economic redistribution as he advocates are designed to promote, indirectly, 'social equality' as distinct from economic equality. Like the professors, Mr. Crosland has no idea how far he wishes the process of redistribution to go; but, unlike them, he frankly and explicitly admits it. Indeed, he says he does not regard this 'as either a sensible or a pertinent question'. 'We need,' he believes, 'more equality than we now have,' and any attempt to be more precise is to embrace 'the vulgar fallacy that some ideal society can be said to exist, of which blueprints can be drawn'. This is perhaps a little startling at first sight, but not unprecedented. It has always been possible to sympathise with the baffled Cromwell, confronted with a demand to explain what he wished to substitute for the episcopal Church of England: 'I can tell you, sirs, what I would not have; though I cannot, what I would.'

Nevertheless, such would-be reformers should not be surprised if their attitude remains, in the last resort, both philosophically and politically unconvincing. Worse than that, it is extremely dangerous. It is not simply that Mr. Crosland, like the professors, would certainly find himself in the unhappy position of the sorcerer's apprentice if his policies really began to gather momentum (and he has made it abundantly clear that 'excessive' equality would be profoundly repugnant to him). The real trouble is that this whole attitude displays the most miserable confusion between ends and means, which is criminal in a philosopher and horribly dangerous in a politician. Certainly Mr. Crosland sins less grievously and often than Tawney, Ginsberg and the rest, who are perfectly capable of elevating a means to the status of an end in the middle of an argument and proceeding with it as though nothing had happened. But the confusion is clearly perceptible to the careful reader.

Mr. Crosland's case for greater equality begins by torpedoing about half the canoes that egalitarians have been so assiduously paddling. Not only is there little or no resentment of wealth as such, but 'if we want more equality, the case for it must rest on statements largely, if not entirely, unrelated to economic welfare'. It then becomes necessary to say what on earth *is* wrong, and Mr. Crosland casts around for a scent. Industrial relations are considered, in which field resentments certainly exist, but little or no attempt is made to show how this is bound up with inequality, or how redistribution of wealth or incomes would improve it.

From this point on, Mr. Crosland's case follows three lines of approach: first that *social* (as distinct from *economic*) inequality engenders class consciousness and social resentments; second, that wealth leads to excessive and unmerited 'privileges' which offend against social justice; and third, that the system is socially wasteful, since it prevents an unknown number of potentially useful people from getting to the top.

I propose to postpone the argument on social class and its implications, which gets us nowhere, and examine the treatment of the 'privileges' of wealth. This is divided under four heads, two of which turn out to be almost indistinguishable and two of which are somewhat cursorily treated.

One section starts with the promising assertion that 'the greater the inequality, the heavier the concentration of power'. But Mr. Crosland, having peered rather dubiously at this proposition, immediately (and somewhat surprisingly) decides to have nothing more to do with it. The professors, who have always been partial to this line, are let down with a bump. 'Authoritarian power today,' says Mr. Crosland briskly and didactically, 'stems less commonly from monetary wealth or private ownership than from position in a bureaucratic hierarchy'. Business executives have too much power, but this is an influence 'which will not be much affected by measures of income-redistribution'. It is just a matter of increasing 'the power of the worker at the point of production'. In other words, this argument is entirely irrelevant to what we are supposed to be discussing.

The discussion of differentials in the rewards from work comes to an equally surprising conclusion. It becomes clear at once that what really bothers Mr. Crosland here is not what is paid for jobs, but whether the people holding them are worth the money. The 'old boy net' is getting the wrong people into jobs, and in the City 'many of the most lucrative posts even now are filled by titled semi-nonentities, or retired soldiers and sailors . . .' 'So long as this continues, the pattern of work-rewards can properly be described as unjust, in that it denies an equal opportunity of attaining certain of the top rewards.' This is completely nonsensical. Even assuming the premises to be correct, it cannot conceivably be the 'pattern of work-rewards' that denies equal opportunity to attain top posts; it is quite obviously the method of recruitment and promotion. Since Mr. Crosland nowhere suggests that altering the level of rewards would result in better men getting the top jobs, this part of the argument is seen to be irrelevant as well as fallacious. As to whether the spread of rewards is too wide, Mr. Crosland confesses himself 'rather agnostic', but is inclined to think it might be. He is, however, in favour of gradually increasing the lower incomes rather than attacking the higher ones, which again runs contrary to the views of the Socialist professors.*

However, Mr. Crosland is right back with them when he comes to discuss the social injustice of the privileges conferred

* Professor Ginsberg is particularly inspiring on earned income differentials. He takes up an idea of the late G. D. H. Cole (another socialist professor), that it is the 'standards of consumption' set by those who enjoy large *unearned* incomes that make top executives so greedy. 'If unearned income were to disappear, or to be greatly reduced, it would become possible to narrow differences of earned income to a very substantial extent without any adverse effects on them as incentives.'[12] Having thus begged no less than three enormous questions and passed on without a blink, Professor Ginsberg reaches his stupendous climax: 'The highest income could be reduced to no more than is at present earned by a highly qualified professional man working as a salaried employee in some branch of public service.' It might, of course, be argued that this *would* result in a kind of social justice; for such executives as did not at once emigrate to the U.S., Canada or Australia would be worth about this sort of salary.

by wealth, especially in respect of the education of the children of the wealthy. And, like the professors, he is a little given to sliding rapidly over awkward gaps in the logic of his argument. He begins with a fine professorial proclamation: 'The present distribution of wealth in Britain is flagrantly unjust; and this is wholly irrespective of the visible pattern of consumption, the effect of redistribution on economic welfare, and even the presence or absence of resentment against the injustice. The only relevant factor is that the possession of great differential wealth still confers an enormous social and economic advantage, however it is spent; and the distribution of this advantage is a matter of social concern.' Well, yes. However, something can be a matter of social concern without being unjust. Moreover, since Mr. Crosland has already expressed his belief that there *is* practically no resentment against wealth as such, and in his subsequent examination of the effects of redistribution on welfare merely concludes that it would probably do no harm, he still badly needs both a proof of injustice and a good positive reason for radical change.

It is not clear whether Mr. Crosland quite realises what he is saying when he asserts that 'the only relevant factor' in consideration of the 'injustice' of the present distribution of wealth is 'that the possession of great differential wealth still confers an enormous social and economic advantage'. After all, *economic* advantage is very nearly a simple *definition* of wealth. This is tantamount to saying that wealth is unjust *per se*, irrespective of its distribution, and would only become just if it could be rendered utterly useless and pointless. Since no one could possibly mean this – or at least believe it to be worth saying – it must follow that it is the addition of *social* advantage that is the crucial point for Mr. Crosland; and indeed my impression is that this is so.

Three possible sources of injustice are then somewhat perfunctorily examined. One is the element of 'unequal opportunity' in the rewards for work, which we have already dismissed as irrelevant to the justice of the income differentials, because it depends on the system of recruitment, which is something quite different. The second is the differential advantages which the tax system offers (although rather less marked since the 1965 Budget) to the owner of capital as compared with the salary earner; this has, of course, nothing whatever to do with the justice or injustice of the present distribution of the ownership of wealth; it is wholly a question of the justice of the tax system.

We are left with one proposition only: 'Inequalities of wealth may be considered unjust . . . if they stem from inherited property, and not from work. This offends against the principle that every citizen should have an equal chance of attaining the highest rewards, and confers a differential advantage related solely to the accident of birth, and not in any way the "fruit of the man's own labour".' Mr. Crosland hastily appends a footnote to point out that the final passage in double quotes is 'not a very sensible phrase'. But nor, it seems to me, is the rest of the quotation.

This 'principle', on which so much hangs, is one enunciated by Mr. Crosland himself in an earlier chapter. 'An equitable distribution (ignoring deliberately eleemosynary payments) requires first that wealth should be a reward for the performance of a definite service or function, and secondly that all should have an equal chance of performing the function, and so of earning the reward. The highest rewards would then accrue to those who, because they possess skills or services in short supply, can contribute most to national prosperity or enjoyment; provided only that the possession of these skills and services should not be artificially (that is, to a greater extent than can be explained by innate differences in talent) restricted to a privileged few.'

Now this looks, at first sight, like a scientific and carefully constructed definition – provided, of course, that we ignore the question of why it should be assumed in the first place that this is what an equitable distribution of wealth 'requires'. But even if we pass over the question begged by the unproved initial assumption, there is surely great confusion here. For what is this 'wealth', the distribution of which we are supposed to be discussing? At one point in the definition it looks as if Mr. Crosland is thinking of rewards in the form of income, which are certainly not 'wealth' as this is commonly understood. Yet the context hardly suggests that this can be so: he must surely be referring throughout to the ownership of accumulated wealth. And this confronts us with a difficulty at once.

It is one thing to say – as philosophers have said throughout the ages – that the possession of wealth carries with it responsibilities and duties, which morality requires should be properly discharged if possession is to be justified. It is quite another thing to say that the possession of wealth is to be considered a *reward* for services performed *before* the wealth is accumulated. This may not be an impossible or totally unreasonable proposition, but Mr. Crosland's treatment of its implications is extremely confusing.

Let us start by recalling that his requirements for an *equitable distribution* of wealth were two: that the wealth accumulated should be a reward for the performance of a definite service or function; and that everyone should have an equal chance of performing the function and earning the reward. Now Mr. Crosland at once admits that his conditions would be satisfied if all private property represented 'the individual's own accumulated savings, the fruits of his personal effort and abstinence'. It must therefore follow, by definition, that an 'equitable distribution' of wealth would have been achieved if all private property were in the form of 'first generation' fortunes – that is to say, if every private fortune had been earned rather than inherited. And this would be so, *entirely irrespective of the size of the fortunes or the way in which they were distributed among the population.* In other words, we reach the inescapable conclusion that – on Mr. Crosland's own definition – 'equity' has nothing to do with equality or distribution of wealth at all. The sole requirement of social justice is that there should be no inheritance of accumulated wealth. It is therefore quite irrelevant if not actually contradictory, for Mr. Crosland to go on to complain that, *in addition* to being unjustly owned because unearned, inherited wealth is also 'most unequally distributed'.

It now only remains to examine the validity of the proposition to which Mr. Crosland's argument has been reduced. Is the inheritance of wealth socially unjust? Mr. Crosland himself regards it as 'a simple moral judgement, . . . not susceptible of proof or disproof; it must be accepted or rejected according to the moral predilections of the reader'. But in that case it has no right to be flaunting itself in a discussion of social justice. It has no objective validity and is not even properly a norm of 'advocative' justice. It is simply a personal statement of what Mr. Crosland believes to be 'fair' and 'right'. Now if he is one of those who hold that moral judgements are purely a matter of emotion, that is one thing; but in that case he really must not expect us to change the basic institutions of our society merely because of his emotions. If, on the other hand, he belongs to that school of ethics which holds that moral judgements may be reached by rational processes, then he has no right to claim that his judgement 'is not susceptible of proof or disproof'. It must be susceptible of one or the other. Certainly Mr. Crosland himself does not prove his claim; but I believe that such arguments as he does adduce are susceptible of disproof.

Let us consider first the remarkable absence of any interest in the way in which wealth is actually *used* by its possessors. It would seem, according to Mr. Crosland's argument, that it is morally right for one man to accumulate a fortune by his own efforts and then to use it for purely selfish and even anti-social purposes, but morally wrong for another to inherit a fortune and use it entirely for the economic and social benefit of the community. But how can this possibly be rational? And if it is not rational, then how can the original proposition possibly be right?

It may, of course, be urged that it is unfair to represent Mr. Crosland as justifying the selfish or anti-social use of wealth, since common sense should tell us that this is wrong anyway. But if this is so, then Mr. Crosland's criteria are inadequate and his argument falls to the ground; we should have to start all over again. Moreover, the moment it is admitted that the way wealth is *used* may affect the morality of its possession, then it at once becomes legitimate to consider how *inherited* wealth is used as one of the criteria in deciding whether inheritance is justified. But Mr. Crosland's argument has no place for this: inherited wealth is wrong *per se*, irrespective of how it is used.

We will now examine the one argument which *is* adduced to demonstrate the injustice of inheritance. In its original form it is stated, as a requirement of equity, 'first that wealth should be a reward for the performance of a definite service or function, and secondly that all should have an equal chance of performing the function, and so of earning the reward'.

Why, as a matter of equity, must wealth be a reward only for a service or function performed in the past? I cannot see that justice or equity requires this at all. Why can it not justly be a reward for a service or function that a man is performing now and will go on performing all his life? If it can – and this is surely as reasonable a proposition as the other – then much of Mr. Crosland's argument falls to the ground. For he would have to demonstrate that there is no useful service or function that a man can render to society through the medium of inherited wealth – and this he could never do.

We are left, after this intolerable deal of sack, with but one half-pennyworth of bread: the 'principle' that no one must be allowed to earn a high reward for performing a function unless *everyone* has an equal chance of performing the function and so earning the reward. This is all that is left. And it is plain, ridiculous nonsense.

'Social justice' has nothing whatever of practical use to say about inequalities of wealth, and equity in no way requires the abolition of inheritance.

There remains only the question of whether social *expediency* requires that we should do something about it. In other words, would society as a whole be better off if we made some radical changes in our institutions to secure greater equality of wealth and to change the pattern of ownership and inheritance?

We have already seen that neither Mr. Crosland nor I (both of us better qualified by experience to judge than are most professors) considers that there is any need to make the changes on the ground of public resentment against either wealth or inheritance. We must therefore judge the desirability of change in the light of the practical benefits it would bring; and this must very largely depend on the form the changes would take, and how society would be left at the end of it all.

Now I happen to agree entirely with Mr. Crosland in his belief that the present distribution of wealth, and the effects of education and class stratification on the tone and temper of society, are matters of grave social concern. But major institutional changes in a society, which could have important and largely unpredictable secondary effects, should not be made suddenly and deliberately unless we are very sure what it is that we are doing and why. In particular, we ought to be sure that we have clearly identified our ends and have not exalted to the status of ends what should properly be considered as means to something else. Further, we should hesitate to make large and deliberate changes if there is a fair chance that society is already moving in the direction of the changes we desire.

I do not happen to believe, on the basis of the experience of other countries as well as of our own, that a totally classless society is either possible or necessarily desirable. At least I should like to know what, if we are to take deliberate action to change the present class structure, the new order would be like. I have no great desire to see society dominated by either a technocracy or a deliberately imposed meritocracy (even if I belonged to it myself). And it does seem to me that in the last twenty years the class structure of Britain has changed perceptibly; we are, slowly but surely, becoming gradually less different and rather more 'the same kind of people'. I am not sure whether this is proving to be a good thing or not. I used to think it was, and it may yet turn out to be. The question is, however, whether we ought to make drastic changes in our institutions to try to speed the process up.

The radical intellectuals feel passionately that nothing is any use unless we get rid of the 'dual system' of private and maintained education. I agree with them that this at least *reflects* social divisions, but not necessarily that it creates them. I also believe that getting rid of it entirely is not necessarily desirable or even possible, and that what we may be able to do about it must be a relatively gradual process. Sudden and radical change imposed by force might well be more socially divisive than the present system. But this is purely a matter of social expediency, having nothing to do with social justice.

As to the pattern of the ownership of wealth, I think perhaps something ought to be done about this, also as a matter of social expediency. And what we do must depend on what we want to achieve rather than on what we want to get rid of. I know that this is an idea utterly repugnant to some socialist professors and probably quite unfamiliar to others, but this is what social expediency – and politics, and common sense – is about.

I am quite sure that what Mr. Crosland wants us to do is entirely undesirable. Ignoring the appalling upheaval that would be caused in the ownership and even the chances of survival of medium-sized businesses, partnerships and farms, he would have us tax away all transmissions of wealth above £50,000 and hand the property over to the State, which would either sell it or administer it itself (using stocks and shares so acquired to influence or control industry). Well, you either have that much faith in the beneficence and efficiency of the State, or you haven't. I haven't. This is a formula for the destruction of individual independence.

What I do believe we ought to do, on the contrary, is to devise a method of spreading the *private* ownership of property more widely among the community, to change the tax system so as to enable many more people to accumulate modest fortunes as 'a reward for the performance of a definite service or function'. There are real grounds for believing that the community as a whole would be better off if *wealth* were to be more widely distributed and the ownership of private property more widely enjoyed. For private property is an essential ingredient of citizenship, enriching the lives of the individual and family, widening the range of choice in living, and opposing a necessary barrier to the encroachment of technique, uniformity and large-scale organisation.

CHAPTER 8

Equality of Opportunity?

The source of inequality of opportunity in our society is not economic but rather what is called cultural inheritance . . . even today much of the transmission of culture, in the narrow sense, occurs through the family, and no system of public education and training can completely neutralise this form of inheritance. . . . The more subtle and profound influences upon the child resulting from love, integrity and family morale form a kind of inheritance which cannot, at least for those above the minimum subsistence level, be significantly affected by economic measures, or possibly by any others. If these influences on the members of the next generation are to be equalised, nothing short of major changes in the institution of the family can possibly suffice. At a minimum such changes would include socialising decisions not only about how children are to be raised but who is to raise them. And this in turn would call into question the very having of children.

Walter J. Blum and Harry Kalven, Jr., *The Uneasy Case for Progressive Taxation*

The desire to eliminate the effects of accident, which lies at the root of the demand for 'social justice' can be satisfied in the field of education, as elsewhere, only by eliminating all those opportunities which are not subject to deliberate control. But the growth of civilisation rests largely on the individuals' making the best use of whatever accidents they encounter, of the essentially unpredictable advantages that one kind of knowledge will in new circumstances confer on one individual over others.

F. A. Hayek, *The Constitution of Liberty*

We have examined at some length the philosophical and logical case for removing inequalities in the name of social justice, and discovered that it is a mirage. There is no way in which the requirements of social justice can be objectively assessed or laid down in detail. It is all a matter of subjective and emotional feeling. The egalitarian is outraged by things as they are, and regards those who are not as insensitive and reactionary. But however certain he may be of the need for redistribution of wealth and income, or of the desirability of curtailing 'privilege', he can neither prove his case logically nor produce a convincing objective assessment of the magnitude of the changes required.

The egalitarians are nevertheless – and have always been – a powerful force in society, and certainly a dangerous one. The fact that they have provided the impetus to many reforms now considered salutary should not blind us to the danger that they represent. It is not simply that some of them are in fact, however deep in their unconscious they have buried the knowledge, moved more by envy than by a fine sense of abstract justice; the truth is that men who are committed by their emotions to demands for radical changes in society, without having any clear idea of where they want to stop and what would be the side-effects of the changes, are always dangerous.

Being powerfully driven by their emotions, they are naturally not amenable to rational argument. Some of them (as we saw in the last chapter in the case of Mr. Anthony Crosland) even admit frankly that their conviction is intuitive and not susceptible of rational proof or disproof.[1] They are also able cheerfully to infuriate their opponents by imputing the most disreputable motives to them. Those opponents who enjoy 'privilege' are of course selfishly defending their personal advantages; those who are 'under-privileged' but nevertheless reject the extreme egalitarian thesis are taunted with accusations of servility and lack of spirit.

Another advantage which the egalitarians possess is that they can reasonably claim that some redistribution of wealth and incomes has produced certain social (and even economic) benefits in the past. When opposed in the present, they smile in a superior way and say, 'Well, of course, the wealthy have always fought for their privileges. These people are behaving exactly as their grandfathers did; but look how much better off everyone is now because of the reforms carried out then. We need still more equality, and we are right now and our opponents are wrong, just as they were before.'

This argument is as hard to rebut as the egalitarians' thesis is to prove. Just as they 'feel' intuitively that more redistribution is essential, so others may be convinced that the process cannot be carried on indefinitely without serious harm being done to the economy and to the structure of society.

But it is not easy to 'prove', nor to say with certainty or authority where the line is to be drawn, however probable it may seem that there is an ultimate point beyond which redistribution is positively harmful. There is not even the comfort of knowing that at some point the egalitarians will be satisfied. Despite the apparent moderation of Mr. Crosland and others, the egalitarians' appetite grows with what it feeds on; as de Tocqueville said, the more equal men become the *more* are the few remaining inequalities resented.

But how deep and general is the resentment, among the people of this country as a whole, at the degree of inequality that remains? Mr. Crosland thinks it is not large, and so do I. It is true that there has been a genuine feeling that the 11-plus method of selection for grammar school education is unfair, but there is little indication that this has amounted to a conviction that selection itself is wrong. It is a reasonable feeling that the age of eleven is too young to make a virtually irrevocable decision about a child's abilities and aptitudes for education, particularly as this decision may vitally affect the whole of his future career.

It is, in fact, to the question of equality of opportunity, rather than to inequalities of wealth or income, that most attention is directed. And since in our society good careers are reasonably open to educated talents, and it is still not impossible for a man to make money if he has plenty of ideas and applies himself to developing them, it is the degree of equality of opportunity in education that comes in for most attention. Everyone agrees that opportunities for the kind of education that leads to a desirable career are by no means equal as between children from different family backgrounds, and most people assert that they believe the inequalities ought to be reduced. The question is, how?

The egalitarians' immediate target is the 'reform' of the present educational system. First, to do away with selection altogether; second, to get rid of the 'dual system', by abolishing independent schools or merging them somehow into the maintained (often inaccurately called the 'State') system. Sometimes they talk as though these reforms would, by themselves, abolish inequalities of opportunity, although most of them must know that they would not. Some of them are aware that their objective must logically be to make social changes going far beyond the reorganisation of education and affecting the whole traditional basis of family life. Nevertheless, the educational system offers an easier target for attack; and, since this is where the egalitarian attack commonly falls, we should consider their case as objectively as possible.

Apart from the contention that the social effects of the present system of privately provided and selective publicly provided schools are manifestly bad, which is arguable, the proponents of change ought to be able to establish three other things if their case is to be considered proven. The first is that their proposals for change will remedy the alleged defects without introducing others. The second is that their new system will in fact increase equality of educational opportunity. Finally, it must be shown that the proposed changes will have in total the effect of improving the general quality of education in Britain without lowering the quality of the education given to the ablest and most intelligent chidren. The proponents of comprehensive schooling and the opponents of the independent schools have never succeeded in demonstrating this.

That the present organisation of education in Britain has many defects cannot be denied. It is certain that complete equality of educational opportunity does not exist; but then it is extremely doubtful whether any system of schooling could provide this. It is not simply a question of differences in innate intelligence and ability, but of the differences in children's early environments. Intelligence is no doubt to a certain extent innate and inherited, and it may be that certain aptitudes are similarly implanted at birth. But there is no doubt at all that the performance of two children with similar intelligence and aptitudes can vary widely if the economic and cultural environments of their early years have been substantially different. The children of well-educated, cultured and prosperous parents will in general tend to do better at school (even at the same school) than those from poorer homes and with more or less unlettered parents. This has been pretty well established as a general rule by various tests and research projects, although there are of course plenty of exceptions. In any case, it is what one would expect, since the influence of parents is important in early childhood in establishing habits of reading, conversation and thought.

It is at this point that the extreme egalitarians take up the argument in the cause of equality of opportunity. And it is important to examine their case with care and without prejudice. To refuse to recognise any merit in it at all is as bad as to accept the whole case uncritically. It is only by identifying what is genuinely wrong about the present system that it becomes possible to test the validity of the egalitarians' proposals.

It has to be accepted that our present educational system does to some extent accentuate the inequalities of opportunity which originate in differences of home environment in early childhood. It may well also be true that in certain cases the system causes the differences in performance and attainment between children of comparable intelligence and ability to widen progressively at each stage of their schooling. This can happen in the following way. An intelligent child from a well-educated middle-class family may well have received the beginnings of an education before he starts at a primary school. He will certainly have had his intelligence sharpened, and may well have learned to read. His vocabulary will almost certainly be larger than that of a child from a home providing none of these advantages. As a result he will probably – although of course it does not always happen – progress faster at school in the early stages than the child from the poorer home. If, as often happens, he maintains this lead, he will probably do better in the selection tests for secondary schooling. However carefully devised the '11-plus' tests may be to measure only 'innate' intelligence, there is no doubt at all that the child whose vocabulary is wider and whose intelligence has been more keenly exercised at home will tend to do better at them. The difference may be that between getting a place in a grammar school and going to a secondary modern school. And unless the grammar school is a very bad one or the secondary modern school a very good one, the difference in attainment between the two children is likely to widen further throughout their secondary schooling. It may well mean the difference between securing a place at a university and never getting a chance of one. And this in its turn may mean the difference between a successful professional career in adult life and a manual, or at best clerical or technician's job.

The egalitarians are rightly anxious to minimise the risk of this kind of increasing inequality between children of more or less equal intelligence and aptitudes. Where many of them go wrong is in trying to impose a perfect solution to a problem which, like most social problems, simply does not admit of a perfect solution. So great is their obsession with the need to eliminate all the factors making for inequality that they have become blind to the dangers which may flow from their own extreme measures and theories.

There are, obviously, two ways in which inequalities can be lessened. One is to improve the opportunities for those who at present have the fewest advantages. The other is to diminish the opportunities for those who are at present 'privileged'. And the first is much more difficult and expensive than the second. The real menace of the extreme egalitarians is that, finding the first method slow and unspectacular, they enthusiastically advocate the second as an urgent measure of 'social justice', heedless of the effects it may have on the quality of education as a whole. Indeed, so clearly do some of them seem to relish the prospect of destroying or depreciating the schools and colleges with the best academic records that it is sometimes hard to believe that they are not motivated either by mere envy or by an actual dislike of outstanding quality.

To remove inequalities by destroying what is good without thereby improving what is second-rate cannot by any stretch of a sane imagination be described as a requirement of 'justice'. Indeed, it may well be thought to be extremely unjust. One can sympathise to some extent with the cry that 'it is not fair' that one child should go to a good school while another cannot; but it is an emotional cry, and a poor basis for constructive practical action. Moreover, even before the need for action is uncritically accepted, it is necessary to examine the demand with some care – otherwise the action taken may well be the wrong action. First of all, the cry of 'unfairness' itself needs to be dispassionately considered.

Let us accept, for the sake of argument, that it is 'unfair' that some clever children from poor homes should not receive the schooling that would make the best of their talents. In fact, not everyone would accept that this violates any genuine abstract canon of social justice, however axiomatic it may appear to radical reformers; let us grant it, nevertheless. Does it now follow logically that it is equally 'unfair' that clever children from more prosperous or cultured homes *should* receive a good and suitable education? Of course it does not. Once the proposition is broken down into its two component parts, no one capable of logical and dispassionate thought could imagine for a moment that the two parts are of equal weight or belong naturally together. Although the egalitarian social reformers have not all been guiltless of a certain intellectual sleight of hand in palming off a false syllogism on the simple-minded, many of them have been genuinely misled by their emotions. Because the spectacle of some clever children receiving a first-class education intensifies their resentment of the treatment accorded to the less fortunate, they have come to believe that access by the fortunate to first-class schooling is wrong in itself. And this is clearly nonsense.

Probably few would openly admit to this absurd belief, but it is implicit in most of what they say. Thus even the normally moderate Mr. C. A. R. Crosland, recently Secretary of State for Education and Science, wrote in 1962: 'These commanding heights of private privilege and social separation (i.e. the public schools) . . . are a flagrant denial of the most elementary democratic claim to equal opportunity, let alone of our wider socialist ideals.'[2] Others go further and say flatly that it is 'wrong' that middle-class parents should be able to 'buy a privileged education' for their children.

It is not wrong at all. It may be wrong that the community, as payers of rates and taxes, should be unable or unwilling to provide a better education for the less affluent – although even this contention has to be examined in the context of the competing claims of other welfare services and of the economic effects of higher rates and taxes. But let there be no mistake about this: if you say that it is wrong that some children should receive a better schooling than the State is able or willing to provide, then you are in fact saying that you want some children to be educated less well than they are being educated now. The folly of this must be obvious. To act upon such a prejudice would be bad for the country and manifestly unjust to a minority of children.

Often the egalitarians, whether from sheer naiveté or from a desire to confuse the issue, maintain that the abolition of selection in independent and direct grant or maintained schools would raise the general level of educational standards. The arguments take a variety of forms. One is based on the assumption that the teachers released from instructing small classes of 'privileged' children would significantly improve the teaching and reduce the size of classes in the country's other schools. This is the most ludicrous of illusions. Even if all independent schools were to be completely abolished, the net effect on class sizes in the mass of maintained schools would be insignificant, even if all the independent school-teachers were prepared to transfer. And to draw on the direct grant and maintained grammar schools would strike a deadly blow at the effective education of the most intelligent children. Nor would the complete abolition of selection in all maintained schools have any significant effect on the size of classes.

Another very popular and ingenuous argument is that the quality of the maintained schools, and the amount of public money devoted to them, would be much higher if the wealthy upper and middle classes had to send their children to them. Then, it is argued, they would not only become aware of their shortcomings but insist upon improvements. Apart from the question of whether it would ever, in fact, be possible to force the well-to-do to send their children to maintained schools if they did not wish to, their power to secure improvements in the maintained system must be considered doubtful. If a Labour Government, together with numerous Labour-controlled local education authorities,* cannot or will not bring about any marked improvement, why on earth should it be supposed that a marginal addition of upper- and middle-class pressure would transform the situation? It is true that many maintained schools have governors or managers whose children are educated outside the system; but in the over-

* They were numerous, at least, before the Local Government elections of 1967.

whelming majority of cases their inability to improve their schools is due not to lack of interest but to the ultimate refusal of the Treasury to let them have enough money to do the job. It cannot conceivably be argued with any plausibility that at the present time it is the parents of 'privileged' children who are holding up improvements in the public sector of education. If the British people as a whole not only wanted markedly better schooling for its children but was prepared to sacrifice other things to pay for it, there is not the slightest doubt that it could have it, whether or not the upper classes were interested.

These arguments are, in short, no more than rationalisations of a prejudice against any form of 'privilege' in education. Indeed, some enthusiasts have gone so far as to say that it is impossible to have a proper system of schooling until 'the taint of money' is removed from it. But provision of education does not drop like the gentle rain from heaven. Sordid as the whole affair may seem to some people, education has to be paid for – in money.

This brings us back to the point made earlier in this chapter. If the taxpayers and ratepayers are not prepared to make financial provision for first-class schooling for all children, then removing the 'taint' of private financial provision can result only in some children being worse educated than they are at present. This is, essentially, what many egalitarians would prefer: but they are often strangely reluctant to say so.

It is, of course, immaterial to this argument whether the taxpayers and ratepayers are right or wrong in their reluctance to provide more resources for education. If it be decided, in view of all the other claims on public finance, that no substantial aggregate increase in the volume of real resources devoted to education is possible or desirable, then there is a strong argument for increasing the amount of private finance devoted to education rather than reducing it. So far from parents who are at present paying for their children's schooling being prevented from doing so, *more* parents ought to be encouraged to make at least partial financial provision for their children's education.

On the other hand, if public authorities ought to be spending still more on education – and I believe that they will have to – it would still be premature to reduce the amount of privately financed provision before the additional public resources have been made available and the expansion is well under way. This is not to say that it would ever be right to reduce it by compulsion – only that it would be foolish as well as wrong to reduce it now.

The question remains whether the abolition of selection in and for all secondary schools would markedly improve equality of educational opportunity without adversely affecting the aggregate quality of schooling. Almost certainly it would not, if the operation were to be carried out in any of the ways which have yet been tried or even suggested. Some of the experiments in postponing selection until the age of thirteen or sixteen may prove fruitful, although the effects of raising the minimum school leaving age to sixteen are as yet unknown. Moreover, the so-called Sixth Form Colleges are an experiment which requires much more time to prove itself before it would be wise to destroy established grammar schools in order to create them. Imposing all-through comprehensive schooling from the ages of eleven to eighteen on all parts of the country, irrespective of the state of their existing schools, would certainly lower academic standards in some places as established grammar schools were abolished. Further, experience of large 'neighbourhood' comprehensive schools in urban areas suggests that they are likely to be both socially divisive and academically lacking in opportunities for the cleverest children.

This is not, of course, to say that educational opportunity ought not to be made more equal than it is, if this can be done without lowering standards of scholarship and attainment. The essential point to grasp is that there is no short cut to this ideal – and above all that there is no cheap and easy way to it. Educational inequality starts well before the stage of secondary schooling, in inequality of environment. This can never be completely eliminated, but we are entitled to expect that some progress will be made with reducing it. The improvement of urban housing will have some effect. In theory, at least, the fact that each new generation of parents will themselves have received a secondary education should reduce the disadvantages of a working-class environment, although the effects will not necessarily be very marked unless the education of non-academically minded children is made more inspiring than much of it is now.

None of this, of course, will help the child who comes from a home with bad or irresponsible parents. Public authorities can do something to mitigate these disadvantages, but nothing less than the destruction or 'socialisation' of the institution of the family could entirely eradicate them. Inevitably there will be some who will wish to go to these lengths in the name of 'social justice' or 'equality of opportunity', but the dangers are too obvious to need emphasising. We must accept, consciously but not complacently, a certain amount of what to some will seem 'injustice', in order to avoid totally destroying the family basis of the social community. As in many other fields, too eager a pursuit of mathematically egalitarian justice can lead to the infliction of great injustice. The pursuit of an unattainable perfection can damage or destroy much that is good. 'Rough justice' is sometimes the fairest kind of justice and the best for the community as a whole.

Certainly every reasonable effort must be made to improve unfavourable environments through slum clearance and better housing. The subnormal and manifestly irresponsible should be discouraged, by all means short of authoritarian methods, from bringing into the world children whom they are incapable of rearing properly in a satisfactory family environment. The power to remove children from bad homes should be used firmly but without undue eagerness to interfere. Casual parents should not be encouraged to believe that they have only to neglect their duty in order to be relieved of responsibility. Indeed, there is a strong case for urging that family responsibility should be more firmly enforced on parents, particularly in the matter of holding them criminally (or at least financially) responsible for their children's delinquency.

All this will be a slow business, and it will take a generation or two before a substantial improvement is made in the environmental causes of inequality of opportunity. But it is the right way to tackle the problem, and the improvements can be made without damaging the prospects of the more fortunate or deliberately destroying the advantages which good parents have won for their children by hard work, forethought and sacrifice.

Meanwhile much can be done within the educational system without destroying what is good. The Plowden Report showed the way to some important readjustments of priorities. We have seen that it is at the primary stage of education that the disadvantages of children from poor or illiterate homes are most serious and most apt to have permanent effects. It is therefore at the primary stage that most needs to be done to offset them. The shortage of teachers is crippling, and will remain severe for many years; it is therefore useless to expect that the overcrowding of all primary school classes will be abolished in the near future. Much can, however, be done to mitigate the effects of the shortage by the use of unqualified teachers' aides and by relieving qualified teachers of as much as possible of the non-teaching work they now have to do. Above all, there is far too wide a disparity between the quality and standards of the best and worst schools in different parts of the country. The Plowden Committee were clearly right to insist that special measures must be taken to raise quickly the standards of the worst primary schools.

The committee also called attention to the benefits which could follow from the selective improvement of nursery school facilities. While the child population is rapidly increasing and pressure on primary and secondary school resources is as great as it is now, it is probably futile to hope that greatly increased resources can be devoted to providing more nursery school places. It is, however, often too readily assumed that nursery schooling can safely be assigned the lowest priority of all. Perhaps the enthusiastic advocates of nursery schools have damaged their case by pressing it too far. It *may* be true – although I personally doubt it – that it would be good for all children to attend a nursery school before going to an infants' school at the age of five; but it can also be argued that the best place for a child under the age of five is in a good home, and that there is no perfect substitute for this. Of course, there are cases, such as those in which the mother has to work, where a nursery school can help to solve a real family problem. But it would be more sensible if the proponents of nursery schooling spent less time in recommending it as an ideal for all children and more in trying to secure the minimum provision necessary to cater for the children whose home conditions make nursery schooling highly desirable. There is no doubt that a year or so at a good nursery school can do much to bring the child from an unsatisfactory home to a state in which he can benefit more fully from full-time primary education; and an extension of these facilities on a selective basis would help to eliminate one of the major causes of inequality of opportunity in education. This is a field in which much of the necessary advance could be secured by voluntary effort rather than by public authorities.

Rejection of the egalitarian solution of universal all-through comprehensive secondary schooling does not imply that there are no reforms that need to be made in our system of secondary schools in the interests of greater equality of opportunity. Certainly selection needs to take place at a later age than eleven, and to be made more flexible, with more facilities for transfer between different types of secondary school. Many local authorities are already making great improvements in their methods of selection.

However, it can also be argued that greater equality of opportunity in education could in some cases be achieved by *more* selection in secondary schooling rather than by less. There are good grounds for believing that the progress of many children of sound intelligence in some secondary modern schools and comprehensive schools is seriously impeded by the presence of children of much lower intelligence, and with a positive antipathy to learning. Not only does the secondary modern school have to take children whose intelligence is barely above the level regarded as educationally subnormal, but the shortage of places in special schools sometimes forces it to take in boys and girls who are not really educable by conventional methods. This is, of course, equally true of the comprehensive school. What is worse, there have been cases in some urban schools where a minority of delinquent and almost uncontrollable youngsters have made such a shambles of a large class that it was virtually impossible for the most devoted teacher to do justice to those who really wanted to learn.

Even where the situation has not degenerated to this extent, it is exceedingly hard for boys and girls who are capable of profiting from a full course of secondary education to remain totally unaffected by the attitude of the remainder. Often the atmosphere of a whole school will be determined by the intellectually immature, but in other ways extremely precocious, youngsters who look forward only to the statutory leaving age and regard the years preceding their emancipation as a tiresome waste of time.

It is probable that a system involving more selection, and more segregation (at least for a certain period of particular children's school careers), would ensure a better education for boys and girls in the 'upper middle' levels of intelligence, and thus reduce the inequality of opportunity as between them and the highly intelligent academic children.

It is not, of course, only in the field of education that steps could be taken to reduce inequality of opportunity without lowering the best standards of quality. Much can be done through tax reforms to enable more parents to give their children a better start in life. Whereas the left-wing egalitarian thinks only of how to prevent the large-scale accumulation of wealth and of how to prevent its transmission by inheritance, which he would do by State confiscation, we should be thinking of how to encourage the moderate accumulation of property and capital by a much larger proportion of the population. To reduce inequality by greatly extending the opportunity for parents to give their children what is now called a 'privileged' start in life is surely a much 'fairer' method than simply to penalise the successful and conscientious without in any way raising the absolute standards of the less fortunate.

Again, while the amount of active resentment against the class divisions of this country is almost certainly much smaller, and its incidence less widespread, than the egalitarians would have us believe, many individuals do feel that there are social barriers which prevent them from rising in the world on their merits. Often – though not always – the grievance is justified. Recruitment to good jobs, and promotion in business and in the professions, is not always carried out purely on a basis of qualifications and merit. But this is not something that can best be put right – or even put right at all – by abolishing the public schools or nationalising family businesses. It will be put right over the years by a process of social change that is already under way, and by the imperatives of competition and common sense.

The widening and improvement of secondary education have already substantially reduced the absolute advantage which the public schoolboy once enjoyed in the competition for good jobs. Moreover, the public school monopoly of university places – in so far as it ever existed – has been broken, and already a university degree or technical qualification derived from other kinds of higher education is becoming the essential prerequisite for a widening range of good jobs. This process is likely to continue, probably at an accelerated rate. Moreover, it is becoming increasingly difficult, as competition is intensified and technical 'know-how' becomes more important, for firms to survive under the direction of second-rate executives recruited or promoted for family reasons or because of their social connections. There are far too many of them still about, it is true; but in the long run their days are numbered.

There are no short cuts to the social millennium, and there is no quick way to abolish inequality of opportunity without inflicting new injustices and damaging the total quality of our society. When Bagehot wrote of philanthropists who have 'inherited from their barbarous forefathers a wild passion for instant action', he put his finger on a menace which has not perceptibly diminished in the last century. The deadly danger of the fanatical apostles of 'social justice' is not that they seek a quick and easy way to abolish inequality, but that the only quick and easy way is to level down rather than to level up; and this cannot fail to have damaging results. The only possible justification for it would be the certainty that popular resentment of inequality was causing so much social friction and so much inefficiency that the forcible and indiscriminate abolition of all 'privilege' would produce benefits to the community as a whole which would outweigh the inevitable loss. And this the egalitarians have never been able to prove – for the simple reason that this situation does not exist.

As with the search for equality, so it is with the pursuit of equality of opportunity. To destroy opportunities that exist, without thereby improving the opportunities of others, is to inflict grave social *in*justice. There are ways to reduce inequality of opportunity, and they should be pursued; but they will take time, and the results will only gradually become apparent. They make no appeal, therefore, to the emotions of the egalitarian fanatic or the chronically envious and embittered social rebel. They offer little material for passionate speeches, nor are they particularly effective in catching votes. But they represent the only sensible path to social reform – the only way that is both effective and morally justifiable.

CHAPTER 9

The Welfare State

Labour has set out to convert into practical reality the Socialist ideal that the best should be available to all.

***Labour Believes in Britain* (1950)**

The ultimate result of shielding man from the effects of folly is to fill the world with fools.

Herbert Spencer, *Essays*

The future of the social services is potentially the most controversial question in politics; but the controversy has remained muffled, never argued loud and clear in public. Basically it is a conflict between two quite distinct philosophies of welfare. Each has from time to time been stated, sometimes in extreme forms, but this has made remarkably little difference to what has actually happened. Changes of government have affected policies only marginally in the last twenty years, without producing any very marked change of direction or scale.

On the one hand the Conservatives have hesitated to make radical changes in the face of a public opinion which, though ill-informed about the issues at stake, has appeared suspicious of any threats to the main structure of the social services. Only after the 1964 election did official Conservative policy appear to be moving decisively in the direction of major changes. Meanwhile the Labour Party, although philosophically inclined to a policy of extending and enlarging the social services, has never felt quite sure of the amount of public support such a policy would command; it has, moreover, shrunk from the prospect of imposing the substantial increases in taxes and contributions that would be necessary.

Consequently the social services themselves have developed more or less haphazard, adapted pragmatically to meet changing circumstances and some new needs, but growing all the time as the country's population increased and its age structure changed. They have been steadily growing into vast permanent institutions, affecting not only the shape and temper of society but the functioning of the economy. They have developed, too, some of the built-in resistance to change that is characteristic of large State institutions.

This is unfortunate, and could in the long run be disastrous, for many of the basic features of the social services system were introduced in a hurry and with only an imperfect idea of what would be their full effects. Some of the aims of the system were conceived rather in terms of past needs than with an eye to a future the outlines of which were necessarily hazy to the official eye. Some of the assumptions on which Beveridge based his recommendations and the Coalition Government made their plans at the end of the war have been proved wide of the mark. Some of the services, too, were designed more to palliate old evils than to abolish them. Meanwhile needs have changed, are changing, and will change still further.

There is thus a danger that the people of Britain might, for want of taking thought for their future needs, find themselves the prisoners of a system that will become increasingly cumbersome and increasingly irrelevant to changing conditions. It is possible that this problem could be resolved without a resolution of the underlying philosophical conflict between the two contrary conceptions of the role of the welfare services, if the cost burden of the existing services grew too great or the public began to fret at the restriction of choice involved in public provision. The indications are, however, that the will to resist the gradual narrowing of choice is already greatly diminished. There is little general apprehension of what is going on or of what the issues in the controversy are.

It is often confidently asserted that the whole structure of the Welfare State has been accepted by the vast majority of the British people as a desirable and permanent institution. This is probably true in the sense that most people appreciate the benefits of the National Health Service, of retirement pensions and of free education, and would never dream of urging their total abolition. Two qualifications must, however, be added to this proposition. First, no other satisfactory system of providing these services has ever been put before people as an alternative. Secondly, because people regard the welfare services in their present form as being essential now, it does not follow that they would regard them as being equally essential, or even desirable, in a quite different set of circumstances in the future. Since very few people have even the remotest idea of what future circumstances are likely to be, the future pattern of the social services is unlikely to be of even academic interest to them. It seems probable that they will have to be forcibly confronted before long with the philosophical choice involved in the two distinct concepts of the social services, and asked to make a choice. This they will not find easy unless the practical implications are spelled out in some detail.

The decision cannot wait very long. It is essential that we should be quite sure, before it is too late, that we have not been misled by the dogma of the Welfare State into creating an over-complicated and inefficient machinery for providing services that could be better and more economically provided in other ways. The machinery of the Welfare State becomes more difficult to dismantle, and less susceptible to radical reorganisation, as the years go by. This is not only because of the political difficulties, but also because of the vested interests created. Not the least of these is the bureaucratic machine itself, which shows the normal tendency to expand in accordance with 'Parkinson's Law' and develops a built-in resistance to radical change. This does not mean that the officials do not plan ahead and try to assess the needs of the future; of course they do, and within the limits of official caution and Treasury economy they often make a very fair job of it. They are even prepared, without positive eagerness but equally without diehard resistance, to make quite considerable changes of principle and method. What they are most unlikely to do is to recommend the abolition or complete transformation of the machine itself, which they and their predecessors have created and of which they are themselves an integral part. It would, after all, be most surprising if they did.

Broadly speaking, there are two conflicting opinions about the future role of the social services. What may be called the 'permanent Welfare State' philosophy can be simply stated. It is based on the conviction that the welfare of families and individuals can best be assured by communal services run or financed by the State, and that this is true for everyone – not only for the subnormal or unfortunate. Circumstances and needs may change, and the relative importance and scale of some of the social services may decline as greater prosperity and the cumulative effects of the services themselves gradually remove some of the evils that they were designed to mitigate. But exponents of this philosophy believe that the resources thus freed should be diverted to expand and improve the other services, and even to provide benefits which have not hitherto been provided by public institutions. The scope of public provision would thus, over the years, tend to increase rather than diminish.

According to one writer, the philosophy of the Welfare State 'assumes that all citizens, not merely the abnormal, the poor, or the lower classes, have certain social needs which cannot be satisfactorily met from their personal earnings, from private or commercial services, from charity or voluntary clubbing together. It assumes that these needs – for education, medical care, income during illness and retirement, and much else – are best provided for by publicly organised services available to all by virtue simply of their citizenship, just as roads, fire brigades, and other communal facilities are used by all citizens'.[1]

Now if these are really the assumptions of the Welfare State, they are far from being permanently acceptable to everyone. Is there really a resemblance of any kind between the building of roads and the provision of an adequate income for those who have retired from work? Would everyone really agree that the whole provision for his retirement can best be made – or can even be made adequately – by publicly organised services?

The fact is that this assumption is made only by those who want to bring such a situation about for socio-political reasons. It is essential that this point should be grasped at the outset, since it is vital to an understanding of the real grounds of conflict. For those to whom social equality is the essence of social justice, it is vitally important that the publicly organised social services should be universally used, and preferable that they should be made compulsory. Compulsion can be secured either by law or by the abolition of the privately provided alternatives. This is the basis of left-wing hostility to independent schools, to private medical practice and 'pay-beds' in hospitals, to 'top-hat' pension schemes, life assurance companies and building societies. For it is a fact – not clearly appreciated by everyone – that there is nothing that more clearly draws social distinctions than the use or rejection of the publicly provided services. The freehold house, the independent school, the hospital private room and the private pension scheme suggest an entirely different world from that of the council house, the comprehensive school, the public ward and the State retirement pension. These represent the distinctions the egalitarian deplores, since he feels that they divide the nation in a way that does nothing but harm.

Those to whom the whole idea of thoroughgoing egalitarianism is repulsive react violently to this conception of the Welfare State. It seems to them simply outrageous that anyone should be forced, simply for the sake of a political theory, to put up with a lower standard of medical care, provision for old age or education for his children than he can afford to pay for as things are now.

Outrage, however, is not in itself an adequate response. It is necessary to be a little careful about how the case is argued. It will not do, for instance, to contend simply that a man has a right to do what he likes with his own money, for this principle has already been so frequently and massively breached that it can hardly be said to exist any longer as a principle at all. To this the *laisser-faire* individualist can justly make two retorts: first, that he has always argued that once the principle was initially breached nothing could logically stop indefinite encroachments upon it; and second, that the fact that a principle has once been breached does not necessarily make subsequent breaches any less offensive. The dilemma, however, is obvious. It would be hard to find anyone today prepared to argue that justice requires that every man should have the right to do as he likes with all his own money. Apart from the demands of taxation for unavoidable public needs, it has long been generally accepted that the use of wealth must be limited by the need to safeguard the rights of others.

But once the right of absolutely free disposition of one's own money has been curtailed, can the right be said to exist any longer at all? It is fatally easy to slip into the assumption that the individual's right to spend his money as he chooses is merely a residual right entirely subject to the prior requirements and policies of the State. And, once that has been accepted, it is easy to conceive of a man's income as being the pre-empted property of the State, which may graciously allow him to keep and spend such part of it as is not required for public purposes.

Now it is obvious from the way in which left-wing politicians – and even some Conservative Chancellors – talk, that this is exactly what they do think. A tax reduction is referred to as a 'concession'; a Chancellor in a position to reduce taxation is said to have such and such a sum to 'give away'. The assumption is that every citizen's income and every company's profits belong, *ab initio* and by right, to the State, which may consent to give some of it back *ex gratia* for the use of the man or the firm that earned it. This may well seem to many people an outrageous assumption, but it is as well to realise that this is the attitude not only of socialists but of many administrators thinking primarily of the financial needs of the State.

There have hitherto, however, been some checks on the application of this doctrine. Most people, even in the Labour Party, agree that some economic incentives are essential to the proper working of an economy that is even partly dependent on the market. The Government must raise enough revenue for its essential purposes, while at the same time ensuring by its fiscal policies that differences of wealth and income do not become so wide as to cause social unrest. It must also prevent inflation and provide conditions that ensure an adequate volume of savings. Beyond this, the freedom of the individual to spend his money on the things he wants cannot, it is felt, be too drastically curtailed. The things he wants must be available on the market, and he must be left free to spend enough of the money he earns to make him feel that it is worth while working to earn it.

Of course there is room for interminable argument about what is a 'reasonable' proportion to achieve this end, and many people would maintain that the proportion at present left to the individual is too small. There can be no certain answer to this, and policy can be determined only empirically on the basis of observed results. Nevertheless, so long as we retain an economic system based more upon the operation of the market than on central planning, the need to provide incentives will to some extent limit the degree of State interference with the citizen's right to spend his own money.

This, then, is one possible limitation on the universal application of the Welfare State philosophy in its extreme socialist form. If all the apparatus of social welfare were to be made egalitarian and compulsory, with all scope for private supplementation outside the State system removed, would this significantly reduce the individual's incentives to earn and save? It is very hard to give any certain answer to this question. To the extent that certain privileges are felt to be part of 'the middle-class way of life', the desire to purchase them almost certainly does provide some incentive to earn and save more. Private pension schemes and life assurance policies, independent schooling for children and private rooms in hospitals combine the attraction of status symbols with the ability to satisfy the not ignoble desire to do the best possible for the welfare and future of one's family. But who could hope to quantify the economic loss, through reduced effort and lack of incentive to the creation of wealth, that might result from the removal of these objects of middle-class endeavour? The attempt is obviously absurd. Undoubtedly great resentment would be caused, and in theory some diminution of incentives would follow; but it is impossible to say what the effects would be. Nor, even if it were possible, can one realistically measure the advantages now derived from the existence of these incentives against what the egalitarians claim are the social disadvantages of the division of societyinto two groups. More middle-class people would emigrate: beyond that, the whole argument is nebulous in the extreme.

Middle-class people themselves – and indeed many working-class people, too – complain of the demoralising effects which they claim the Welfare State services are having among some sections of the working class. There has been some talk of the 'cynical exploitation of the Welfare State' by the workers. A typical exposition of this thesis was contained in one of the earlier manifestoes of a right-wing body called the National Fellowship: 'The Welfare State has gone too far. It is breeding a nation of idlers. Families and individuals should stand upon their own feet. National Assistance should only be available in cases of genuine hardship.'

To say that the British are a 'nation of idlers' is of course the purest hyperbole, and misses the real point. It is no doubt perfectly true that it is today easier to be feckless and irresponsible without actually starving than it was fifty years ago; but it is as well to remember that for those without private means it is nearly always much more comfortable to work for a living than not to do so. Certainly there are people who 'exploit' the Welfare State, in respect of medical certificates, sickness benefit, supplementary benefits and council house subsidies. But society has always contained a proportion of people who are idle, irresponsible or unscrupulous, and no doubt there were those who exploited private and monastic charity long before the advent of the State social services.

That there is some laxity in the administration of the social services, particularly in respect of supplementary benefits and the issue of medical certificates of sickness, is true; to the extent that it is, it is in administration that the cure lies. Sometimes, as in the case of the much publicised 'abuses' of the National Health Service for foreigners, the loss is too small to justify the administrative cost and the inconvenience to genuine users of the service that would be necessary to stop all the loopholes. But in any case it is not easy to prove – however deeply convinced some people may be of it on general principles – that the mere existence of the opportunities provided by the Welfare State has greatly increased the number of idle, irresponsible and unscrupulous citizens in Britain. Even if it had had some such effect, the harmful results might still be insignificant in relation to the real benefits conferred on the deserving.

It might well be, too, that such irresponsibility and exploitation as exist are due to a deeper malaise; it could be argued that the Welfare State is no more a cause of idleness and irresponsibility than the existence of a bank is a cause of burglary. They are in part due to the same causes that have produced cheating and petty dishonesty among employees, as well as the growth of more serious crime.

Just as the football pools are the poor man's Stock Exchange, the social services are to some what the expense account is (or used to be) to the business executive. Tightening up the administration and the benefit provisions of the social services would no doubt, like reducing the tax concessions for the business executive's 'expenses', reduce some of the symptoms; but it would scarcely cure the disease. It would make it more difficult to exploit the social service funds – probably at the cost of irritating restrictions and formalities for the innocent majority of citizens – and marginally harder for unscrupulous workers to cheat their employers. But so long as the impulse was there, other methods would certainly be discovered. It is not so much the temptation of the means that needs to be removed as the causes of the willingness to abuse them. These are all part of a 'class war' being waged throughout industry, and for which management must presumably bear some responsibility. Some of the remedies lie in the field of industrial relations.

In fact, complaints about 'exploitation' of the welfare services miss the real points at issue. The actual abuses of the system are not substantial enough to justify, by themselves, the scrapping of the system. The real question is whether the system itself is the most efficient way of getting certain things done. Unfortunately, of course, there is no unanimous agreement even on what are the things to be achieved.

The opponents of the Welfare State philosophy base their opposition on two main theses. The first is that the services necessary for welfare can often be more efficiently provided without the immense organisation that an all-embracing State service requires. The second is that the present system seriously restricts freedom of choice for many people and weakens personal and family responsibility. They do not deny that the State services have in fact widened the range of choices available to some people, and enabled them to discharge some responsibilities which they could not otherwise have managed. They believe, however, that circumstances have changed, and are changing, to an extent that has put the possibility of personal provision within the reach of many more people than before. Increasing prosperity, if it were coupled with increasing confidence in the future, might enable some of the Welfare State services to be replaced by the ability and willingness of individuals to save and pay for their own security and services through methods chosen by themselves from between genuine available alternatives.

Of course the services, and the needs for which they are designed, differ widely, so that there is no reason to suppose that the same principles must be applied equally to all of them. Retirement pensions and education, for example, have very little in common; it is one thing to compel parents to send their children to schools of recognised efficiency, but quite another to force them to save through a State pension scheme. The provision of housing by local authorities for letting to tenants, especially at rents subsidised from rates and taxes, is something else again.

What we have to do is to take an impartial look at the arguments both of the apostles of the total Welfare State, who would have all the social welfare services wholly and compulsorily provided for everyone by the State or its agencies, and of those who believe that the Welfare State has 'gone too far' and ought to be encouraged to wither away. This is inclined to degenerate into an all-or-nothing controversy, in which neither side is prepared to concede a single point to the other. Yet it is at least possible that neither side is wholly wrong over the whole field.

The strongest argument for examining the whole system now with the greatest care is that it will become less and less easy to change it as the years pass. Both psychologically and institutionally the system will become increasingly accepted and less susceptible to change. The transfer of responsibility from individuals and families to the State and its agencies will continue to proceed with general agreement – or at least without overt opposition. The philosophy of the total Welfare State will win by default.

If the full egalitarian *theory* of the Welfare State were to be accepted in this country the results would, I believe, be disastrous. It is one thing to argue that health, education and social security services can be provided efficiently for the majority only by the State and its agencies, and that the services can only be fully effective if everyone contributes to them. The argument stands or falls on the case made out for the unique *efficiency* of comprehensiveness: if that thesis cannot be substantiated, then compulsion cannot be justified, and everyone must be free to use privately organised alternatives to the State services if they wish. But it is quite another thing to seek to justify comprehensiveness and compulsion on grounds of social egalitarianism. This argument amounts to the enforcement of uniformity irrespective of whether the results are efficient and irrespective of comparative costs. The proponents of this thesis are frankly prepared to destroy freedom of choice, and even to deny a better standard of service to a proportion of the population, simply for the sake of an ideological doctrine. At best, they put forward a hypothetical case for the beneficial social results of egalitarianism, which they cannot prove, and which many people believe to be completely imaginary.

We discussed the myth of 'social justice' at some length in Chapter 7, and came to the conclusion that equality cannot possibly be justified as an end in itself, but only as a matter of social utility or expediency. It must be clearly shown that either inequalities are so widely and deeply resented as to threaten the stability of society or the efficiency of the economy, or that the aggregate quality of the nation's life and welfare would be substantially improved by the enforcement of equality at all costs. On neither of these grounds can a case be made out for the compulsory extension of the Welfare State. The amount of discernible resentment is very small. In present circumstances, too, it is clear that most of the proposals for reducing the existing inequalities between publicly and privately provided welfare services would actually reduce the total quantity and quality of the services. They would involve destroying the high quality of private provision, without appreciably improving quality in the public sector.

On the other hand, the case for retaining a private sector – in education, health services, housing and provision for old age – is overwhelming. It can (although it does not follow that it always does) act as pioneer, pace-setter and yardstick, providing both competition in service and quality and an alternative area for experiment and innovation. It is essential to the professional freedom of the people running the services that there should be alternative employers to the State. It is also important for our culture and the quality of our life that there should be something available which is superior in quality to services which are always in the last resort limited by the availability of public money. This is not to say that private provision should necessarily be subsidised, although there may be sound reasons for encouraging by tax concessions both home ownership and the use of private services which reduce the volume of public expenditure. These decisions must be taken *ad hoc*, in the light of prevailing conditions. The essential point is that the availability of private provision must not be deliberately destroyed or reduced by government action dictated by an egalitarian ideology.

It is desirable, as I have already argued, rather to extend than to contract the area of free choice for individuals and families. Diversity, rather than universal dependence on the State, is desirable in itself. Unless it can be proved – and in most cases it cannot – that provision by a single State agency is overwhelmingly more efficient and less costly in aggregate to the community, then there is everything to be said for competing private agencies subject to the discipline of a free market.

How then ought the publicly provided services to develop? While it is possible to apply the same philosophical yardstick to all of them, it does not follow that all will, or ought to, develop in the same way. The possibilities of alternative privately financed provision are not the same in every case. Nor can one apply the principle of 'selectivity' in the fields of health and education in anything like the same way that is possible for social security, pensions and housing.

The alternative lines of development in the health services are few. The hospitals will remain under the control of some kind of public body; whether this should take the form of regional hospital boards, or whether control should ultimately be transferred to local authorities, involves no major question of principle. The important question is whether all patients should be required to pay a charge for board or for professional and nursing services. It should be realised that to insist on this would in fact not significantly enlarge the area of personal choice; indeed, in some cases it would actually narrow it. For it is already open to anyone to insure himself and his family with one of the medical benefit groups, and to make use of private consultants, nursing homes or pay-beds in hospitals. The question is whether making this compulsory by statute, or virtually compulsory by demanding payment for hospital services from all but the poorest, would be worth while in terms of administration and saving of public money. Probably it would not, nor is it very likely that the resulting service would be on balance markedly better. But there is as yet no certainty about this.

There is clearly more to be said for putting the general practitioner and pharmaceutical services of the N.H.S. on to a basis of charges financed by personal insurance. A possible method would be to make medical insurance on the lowest contribution scale compulsory – except perhaps for the poorest – and giving tax concessions to encourage supplementary provision at a higher rate. This would enlarge the area of choice for many people and reduce the cost of the services to public funds. The scheme could be made administratively simpler than the existing one.

This solution is often advocated on the grounds that it would act as a deterrent to unnecessary calls on family doctors and wasteful prescribing of expensive drugs. Certainly it would have this effect, but too much should not be made of the argument. It is at least debatable whether we want to risk financial deterrents to cases of genuine medical need, and great care would have to be taken to ensure that this danger did not outweigh the desirable savings.

By far the strongest argument for freeing the family doctor from State employment is that the service may ultimately break down if we do not. Discontent with the present situation is very strong in the medical profession, and the rate of emigration of young and middle-aged general practitioners and hospital doctors is alarmingly high. We are only just compensating for this by employing very large numbers of Asian immigrant doctors. There is no doubt that most doctors would welcome the greater freedom of private practice, *provided that they did not feel that cases of genuine need were being kept from them by financial deterrents.*

In education, the essential thing is to preserve the area of free choice and private provision that we already have, and to defend it against the assaults of the egalitarians. To extend the area is much more difficult. It is by no means impossible, and the logical arguments for some kind of 'voucher' system can be made to sound extremely convincing.[2] The most common version of the scheme is that under which parents of school-age children are given State vouchers, generally for a sum of money equivalent to the cost of educating a child in a maintained school for the appropriate age-group. These can either be presented in full payment for education at maintained schools to be chosen by the parents, or can be used in part-payment of fees at independent or direct grant schools (the State paying the cash value of the vouchers to the schools). It is hard to see how this scheme would result in any saving of public money, as some of its proponents claim, unless the value of the voucher were fixed well below the cost of education at a maintained school. If it were not below this level, the net result would be a subsidy to parents already sending their children to fee-paying schools.

The argument is strongest in terms of increased parental choice, but it scarcely seems as strong as it is often claimed. No doubt a marginal number of additional parents would be encouraged to send their children to independent schools, since for some the part-remission of fees through the voucher would make enough difference to swing their choice. Whether this would justify what would almost certainly be a considerably increased amount of administrative work is doubtful: much the same result might be achieved by the much simpler method of admitting more schools to the State's direct-grant list. It is hard to see how freedom of choice could in practice be significantly increased in the maintained sector, given the very great pressure already existing on school places. The tendency might well be for the worst schools to become worse, and for the better schools to be forced into rapid expansion, which would be both costly in capital expenditure and awkward to administer.

In the field of social security and pensions there is clearly considerable scope for the extension of private provision and supplementation. The right policy for the immediate future would seem to be to give every encouragement to industrial pension schemes and private contractual saving, through tax concessions in particular, while resisting all pleas for the extension of the State system. Once a start has been made, for example, with the Labour Party's plan for earnings-related retirement pensions, it will be extremely difficult to reverse the trend. On grounds of public expenditure, freedom of choice and independence from State-controlled uniformity, it is clearly better to encourage private provision of higher retirement pensions than to extend the State scheme beyond a basic flat-rate minimum. Meanwhile, whenever it is thought possible to devote more resources to social security benefits, the additional resources should be devoted selectively to raising the living standards of those most in need before increasing flat-rate benefits for all.

Family allowances should, for the present, be retained, since to abolish them would certainly start irresistible pressure for inflationary wage and salary increases – which would be granted to bachelors and childless men as well as to parents. It might be possible to devise a selective system for family allowances, however, or even to transfer them from the State to industrial insurance schemes.

We come finally to housing. At present we have a situation in which local authority housing, originally designed to meet the needs of the worst-off, has become too expensive for many of the poorest people. The first step should be to abolish subsidies on houses, and give help only to needy tenants. This would reduce the incentive to occupy council houses for those who can afford to buy their own houses or rent privately owned accommodation. Tax concessions for home-owners and private landlords should be increased rather than diminished, and every effort made (by means of grants and loans) to encourage the repair and rehabilitation of older houses. Hitherto, private landlords have been discouraged from expanding their share of the market for rented houses and flats because of the Labour Party's devotion to rent control. There now seems some hope that the switch from rent control to a 'fair rents' system may ultimately produce a situation in which the private landlord may be encouraged to expand.* If not, the aim should be to encourage the expansion of independent housing trusts and associations, free from local authority control.

The object of all these proposals is not to destroy the social services but to restrict provision to those areas where it is most efficient. The aim is to free as many people as possible from the need to rely entirely (or even mainly) on public authorities, to restore a greater degree of family responsibility and initiative, and to increase their freedom of choice by expanding the amount of private provision. At the same time, by reducing the pointless redistribution of funds where no net benefit is secured, it should be possible both to lower administrative costs and concentrate help where it is most needed.

The day will no doubt come when it will be possible to reduce the mass of tax and rate levies, National Insurance contributions and flat-rate benefit payments involved in the present redistributive system almost to nothing. It is theoretically possible to plan a computer complex which will reduce each individual's liabilities and claims to a single net payment either to or from the State. There are dangers in the centralisation of information and decisions, and perhaps less scope for flexibility in administration and sympathetic treatment of borderline cases, so that it may well be undesirable to 'rationalise' the system to the full extent which technology will one day make possible. Nevertheless, there is considerable scope for simplification.

* Strict control will be needed, in the case of both new owner-occupied and rented houses, over design and layout. The standards are often markedly lower in the cheaper private developments than in council building.

It will be remembered that in Chapter 1 we examined the processes by which the relationships and responsibilities of the family have been altered and confused, so that the institution itself no longer seems to have any clear philosophical grounding. It is obvious that an indefinitely continuing extension of the Welfare State, such as is desired by some people for ideological reasons, would progressively encroach on the independence and responsibilities of the family group; it would seem to follow that those who advocate an opposite policy, such as that sketched above, must be prepared to justify on some general grounds their intention to defend the family against these encroachments and if possible restore some of its responsibilities.

In the last chapter, too, we noted that there is today some ideological pressure to 'socialise' the family in the interests of 'equality of opportunity'. If it is considered 'unfair' that a child should get a bad start in life because of an unsatisfactory family background, it seems logical to remove the unfairness by trying to eliminate the inequalities that originate in the home. It is clear that we must firmly resist the emotional arguments of those who seek a short cut to equality of opportunity through the removal of the benefits enjoyed by those they call 'privileged'. The only justifiable policy is one aimed at improving the conditions of the less fortunate, relatively as well as absolutely.

This can be done in two ways. It can be achieved through the machinery of the social services, including policies designed to improve bad housing conditions and inadequate schools; but some results can also be achieved by creating conditions in which people can be better enabled to help themselves. The objective should be to secure the right blend of both methods. Some people will never be able to do much for themselves, and for them the social services must bear most of the burden. Yet it should never be summarily assumed that they can do *nothing* for themselves, or they will too easily come to believe it and become actually incapable; sometimes the will to self-help and the capability of pursuing it can be stimulated and increased by the right conditions and encouragement. At the same time it is essential to resist the tendency to believe that because *some* people need help *everyone* must be offered it (or even compelled to accept it). It is not just that there will always be people – perhaps many more than is generally supposed – who will resent being compelled to pay taxes and contributions in order to have done for them things they would prefer to organise for themselves. The greater danger is that many more people will suffer a gradual weakening of their will and ability to look after themselves and their families independently in their own individual way.

Family responsibility is being eroded in two ways. First, the opportunity for choice and individual action is being gradually removed. For many – if not most – families, it is becoming impossible to choose the school to which their children will go to be educated. The destruction of the market in privately provided rented accommodation, with the consequent growth of the proportion of council houses, is removing even the choice of a home from many families, making them dependent on the decisions of local authority officials and committees. This can also split families up, forcing children to move to other areas when they marry. The sphere of the family doctor, chosen by the family and personally familiar with their circumstances and relationships, is being gradually contracted.

The second trend is quite different, and even more dangerous. The things we have just considered result for the most part from policies ostensibly pursued in the interests of families, since they are regarded as being the most efficient ways of providing certain services; the adverse secondary effects have not been adequately appreciated. But there is also a tendency to weaken the institution of the family quite deliberately, in the interests of individual members of the family. This is seen in the desire to 'socialise', as far as is possible, the family in order to minimise the inequalities arising from different family backgrounds. That tendency must be firmly resisted on philosophical grounds. Any benefits which may possibly accrue to a minority of individuals are likely to be far outweighed by the loss of independence and individuality by the majority. Independence in the 'private sphere' is almost an end in itself for humanity, and it is certainly not something that should be taken from the majority in the interests of a few. Again, diversity is the source of creation and progress, which are inevitably stifled by an imposed uniformity.

The deliberate attack on the family institution takes other, more controversial forms. The moral attitude towards marriage, and towards the responsibility for procreating and bringing up children, has been changed by the deliberate propaganda of 'liberal reformers'. The argument about cause and effect tends to run in a circle, but two things are pretty clear. The more or less continuous pressure to make divorce and remarriage increasingly easier has been entirely based on arguments of the 'hard case' type, and its proponents have generally purported to be seeking only to legislate for the exceptions rather than for the majority; nevertheless, they have clearly been taking a much looser view of the marriage bond and of family ties than used to be conventional, or they would not have been prepared to risk the obvious consequences of making divorce so much easier. For the consequences *are* obvious. What has been happening has gone far beyond permissive legislation to legalise an already widely prevalent attitude. The attitude itself has been spread wider and wider by the ready availability of the escape route and by the example of those who have previously taken it. It is not simply that the knowledge that marriages can be dissolved with comparative ease encourages some couples to get married more 'lightly and unadvisedly' than might otherwise have been the case; what is much more important is that it greatly weakens for some people the determination to surmount the difficulties that arise in every marriage and to make the marriage work.

The result has been an enormously increased number of dissolved marriages, broken homes and children deprived of a solid family background. It has become much easier (and inevitably, in consequence, more common) for middle-aged men to desert their wives for younger women and to start a second 'family', often leaving the first in financial as well as other difficulties. The 'liberal' argument in favour of all this takes two forms, both sentimental and superficial. One is that it is better that an unhappy marriage should be dissolved, so that the two partners can have a fresh chance of 'finding happiness'; this argument ignores the fact that it is very much easier for the middle-aged husband to remarry to his satisfaction than for the middle-aged wife, especially if she has children. The second argument is that it is worse for children to be brought up in an unhappy home than for bickering parents to be separated; however sensible this may sound in theory, it is very far from being always proved true in practice. All in all, it is at least extremely doubtful whether the sum total of human happiness, taking that of husbands, wives and children together, has not been actually diminished by the changes that have taken place. It is probable that for every happy new marriage that has followed a divorce, two or three marriages have been dissolved which with patience and courage could have been made to survive and succeed.

There are those who argue that the gradual changes that have taken place in the status of the family have been inevitable, since the family is an economic and social institution that must necessarily change in conformity with alterations in economic organisation and social conditions. To some extent this is obviously true: it is at least open to question whether the family pattern suitable for the patriarchal nomadic tribe or for small-scale peasant agriculture is necessarily the most suitable for a sophisticated urban civilisation. On the other hand, the argument begs at least as many questions as it answers. For example, if economic and social changes have produced pressures on the family which have had on balance a bad effect on individual men, women and children, does it follow that we ought to encourage still further adaptive changes in the family institution? Is it not possible that it is the organisation of the economy and of society that is wrong?

When we come to answer the fundamental question, what is the purpose and function of the family, it becomes clear that there are certain functions which have not changed significantly. What *has* changed is that there are now other institutions which purport to be able to offer an alternative method of performing some of these functions.

The family is no longer an indispensable economic unit, nor does it now provide the basis of a system of government and defence, as it did in some past civilisations. However, its primary functions are still to provide for the nurture of children, to enable the community to identify someone who can be held legally and morally responsible for the children's welfare, and to provide the domestic and financial security which a woman needs if she is to be able to bear and rear children satisfactorily. A scarcely less important function is to forge links of affection and responsibility which will ensure that members of the family are properly looked after when they are unable, owing to age or sickness, to look after themselves.

Now it is precisely these enduring functions of the family for which the theory of the Welfare State purports to provide alternative machinery. This is often dignified by the title of 'communal provision'; the title is, however, wholly misleading, for services run by central and local government officials are not at all the same thing as the care of those in need of help which is provided personally by members of a genuine community. Since only very small communities are likely to be sufficiently closely knit to make this kind of care possible,* it is obviously desirable that there should be some machinery available as a 'safety net' for those who cannot, for one reason or another, be properly cared for by their families. But this can never, despite the arguments of those who maintain that it is 'more efficient', be a really adequate substitute for the care which is based on the genuine love and responsibility of a united family. It is therefore important that people should not be persuaded that it is. It is possible to feel compassion for a married couple, perhaps with children, who are called on to look after an elderly relative, and it is only right that they should be given all the help that is possible. But it is not right that they should be encouraged to believe that the ultimate responsibility is not theirs but the State's. The end result of weakening the sense of family responsibility, whether the responsibility be towards a wife, children, or parents and grandparents, is to destroy something that is truly irreplaceable and to reduce the sum of human happiness.

The family home, with its family connections extending to other households, is the basic unit of the community, and no

* Although still more could be done by voluntary effort, especially for the old, than at present.

genuine community is possible if the family is destroyed. Both in our social service and housing policies and in our attitude towards marriage and divorce and individual responsibility for the family, we must seek always to strengthen rather than weaken it.

CHAPTER 10

The Transitional Economy

The problem . . . lends itself most readily to two types of treatment: it can be made the object of a highly technical scientific study, in which varying interpretations of different sets of statistics are carefully weighed, and a small grain of certainty laboriously winnowed from the chaff of speculation; or the writer may start from certain implicit assumptions, treating his own qualitative judgments as self-evident facts and proceeding to the solution of problems which he has himself invented. Neither of these methods would be wholly satisfactory in the present context.

Roy Lewis and Angus Maude, *The English Middle Classes*

Practical men, who believe themselves to be quite exempt from any intellectual influences, are usually the slaves of some defunct economist. Madmen in authority, who hear voices in the air, are distilling their frenzy from some academic scribbler of a few years back.

J. M. Keynes, *The General Theory of Employment, Interest and Money*

There are two serious problems which arise from a state of full employment in a more or less free economy. One is the danger of demand inflation, leading to rising prices which in their turn provoke wage increases leading to still higher prices. This process, besides causing great hardship to the economically weak, also leads in certain circumstances to serious balance of payments difficulties. The other besetting problem of the free economy in a state of full employment is the difficulty of securing the optimum (or even a rational) balance between private expenditure on goods for consumption and communal expenditure on services and on things which endure for useful purposes.

Of the two problems – despite a widespread conviction to the contrary – the second is the more difficult to resolve. This is so, not only because demand inflation is largely a political problem and one relatively easy to control given the requisite willingness and courage, but because some people deny that the second problem even exists at all in any meaningful sense.

In addition to these two problems, consideration of our present economic difficulties is complicated by the fact that much of the popular theory that is supposed to explain them is still based on assumptions from which reality is increasingly divorcing itself. This is not simply a matter of the post-war tendency to apply Keynesian remedies to situations which Keynes scarcely contemplated, for the worst excesses in this direction have now been somewhat crudely corrected. There have been many other changes with which theory cannot yet cope. Competition is taking forms very different from the simple concepts of economists. The actions of governments create situations and produce secondary effects which are often alien to theory and highly disruptive of attempts at prediction. Above all, the increasing tendency of production to become a law unto itself – to produce what its own necessities seem to require rather than what the necessities of consumers would otherwise effectively demand – has results which are still imperfectly appreciated.

It is true that a change has come over economics itself, apart from the change in the facts with which it has to deal. The first stirrings of change were perhaps perceptible when Keynes showed that the classical theory of economics was correct only in a set of circumstances which had never been achieved. Economists began to look at the facts of life with a new eye, and statistics became more important than the operation of the 'invisible hand'. The science of econometrics began to get off the ground, and the publication in 1940 of Colin Clark's *Conditions of Economic Progress* was a portent. The cult of Growth had begun.

The new economist has available to him an ever increasing quantity of data, together with rapidly improving techniques of measurement and calculation. He is increasingly able – though by no means as yet perfectly, and not always very quickly – to find out what is actually happening, or at least what was happening fairly recently. By the application of mathematical techniques to his data, he is able to perceive and explain relationships and processes, which in turn encourages him to extrapolate and predict. This naturally reawakens in him the economist's primeval yearning not only to advise but actually to influence events. From predicting the consequences of proposed actions it is but a step to the recommendation of alternative action. And the increasing complexity of the economy makes it increasingly hard for the non-economist to understand what is going on: not only the government but large organisations – companies as well as trade associations, trade unions and the like – must have their teams of economic advisers. These are increasingly technicians rather than theorists. Messrs. Balogh and Kaldor were old-fashioned anachronisms, among the last of a dying and already irrelevant species. They still had theories.

We have already noticed the extent to which politics and economics are becoming co-terminous. Increasingly it is the economic policies and performance of governments and parties which form the staple of political discussion and which determine the results of elections. Conservatives are apt to bewail this process, attributing it to the increasing influence of socialism. In effect, they diagnose the process as one of increasing interference by the State – by governments – in the working of the economy; since this is, in these terms, a deliberate and voluntary process, which they deplore, it is represented as reversible. But this is based on a questionable assumption. Is it not in fact much truer to say that the economy has been interfering in – indeed swallowing up – politics than that the reverse is true?

Whether one approaches this problem from the point of view of J. K. Galbraith's *The Affluent Society* or of Jacques Ellul's *The Technological Society*, the answer is much the same. In Galbraith's diagnosis the pressure comes from an obsolete economic theory which poses as the overriding aim the maximum production of goods, which in its turn requires the stimulation of maximum consumption. Ellul sees an unremitting pressure – indeed a semi-automatic process – towards the full and 'efficient' exploitation of the resources and capacity of technology in industry, which requires the economic 'techniques' of the State to complement them and give them due scope. The explanations of the motives differ, but the results are very similar and conform to what is readily observable.

In Britain, at any rate, the official policies of all three

political parties accept the stimulation of 'economic growth' as the primary task of government. They propose to set about it in slightly different ways, but the primacy of the objective is assumed. Economic growth will provide the 'good life' for the people.

At the same time, however, the economic slogans of the parties have to a large extent ceased to be relevant to the economic realities. The Conservative and Liberal parties, while accepting the need for some measure of State intervention for social purposes – not only to maintain full employment but to provide for the social services and to protect the weak and unfortunate – still claim that economic growth will best be achieved through 'competitive free enterprise'. Mr. Enoch Powell, acting as the conscience of the Conservative Party in this matter, keeps it up to the mark with speech after speech extolling the unmatchable and irreplaceable virtues of the market economy.

It is sometimes said that Mr. Powell has resurrected the doctrines of Alfred Marshall, and preaches the pure milk of classical economic theory, as though Keynes had never been. It is, however, instructive to recall what Keynes himself had to say in the 'concluding notes' to the *General Theory*. After pointing out that the tacit assumptions of the classical theory 'are seldom or never satisfied', he conceded that, 'if our central controls succeed in establishing an aggregate volume of output corresponding to full employment as nearly as is practicable, the classical theory comes into its own again from this point onwards'. There would still remain, he insisted, 'a wide field for the exercise of private initiative and responsibility', within which 'the traditional advantages of individualism will still hold good'. There follows this remarkable paragraph:

> Let us stop for a moment to remind ourselves what these advantages are. They are partly advantages of efficiency – the advantages of decentralisation and of the play of self-interest. The advantage to efficiency of the decentralisation of decisions and of individual responsibility is even greater, perhaps, than the nineteenth century supposed; and the reaction against the appeal to self-interest may have gone too far. But, above all, individualism, if it can be purged of its defects and its abuses, is the best safeguard of personal liberty in the sense that, compared with any other system, it

> greatly widens the field for the exercise of personal choice. It is also the best safeguard of the variety of life, which emerges precisely from this extended field of personal choice, and the loss of which is the greatest of all the losses of the homogeneous or totalitarian state. For this variety preserves the traditions which embody the most secure and successful choices of former generations; it colours the present with the diversification of its fancy; and, being the handmaid of experiment as well as of tradition and of fancy, it is the most powerful instrument to better the future.[1]

It might almost be Mr. Powell speaking – or even Dr. F. A. Hayek. What is more, it is certainly true. The question is, what relation does it bear to the realities of today?

Let us take, for example, 'the advantage to efficiency of the decentralisation of decisions'. Not only is decision-making becoming more and more centralised over a widening range of industry, but its advocates continually insist that this centralisation *is essential to efficiency*. There is also 'the field for the exercise of personal choice'. Now there is a sense in which this can be said to have widened and to be still widening; but it is a rather special sense. It is true that there are far more different articles of consumption that have been brought within the reach of the average wage-earner. Increasingly, however, these tend not to be articles which he consciously 'wanted', or would have chosen, but articles designed to meet the convenience of their producers and for which an artificial demand has been laboriously created by the lavish use of advertising. Meanwhile each article tends to become increasingly standardised for the convenience of mass production, with a diminishing range of models or qualities to meet individual tastes and preferences.

Even where there are 'competing' firms in the market, the tendency is to produce much the same product in much the same limited range of models and qualities, and above all at much the same price. Production is more and more geared to meet the statistical average of demand. The result is often to bring a higher quality article within the reach of those of modest means, but to lower the quality available to those of moderate means. In the case of many articles of everyday use, what used to be considered normal good quality by middle-class people is now available only at very high prices to the rich. Many simple articles for household use, which were once produced in fairly small quantities from cheap materials, are now either not produced at all or are produced only in more expensive materials or with the addition of some 'gimmick' which adds to the price while detracting from the utility. Quality of some kinds of product tends to become standardised at a low average of mediocrity, with a flashy but often inferior finish and a high frequency of production defects.

And all the time the number of 'competing' firms is diminishing. Individual enterprise still brings new small firms into existence to exploit a new product or a new technique, but it is becoming increasingly rare for them to retain their independence once they have become established. Apart from the occasional maverick and the man operating on the smallest scale, the individual entrepreneur is becoming a creature of the past. The trend will continue until the tax system is changed, to make enterprise worth while.

The executive experts in control of large firms are not fond of taking risks. They would consider this a breach of duty to their shareholders. Galbraith was perfectly correct in his analysis of the psychology of the executive of big business.[2] His aim is above all security, to be covered against every kind of risk and uncertainty. He will try to secure his raw materials and components, and even his sales outlets, by vertical combination. Only in exceptional and desperate circumstances will he relinquish his skilled labour during a recession of demand for his product, in case he cannot get it back when business improves; he will rather resort temporarily to short time and work-sharing. He will nearly always seek to avoid price competition, by making agreements with his rivals. If competition becomes too keen, and his share of the market cannot easily be increased by advertising and hard selling, he will seek first to divide the market by agreement and then explore the possibility of merger or takeover. His ideal is a nice steady growth of production, and he is all for a government that will guarantee him steady and uninterrupted economic growth.

All this is very far from the ideal operator envisaged by Keynes and by Mr. Powell. Today's manager is concerned to make the consumer want what he produces rather than to produce what the consumer wants. He is not passionately anxious to make a better product so long as he can hope to go on selling what he now produces. He is not at all independent-minded, and not particularly enterprising. As for being the 'handmaid of experiment' and 'colouring the present with the diversification of his fancy', the very idea is enough to give him nightmares.

All this is as disturbing to Conservative enthusiasts for free-enterprise capitalism as a well-backed racehorse that stops to graze halfway down the course. To socialists it often appears to afford satisfaction, for it seems to improve the chances of their own horse. Their arguments are, of course, as irrelevant as those of their opponents. Some say, 'Since your capitalists display none of the qualities which you claim are the cardinal virtues of your system, we will nationalise the wretched fellows, and then they will have to work in the national interest.' Everyone else knows quite well, of course, that the result would be to make the whole industry even more cautious and unenterprising than the big firms are now, besides removing such competition as now exists and preventing new entrants to the industry from introducing any new ideas at all. Others, however, take a slightly different line. 'If your capitalists,' they say, 'refuse to be enterprising, then we will force them to be enterprising (in the national interest, of course) by making them conform to a National Plan.' But the joke is that a 'national plan' (of the right kind, of course) is exactly what many big businessmen want. It has nothing whatever to do with being enterprising; the idea is to secure the nice steady economic growth required to give them a nice steady growth of production.

Yet here is Mr. Powell, together with a large section of the Conservative Party, inveighing against government intervention and planning, on the grounds that they prevent free enterprise from having the scope for the things which (presumably) it desperately wants to do if it is given a chance. Other Conservatives have spotted the snag, and now speak of the possible need for partial or 'indicative' planning – a setting of the framework, so to speak, within which free enterprise can be enterprising. This, which used to be called 'liberal interventionism' in America, is not very far in theory from what Keynes was advocating. The question is, has it any practical meaning now?

Mr. Ernest Marples, who knows something of the potentialities of modern technology, is confident that massive economic growth is possible in Britain if British industry will only take advantage of the newest technical methods available. It is not always clear whether he believes that British industry actually would take this advantage, if government were simply to provide the right economic 'climate' and the right fiscal incentives: or rather, it *is* fairly clear that this is what he would like to believe and even feels that he ought to say. Occasionally, however, a faint note of impatience is discernible. British industry, we gather, will have to pull up its socks if it doesn't want to be left behind by the foreigners. And if it doesn't pull up its socks, well . . . there is a dark suggestion that ways can probably be found to make it (in the national interest, of course). Tariff protection, monopolies, restrictive practices, price agreements – all these could do with looking into.

Mr. Powell, sternly confident that free consumer choice and more or less untrammelled free enterprise will do the job if given half a chance, would no doubt go along with much of this. He approves of the government removing the obstacles to free choice and competition, so long as it does not then try to do anything helpful. This, by definition, would be bound to fail – or at least be less effective than what the market would contrive if left to itself.

Meanwhile, many rank-and-file Conservatives (like many rank-and-file businessmen) are equally unmoved by Mr. Marples' technology and Mr. Powell's militant economic liberalism. If there is, they feel, anything wrong with things as they are, it is due to too much government interference and to all this nonsense about planning.

Things are just as confused on the Labour side of the fence. Mr. Wilson is addicted to extraordinarily vague dissertations about 'purposive planning' (though it is hard to see how anything that had no purpose could possibly be called a 'plan'), and sometimes about 'purposive intervention' (as if his alternative course of action would be to intervene without any purpose at all). At the same time, he is just as enthusiastic about the technological revolution as a means to economic growth as is Mr. Marples; in fact he pre-empted this line with some inspiring speeches in 1963 and 1964 which did much to win him the 1964 election. It is true that in office he has done very little about it; but this is possibly due to the fact that before his plans had had time to mature his government was cutting back investment so savagely that it might have seemed in poor taste to urge industry to modernise itself in a hurry. Many of his trade union followers, however, are very dubious indeed about all this technology: it sounds altogether too much like automation, and everyone knows that automation means good honest craftsmen being replaced by computers.

It is, indeed, all very confusing. But it is not really so funny, after all. When you have, not only inside one political party but inside both, spokesmen advocating economic policies which are almost certainly incompatible, one wonders what is likely to be the result of trying to enforce them. Sooner or later we have got to make up our minds about growth, planning and technology; and the decisions we make will determine the whole nature not only of our economy but of our society for many years ahead.

We need not waste time discussing the question of whether further nationalisation of industry would help to solve any of our economic problems, since all sensible people are agreed that it would not. If what is needed is a reversal of the trend towards monopoly and away from competition, then the forcible creation of new monopolies would clearly be folly. If, on the other hand, we need still more concentration in order to achieve further economies of scale and more efficient use of new large-scale processes, the desired results are likely to be more efficiently secured by allowing the concentration to proceed, as at present, through the pressures of the market rather than by imposing a rigid pattern from above. If what we need is more enterprise, a greater readiness to take risks, more courage and ruthlessness in scrapping the old and substituting the new, then we know from experience that nationalisation will not provide it; innovation will be slow, costly, and interrupted by changes of government economic policy.

The real question is this: have we any effective choice about the way in which our economy will develop, about the objectives of economic activity, and about the relationships between government and economic activity that these will involve?

It is not quite such an easy question to answer as it sounds. Of course there is a sense in which we can be said to have complete freedom of choice, but we have ourselves deliberately limited it. First, it is limited by the need to maintain full employment, and this is a much bigger limitation than might be thought. We have become so used to regarding this as the first and overriding object of economic policy that we may not immediately see how completely it reverses what might otherwise seem to be the logical order of things. 'Natural man', if we can any longer conceive of such an abstract being, would work only to produce what he needed to use or consume. It would never occur to him, surely, that he had to keep on producing things simply in order to keep himself *working*. But in the modern industrial society the 'job' is everything, for without one the individual cannot live the same sort of life as his neighbours. He must either starve, or live on such doles as society decides to allot him. Instead, therefore, of applying to the productive process whatever quantity of labour is required to provide for the community's needs, we try to organise it so that every man or woman who needs one has a 'job' – however pointless or trivial may be the job and what it produces.

Now this may, and clearly often does, involve a considerable distortion of what people might decide would be the 'ideal' scheme of production if they were thinking only of the 'worth' (however defined) of the things to be produced. This reversal of the normal order of things is illogical enough, but the secondary effects can be almost ludicrously improbable. Having set out to stimulate a level of production adequate to absorb all the available labour and give a job to everyone who wants one, we sometimes (either through technical miscalculation or an excessive desire to please on the part of politicians) apply too strong a stimulus. Then we announce that – of all things! – there is a *shortage of labour*. Not only do employers start trying to bribe other employers' workers away from them, but we bribe into employment additional women who would be much more usefully occupied at home, and even start importing workers from overseas. It is true that this never lasts for long without a 'crisis', after which we try desperately to reduce the number of 'jobs' available, but after a time it all starts again. And it is no good passing this off as a mere miscalculation, or a failure of economic technique not yet properly developed. The truth is that the whole principle of the thing is plain nonsense.

There can only be such a thing as a 'shortage of labour' in very rare and exceptional circumstances. There can of course be shortages of workers with particular skills, or of workers in particular places, but this is not the same thing at all. Some shortages of this kind are always likely to occur, but they can be minimised either by proper forethought and planning or (in time) by the operations of the market. In what circumstances would it be reasonable to speak of a total shortage of labour? In wartime, certainly, when the nation is fighting for its life and may well find it hard both to man its armed forces and to do in time all the other things necessary to ensure its survival. Also, perhaps, after a war, when a great national effort may be needed to reconstruct and rebuild. Less convincingly, but still just possibly, we might conceive of the need for a great national effort directed to a limited purpose: for example, to modernise all our industries in one fell swoop; to clear away all our slums and modernise all our older houses; to provide enough good modern hospitals, and so on. But of course it would have to *be* a great national effort, consciously and voluntarily directed to a specific end for which people would be prepared to make sacrifices of convenience and consumption, and above all of limited duration. It is not in nature for people to be making a great national effort for ever. But, in the name of reason, how is it possible to speak of a total shortage of labour when the overriding aim of our economic policy is simply to provide jobs for those who want them? The whole idea is crazy.

Let us not be under any illusions about this. You will hear people trying to disguise the essential lunacy of the thing by seeking to persuade you that it *is* all a 'great national effort'. It is the 'battle for exports' or the 'struggle to build a new and better Britain'. This is sheer nonsense. We only need to export in order to pay for our imports; and the high level of imports is due to the inflation of the economy into a state of so-called labour shortage. The need for more exports cannot possibly prove that there is a total shortage of labour. As to the 'struggle to build a new and better Britain', if we are really all locked in a united and enthusiastic national effort to this end, why in God's name are thousands of people being employed to produce plastic flowers to put in detergent packets, plaster gnomes to put in front gardens, and paper hats with 'Kiss me quick!' on them to put on girls at Blackpool? Are these things essential components of the new and better Britain?

Do you still believe that there is, or was, or can be, a shortage of labour? Or do you accept that, when this cry goes up, we have (a) forgotten what it was that we set out to do, and (b) got into a silly inflationary muddle which can be sorted out much more simply and sensibly than by luring mothers from their children and importing bewildered Pakistanis (with their wives and children) to freeze in Preston? If there are still any lingering doubts as to whether it might not, nevertheless, be possible to speak of the labour force being inadequate 'to do all the things we want to do', you have only to ask yourselves whether all the things we are producing are in any meaningful sense things we 'want' – or want enough to go to all this trouble and inconvenience and social dislocation. In fact, you know that many of them are not things that anyone consciously wanted at all before they were produced; being persuaded to buy them is not at all the same thing.

Some such notion as this was clearly floating through Mr. Harold Wilson's mind when he made his famous speech about 'our candyfloss economy' before the 1964 election. Yet it must have been a very vague and nebulous notion, not thought through to any logical conclusion at all. For, if it had been, you would have expected a Prime Minister dedicated to 'purposive planning' to have taken steps to produce economic conditions in which workers would have poured out of the candyfloss factories and into jobs more intimately related to the task of building the new and better Britain. But not a bit of it. The new Labour Government settled down to run an inflation which caused the cries that there was a total shortage of labour to rise to an unprecedented volume. All the most knowledgeable economic commentators wrote about it in all the best newspapers and journals. Finally, Mr. Wilson's government had the most original idea of all. They devised a Selective Employment Tax which provided that the manufacturers of candyfloss – and plastic flowers and gambling machines – should actually be *paid* 7*s.* 6*d.* a week by the taxpayers for every worker they could manage to employ. In fact, however, this was not quite the last indication of Mr. Wilson's state of mind, or of his conception of how to intervene purposively in the candyfloss economy. For, when he at last announced that there was to be a 'shakeout', a 'redeployment' of labour, his government hit the economy with all the crudest, bluntest and least selective deflationary weapons at their disposal. The first mass dismissals of workers were in motor car factories producing largely for export.

So it seems likely that, if Mr. Wilson really thought about the matter at all, he was still guided by what J. K. Galbraith calls 'the conventional wisdom' – which means he had got his ideas back to front.

At any rate, it should now be clear that some very odd things are liable to happen when we decide to run our economy with the overriding objective of 'maintaining full employment'. Can we prevent these disconcerting things from happening? Yes, we can. We can refuse to be taken in by all this nonsense about a shortage of labour. And we can insist that our politicians curb their excess of zeal and stimulate employment only to a level substantially short of that at which employers (and economists) start screaming about a labour shortage. In other words, we can insist on controlling inflation. It can be done.

Nevertheless, it will still remain true that the acceptance of full employment as the chief end of policy – however humane and politically essential this acceptance may be – represents an illogical reversal of the natural order of things. We are thinking of production as a means of creating jobs, rather than of work as a means of doing or creating useful things. The extent to which the idea of 'the job' as the central – and indeed total – object of the whole productive process has taken root in Britain was clearly shown by the outraged cries of the motor car workers 'made redundant' (or 'purposively redeployed' or, not to put too fine a point on it, sacked) in the 'shakeout' of 1966. They bluntly asserted that it was the duty of the government and of the car manufacturers to arrange things so that they retained the jobs to which they considered they had acquired a prescriptive right – irrespective of the demand for motor cars or the possible economic advantages of their being employed elsewhere.

Let me say at once that I am not intending to be in the least censorious about the attitude of these workers. It is the logical outcome of the prevailing conception of the purpose of economic activity. Moreover, I can perfectly sympathise with their desire to have a job as secure and enduring as that of, say, a civil servant or a schoolmaster. There ought to be more such jobs in industry than there have been, for totally insecure daily or weekly work is no kind of basis for a decent life. This is what contracts of employment were designed to prevent, together with the movement (which started in America) towards the 'guaranteed annual wage'. Of course both these devices complicate and distort the 'free operation of the market', making redeployment to meet changes in the relative demand for labour by different industries both slower and more difficult to achieve; they thus reduce the efficiency of industry by an amount which may or may not (we shall no doubt discover in time) be more than matched by a gain in efficiency from the zeal and loyalty of workers who have been made to feel secure.

However that may be, it should be clear that in this respect, too, things have not worked out quite as Keynes imagined they would. The State's intervention for the sole purpose of ensuring full employment has not left the ring clear for the operation of a free market to produce the results he thought desirable. Not only has the making of decisions become less, rather than more, decentralised; not only has consumer choice not, on the whole, become freer and wider; but the very acceptance of the full employment objective has produced additional distortions of the free market process. It is becoming geared to the production of jobs rather than of things that people want. And it seems to me that this will be exactly the same whether we try to make the operation of the 'market' freer and more effective or whether we decide to try wider and more detailed 'government planning'; in both cases the determination to secure full employment by government action will condition the whole productive economy.

A question that will no doubt occur to many people at this stage is, does it matter? Is not all this somewhat hair-splitting and pointless? We are all agreed that for reasons of humanity, as well as because of the pointless waste of labour that is unemployed, we must have full – or at least fairly full – employment. So must we not lump the consequences, having mitigated the worst of them as best we can?

But the answer is that it *must* matter that a whole nation – and indeed a whole world – should set out with pride, enthusiasm and the best of motives to turn the whole logical order of things upside down. It literally does not make sense, and it is utterly unnatural, to think of jobs as an end in themselves, of production as a means to create work, rather than of work as a means to create needed things. And if anyone imagines that it 'comes to the same thing in the end', the answer is that it is precisely in the end that it will not – and cannot – come to the same thing. The more ingrained the idea and its implications become, the longer its results are allowed to shape (or distort) the development of our productive economy, the more certainly we shall be creating a society dedicated to sterile consumption and pointless futility. If you go on long enough with your ideas back to front, you get stuck like it.

The question is whether there is anything we can do about it. Are the pressures too strong, the old attitudes too deeply ingrained? Let us try to analyse just what is behind them.

There are two arguments commonly regarded as overwhelming in favour of government economic policies directed to the maintenance of full employment. The first is that involuntary unemployment is bad for the individual – not only because it depresses the material living standards of himself and his family, but also because it is psychologically demoralising. The second is that unemployed labour is a waste of the community's resources: it results in a loss of goods for consumption, and in addition means that the economy can provide only a lower standard of community and social security services than would be possible with full employment.

The second argument is not nearly so good as it looks. It rests on the implicit assumption that *all* economic activity is good in itself, irrespective of the need for what results from it and the usefulness or intrinsic worth of its products. Judged by these standards, it can be argued that a fair proportion of the community's resources are being wasted now, and that there would be no great harm done if fewer people were employed in making or doing relatively useless things. As to the provision of community and social services, a decision to divert more resources to these can be taken by the community at any time, irrespective of the level of economic activity as measured by the volume of employment. The argument in fact assumes its own conclusions; for the only possible justification for saying that all economic activity is good in itself, however apparently useless its other results, would be that it was neccessary in order to provide people with jobs.

The first argument, which asserts the harmful effects of involuntary unemployment on the individual, is of course much stronger. Given existing attitudes towards both employment and public expenditure, it is almost unanswerable. Yet these attitudes, which are to a great extent hangovers from an earlier age with different problems, might possibly not endure for ever. For the argument does rest on two assumptions of its own. The first is that idleness is morally bad in itself, and that work is both virtuous and good for people; the second is that people who cannot at any given moment find employment in the economy must necessarily spend their time in 'useless' idleness.

Neither of these assumptions is necessarily sound. The first derives from the 'Puritan ethic', and is almost completely illogical in that it takes no account of the nature or usefulness of the work done. Would the Puritan consider it 'virtuous' to work on the production of gambling machines, for example? Again, what is it about work that is supposed to be 'good for people'? There is, certainly, the satisfaction of being self-supporting and of supporting a family by one's own efforts. But this is not an argument in favour of work for its own sake, but only an assertion that a normal man finds it more satisfying to be useful and independent than to be shiftless and irresponsible. Surely work can only be 'good' for people if the work passes one of two tests: either the process must be physically or mentally healthy and stimulating in itself, or it must provide satisfaction through its creativeness or through the knowledge that it is useful. Quite a lot of the work being done today passes neither of these tests. And the second assumption – that the alternative to employment in the economy is 'useless' idleness – is equally invalid. There are plenty of 'useful' things crying out to be done, which do not get done even when there are people unemployed. Many of them could be done by untrained people and for short periods. The assumption only means, in effect, that we do not know how to organise our affairs properly.

There, of course, is the rub: how to organise our affairs properly. We began by asserting that it is an illogical and unnatural reversal of the rational order to treat production as a means of creating jobs, and to make the creation of jobs the overriding objective of national economic policy; and it is clear that, so long as we adhere to this order and obey this imperative, we shall not achieve a pattern or organisation of economic activity and human effort that anyone would judge to be anything like ideal by any rational criterion. But is it not also clear that we could not reverse the order, or achieve the 'ideal' pattern, through the operation of the market economy as it is at present developing? In theory, the operation of the market is supposed to produce the things that are most 'useful' and the things that people 'want'. In practice, as we have seen, it falls far short of any rational ideal by the test of usefulness; and as people's expenditure moves from the sphere of necessities into that of 'luxuries', the market is tending more and more to create wants for the sake of filling them rather than to minister to wants that are felt.

It will be asked why it should not be possible to arrange things better. Surely it would not require a great deal of planning to set about things in a rational way and to establish a reasonable order of priorities? In fact, this is what a great many people convinced of the practicability of economic planning do believe. The trouble is that experience does not so far suggest that the advantages outweigh the disadvantages, which are considerable. For it does seem that we cannot secure the real improvement we want by any modest measure of 'indicative' planning of the economic framework. We can 'achieve' full employment, and perhaps a more satisfactory allocation of resources to those community services most in need of it. But within this broad framework the decisions about priorities of production and employment will be made by the market, which is to say increasingly by producers rather than by consumer demand. The moment an attempt is made to interfere in any detail with this, the imperatives of planning will begin to take command. So complex are the interrelations of the modern economy, so diffuse and unpredictable the secondary effects of government intervention at any point, that more and more details of the economy will have to be 'planned' in order to prevent chaos. Indeed it is logically almost impossible to stop short of the detailed control of employment and labour movements. So crude are planning techniques in their present stage of development that mistakes will certainly be made from time to time in forecasting and in assessing future needs; and these mistakes, because they are mistakes of central planning for the whole economy, will have very widespread effects, from which additional secondary effects will spread out like ripples. We know that this is true, because it always happens; it has happened in this country, where planning has been tried only on a fairly modest scale, but it has also happened in communist countries where governments have had the widest and most complete powers over everything.

Economic planning, on anything like the scale that is necessary to secure a more rational use of resources for the priorities of production and community services, would have to be as all-embracing as it is in wartime. Yet we know that the planning techniques used in the last war were pretty crude, and that the rough-and-ready results were often extremely wasteful. Moreover, they involved limitations of personal freedom that would scarcely be acceptable in peacetime, without the overriding sanction of a 'great national effort for survival'.

Of course, statistical and forecasting techniques have been improved since then and are likely to improve further. There will always be plenty of people who will assert the possibility of efficient planning to secure rational priorities, and from time to time there are bound to be governments which will experiment with it. Indeed, it seems certain that the conviction of ultimate success will remain undimmed. Nor is it yet possible to say that ultimate success will be denied them, although for a long time the experiments are likely to be crude affairs and doomed to failure. But it is certainly impossible to be sure that the techniques, aided as they will be by increasingly subtle and complex computers, will not one day succeed in doing what men think they want done. How much they will have sacrificed to this in personal freedom and scope for individual initiative it is impossible to tell. Yet I am sure that men will not indefinitely be content to leave uncontrolled the purposes for which their productive efforts are made. It will not always seem an adequate object to provide everyone with jobs, irrespective of the total utility of what the jobs produce.

That this will conflict with the ideals of personal freedom and consumer choice is obvious. However, the conflict is still being discussed in terms that have become almost meaningless. For the choice is presented as one between an increasingly encroaching State and a system of markets and free enterprise with effective consumer choice. But the technological necessities of production, even in the free sector of the economy, are increasingly narrowing the scope of consumer choice and putting pressure on government to control the economy. Thus it would seem that the most likely effect of making industry still 'freer' would be to give it a green light to speed this process up.

The disconcerting prospect is thus that whoever wins – the

State or the technocrats of productive industry – the scope of freedom and consumer choice will continue to be narrowed. It is thus almost impossible to regard the conflict, as it is conventionally portrayed, as being particularly meaningful – or even as being the right conflict to study. The real conflict is surely that between personal freedom and consumer choice on the one hand, and the encroachments of technique (whether under the auspices of the State or of 'free enterprise') on the other. We shall consider in the next chapter what it might be possible to do about it.

CHAPTER 11

Towards a Synthesis

If we continue to believe that the goals of the industrial system – the expansion of output, the companion increase in consumption, technological advance, the public images that sustain it – are co-ordinate with life, then all our lives will be in the service of these goals. What is consistent with these ends we shall have or be allowed; all else will be off limits. Our wants will be managed in accordance with the needs of the industrial system; the policies of the state will be subject to similar influence; education will be adapted to industrial need; the disciplines required by the industrial system will be the conventional morality of the community. All other goals will be made to seem precious, unimportant or anti-social. We will be bound to the ends of the industrial system. The state will add its moral, and perhaps some of its legal, power to their enforcement.

John Kenneth Galbraith, *The New Industrial State*

The power of custom is enormous, and so gradual will be the change that man's sense of what is due to himself will be at no time rudely shocked; our bondage will steal upon us noiselessly and by imperceptible approaches; nor will there ever be such a clashing of desires between man and the machines as will lead to an encounter between them. . . . And should we not be guilty of consummate folly if we were to reject advantages which we cannot obtain otherwise, merely because they involve a greater gain to others than to ourselves?

Samuel Butler, *Erewhon*

In the modern world, the most dangerous form of determinism is the technological phenomenon. It is not a question of getting rid of it, but by an act of freedom, of transcending it. . . . The first step in the quest, the first act of freedom, is to become aware of the necessity. . . . If man were to say: 'These are not necessities; I am free because of technique, or despite technique', this would prove that he is totally determined. However, by grasping the real nature of the technological phenomenon, and the extent to which it is robbing him of freedom, he confronts the blind mechanisms as a conscious being.

Jacques Ellul, *The Technological Society*

I had written the last chapter before the publication of Professor J. K. Galbraith's penetrating and entertaining book, *The New Industrial State*. I have nevertheless resisted the temptation to rewrite what has gone before.

It is impossible to ignore Galbraith's message, and almost impossible to deny rationally its essential truth. The shocked reaction of most businessmen and many conventional economists – predicted by Galbraith himself in the book – arises from one or other (and in some cases from all) of three causes. Some resist the message because it involves so radical a change in much of conventional economic theory, and so new a view of certain established economic institutions, that it would be altogether too disturbing to accept it. Some have failed to understand – or have deliberately ignored – the fact that Galbraith is dealing with only a limited sector of the industrial economy, namely that increasingly important sector dominated by the large and 'mature' corporation; they have sought to demonstrate the unreality of his observations by reference to that other sector of the economy where the scale of enterprise is small and entrepreneurs and market disciplines flourish. Others have simply failed to perceive what has been going on around them.

That the large industrial firm has moved out of the field of entrepreneurial capitalism into the control of salaried expert managers, largely divorced from ownership, has been recognised for many years. Indeed, the recent history of major 'takeover' battles in this country* has shown that the ownership of very large firms can be brought under the control of the managers of other large firms without the managers spending any of their own money at all. What has not always been recognised is the extent to which the process has been gathering speed. It has been estimated that in the United States large corporations are now responsible for between half and two-thirds of all the industrial and commercial activity in the country. The proportion is certainly much smaller in Britain, but it is growing rapidly. Another feature of the situation which has not been clearly recognised is the radical nature of the economic, social and political changes which this trend brings with it.

The requirements of modern large-scale production techniques, says Galbraith, include the planning and management of demand as well as of the supply of goods. It is essential to

* The cases of the General Electric bid for Associated Electrical Industries and I.C.I.'s 'near miss' with Courtaulds are obvious examples.

'efficiency' that the unpredictability of consumer choice should be as far as possible eliminated. Market research is undertaken not only to determine what the consumer 'wants', but also to obtain the information about consumer psychology and motivation required to plan the appropriate sales campaign for the product. Over a wide field, the consumer is no longer 'sovereign' in the old sense assumed by the classical economic theory. He is to a large extent managed by the producers themselves. In particular, it is essential for the producers of consumer goods to ensure an adequate, and indeed increasing, demand for their products if their resources and capacity are to be efficiently employed. This requires two things. First, the media of mass communications must be employed to create the right psychological climate – one in which there is an obsessive preoccupation with the enjoyment of goods and services. Second, the State is expected to pursue economic policies designed to foster 'growth'; not only must total consumer demand be kept at a level adequate to absorb the products of industry, it must also be encouraged to grow steadily and predictably.

The stimulation of consumer demand is also important for another reason. Efficient planning of the industrial process requires that the supply and performance of labour be predictable. There must be the right incentives to persuade employees to work regularly and for long enough hours. It is of no use to provide monetary incentives, in the form of high wages and bonuses, if there comes a point at which the worker decides that he does not need any more money and prefers to absent himself from work. It is therefore essential to persuade him that there are more and more exciting things available for him to buy if he only had the money. Even 'leisure' has to be made more expensive.

We have not suffered in this country from the violent contrast between 'private affluence and public squalor' which Galbraith, in *The Affluent Society*, attacked as characteristic of the United States. Nevertheless, the fact that we have, by fairly general agreement, become accustomed to allotting a higher proportion of our national income to the public provision of welfare services has not been without disadvantages of its own. Because this process was greatly accelerated after the second World War, under a Labour Government in effective power for the first time in the Labour Party's history, the institutional organisation of the British Welfare State was already becoming an anachronism when it was being set up. The principle of universal (and in most cases compulsory) provision of welfare services is not necessarily the best system for an affluent society. Moreover, as we have seen, the promise of universal provision resulted in the available resources being spread widely over a field in which it was impossible to do everything properly. A political unwillingness to assign lower priorities to certain services in order to improve the standards of other services led to inadequate provision in some sectors.

In addition, the creation of a vast machinery for State provision of welfare services involved the centralisation under State control of some services which might have been better provided under a system of competing agencies. (This problem was discussed in Chapter 9.) The chief objection to the system which has grown up in Britain is that – largely as a result of the left-wing Welfare State philosophy – the determination to help people by collective public provision has been accompanied by an almost equal determination to prevent people from helping themselves.

Both economic and social trends, therefore, have been in the direction of reducing the scope and freedom of individual choice and action. It is by no means impossible to reverse this trend in the social field; but, as I suggested in the last chapter, our freedom of manœuvre is much less in the economic field.

Jacques Ellul, in *The Technological Society*, argues strongly that the process of technological innovation and its accompanying increases in the scale of organisation lead to almost irresistible pressure to eliminate the unpredictability involved in free individual choice. Only by a great effort of the human will, he maintains, can the pressures of technique be 'transcended'. Galbraith makes a similarly powerful case, but concludes on a note of greater optimism for the future. Recognising that industry, together with the other interests adhering to the 'conventional wisdom' of economics, has become inextricably involved in the policies and programmes of governments and achieved a marked influence over them, he dumps the responsibility for reversing or modifying current trends firmly into the lap of the educated intellectuals.

This is unlikely to appeal to everyone as a very hopeful prescription. The influence of intellectuals in politics has been generally regarded as a somewhat mixed blessing. They have often shown a diffuseness of aims, together with a vagueness of comprehension of the purpose and working of institutions, which has been far from reassuring.[1] Nevertheless, the proposition is worth considering.

Some intellectuals, of course, are on what Galbraith would no doubt consider the wrong side. Many of them are dedicated to theories of planning and the virtues of technique. Most intellectuals do, however, show a healthy scepticism about the material calculus and the social merits of the industrial system. If the politicians are unanimous in their advocacy of 'the present agenda . . . which associates all progress with percentage increases in Gross National Product or percentage levels of unemployment',[2] then politicians will be increasingly powerless to cope with the rising volume of dissent and discontent which current preoccupation with economic growth and material consumption is beginning to provoke, especially among younger people. The focusing and leadership of this dissent can only, it would seem, be undertaken by the people – in all political parties – who are temperamentally and philosophically inclined to resist the ultimate demands of technique.

It must not, however, be thought that the virtues of unlimited consumption are being challenged in Britain only by the young or by the highly educated. There is a certain scepticism apparent among manual workers of all ages in respect of the 'values' of the consumer society. This shows itself in two ways. There is first the fact that many workers simply refuse to behave in the way which the system requires if it is to work 'efficiently'. After a particular (but generally almost unpredictable) level of weekly earnings has been achieved, some tend to prefer leisure for the rest of the week – or at least absence from the regular job – to the effort involved in earning more. It is sometimes argued that it is the incidence of income-tax, which falls at a higher rate on the top 'slice' of earnings, that is responsible for this. No doubt it is a contributing factor, but there is clearly more to it than this. There is also a tendency to sit much more loosely to the job than was possible in the days before full employment became the norm. Workers are more liable to change jobs at the first onset of dissatisfaction with their work, and often prepared to strike for what appear at first sight to be comparatively trivial reasons.

The conventional reactions of the advocates of 'discipline' miss the point at issue. It may be – although the events of 1967 do not suggest that it is so – that these tendencies would be halted by a higher proportion of unemployment. It is certainly possible that a more restrictive attitude towards the payment of social service benefits would have some effect on the willingness to cease working. Nevertheless, neither of these prescriptions would have any effect on the underlying attitudes towards the workers' jobs and the attractions of the incentives offered to higher output: and it is clearly these which have to be altered if technology is to develop its full potential. As we have seen, this demands that the workers in industry should show a constant and predictable desire to earn more money as a reward for regular attendance and higher output.

Ironically enough, the unwillingness of so many workers to conform to this pattern is largely the fault of several generations of British employers. The determination, from the industrial revolution until very recently, to keep labour cheap and earnings low has created a climate in which employers have shown a marked resistance to the 'efficient' use of technological developments, while the workers have not for the most part been brought up (as they have in the United States) in a climate in which high earnings and high levels of consumption are considered to be normal and worth working intensively to achieve. That the old attitudes survive over a large part of the field on both sides is shown by the conservatism of the older craft unions and the superficiality of the economic arguments adduced for the importation of large quantities of cheap coloured labour into Britain in the 1950s and early 1960s.

While the enthusiastic advocates of 'modernisation' and

technological efficiency have no doubts at all that these attitudes are economically wasteful and socially damaging, there is not much comfort in them either for the sceptic or for those less dedicated to the material calculus. Indeed, one cannot avoid an uneasy suspicion that we may simply be getting the worst of all worlds.

Scepticism about the ultimate value of a policy of economic growth for growth's sake does not imply a belief that economic stagnation has anything to commend it. It is a perfectly respectable and prudent attitude to be suspicious of change – particularly of change that is rapid, fundamental and deliberately imposed. It is quite another thing to seek all the time to stifle innovation. To regard all innovation as a threat is to fail to perceive that it often offers opportunities. Innovations that have been tried, proved, adopted and absorbed are the motive power of evolutionary change. And this kind of change is – or should be – constant. At present, the diversity of innovation produced by many pieces of small-scale enterprise is being stifled by the taxation system.

At its best, the challenge of innovation can produce a continual state of creative tension between innovators and conservatives. What we seem to have achieved is a state of psychological warfare, devoid of compromise or common sense, in which both sides are locked in rigid attitudes of incomprehension. For those on the one side, technological innovation and the institutional changes necessary to permit its maximum exploitation are almost ends in themselves; so convinced are they that the results must be beneficial to humanity that they have not tried to understand the nature and implications of these results. For those on the other side, the immense dangers of the total triumph of technique are so obvious that technology has become something to distrust and oppose in itself. There is perhaps even less hope of beneficial progress in this attitude than in the other.

It is not only the fact that each side has settled down to an 'all or nothing' war that makes it exceedingly hard to see a middle road between the two positions. There is actually a sense in which both sides are right to insist on the impossibility of compromise. The technologists *know* that they must have a *carte blanche* to develop the full potential of their techniques, since anything short of their full development is inefficient and wasteful, causing human 'welfare' to fall short of its possible maximum. Moreover, once technique has begun to take over one sector, its effects start to spread out in widening ripples: its imperatives demand the taking over of neighbouring and cognate sectors, in order to eliminate unpredictability and ensure the smooth planned running of the whole complex of interacting and interrelated activities. Similarly, the opponents of technique recognise the imperatives, and *know* that there will be in the end no impermeable frontiers to the claims and influence of technique.

This is the sense in which Jacques Ellul maintains that the 'middle way', the way of 'liberal interventionism' or 'indicative planning', 'presupposes a spiritual revolution that has not yet even begun'.[3] This is something more than a matter of unravelling the confusion between ends and means, of looking beyond 'know-how' with a desire to know 'what' and 'why'. It is even more than the need to think about ultimate objectives in moral terms. It is something which goes beyond an 'attitude of mind', and demands a reawakening and reorientation of the spirit of Man.

This will be thought a very high-falutin' and unpractical way of approaching a socio-economic problem. On the contrary, it is those who ignore or deny this neccessity who are being unpractical; for the conflict cannot be satisfactorily resolved without it, and unless the conflict can be resolved we shall not only be deprived of many of the real benefits of technique but be condemned to a long and frustrating period of social conflict.

I have already touched, by implication, on what is needed to stimulate this reawakening. It is the regaining of confidence. Confidence, first, in the real possibility of a significant future for ourselves and our posterity; perhaps even more important, confidence in the possibility of *individual participation through action* rather than mere conformity in behaviour. If it is true that most people cannot see a stimulating future for themselves unless they can see the possibility of a great future for their country, it is equally true that they will not bestir themselves in their country's interests unless they can see a meaningful and active role for themselves within their country. People will only do great things if they believe that there are great things to do.

What is obvious is that the aspirations involved must go well beyond, and much deeper than, a total concern with material welfare and the efficiency of techniques. They will not be too easy to reawaken, since the tradition has been weakened and the standards obscured. It may indeed take a generation to accomplish, and it will certainly require both a change of aim and direction in education and a considerable achievement in communication on the part of those who set out to effect the transformation. The knowledge that it will take a long time should not cause either surprise or discouragement since the malaise itself is of long standing – certainly much intensified since the war, but going back in its origins well before it. This is a task in which 'a wild passion for instant action' has nothing to commend it; it requires patience, understanding and a comprehension of the perspectives of social development.

This is not to say that it is not possible, as well as desirable, to make a start with the process of conversion now. Indeed, two things make it important that the message should be disseminated as widely as possible now. The first is that the present generation of disenchanted young people, many of them conscious of a frustrated idealism, should be made aware that there is a constructive alternative to the aims and policies which they find unsatisfying in the world today. Mere exhortation will not move them: they must see the possibility of personal commitment and constructive action. The second reason for beginning the campaign now is that the technocrats are all the time consolidating their positions and perfecting their techniques of conditioning people to accept their terms of reference.

Both sides in the confrontation between the technocrats and the anti-materialists will have to make some concessions in aims and attitudes. They will always and inevitably confront one another in a state of tension: the task is to make the tension a genuinely creative one rather than a deadlock of frustration and suspicion. Probably nothing will ever stop the extremists and enthusiasts on both sides from saying things which arouse suspicion and make accommodation difficult. Some technologists – particularly Marxist ones – will always give the impression that our environment and our own destiny must be handed over lock, stock and barrel to the experts if our best interests are to be properly looked after. Some reactionaries will always talk as if everything mechanical and every attempt to organise anything efficiently is a desperate threat to be resisted to the death. The sensible majority can be brought to realise that neither side can impose its terms – and must not, indeed, be allowed to impose its terms – wholly and without compromise on the other. They can be brought to live and work creatively together if both are prepared to accept the discipline of certain limiting principles. That means accepting the philosophic basis which provides the ethical framework within which choices of ends can be made and the comparative costs of alternative means assessed.

This brings us to the heart of the matter. It is in the assessment of these comparative costs, and in the decisions as to the price we can afford to pay for the advancement of technology in some sectors and its limitation in others, that the real problem lies. Backward as Britain is in the development of advanced techniques over much of industry, assessments and decisions of this kind are already being made all the time. The trouble is that they are being made for the most part in a very haphazard and rough-and-ready kind of way. This is partly because so many of the factors involve apparently abstract values instead of costs which are quantifiable and measurable with existing techniques; partly because the judgements are too often being made *ad hoc*, under the pressure of immediate necessities and without any recognised principles to guide the decisions towards a common end.

Where the physical environment is affected, there has grown up a body of town and country planning precedents from which certain principles can be deduced. These tend, however, to be concerned chiefly with small-scale developments, and the really large decisions (like the Stansted one) are too often taken without any apparent consistency of principle and justified by unconvincing references to the 'national interest'.

Two points need to be made here. The first is that appeals to the 'national interest' are quite unacceptable as the sole justification for developments which may permanently alter the physical environment or change the conditions of life of a substantial number of people. The case has to be developed in detail, the alternatives made explicit, and the advantages and disadvantages openly displayed. Second, the 'national interest' is often very superficially defined in these cases; it is sometimes possible to argue that the real long-term national interest would be better served by a different decision.

Certain principles are clear. It must never be forgotten that the countryside and our towns and villages are not ours alone to destroy or change entirely as we will. Governments and industrialists have to remember that these are the environment in which people live, and that major changes may be permanently unsettling or even destructive of a valued way of life. But over and above this, the land and scenery, together with the best buildings of the past, are a trust which we hold for posterity and for the care of which we shall be held responsible by posterity. Also, we must distinguish between changes which are permanent and destructive and those which leave no lasting scars and can be later reversed. For example, there are always arguments going on about the disfiguration of the countryside by overhead power lines, and indeed it is necessary to site them with the utmost care and to be prepared in exceptional cases to bear the high additional cost of putting cables underground. But pylons and cables are quite transitory objects in the landscape. They may be ugly now, but they will not be there for ever – any more than the television aerials which disfigure so many good houses and urban skylines. Ultimately, a more efficient and sightly method of power transmission will be evolved, and the wirescapes will disappear without the slightest trace that they have been there.

Again, it is of the utmost importance that those who plan environmental changes should not only take account of their effects on the lives and amenities of local residents but should preserve as far as possible local control over the planning decisions involved. People need to feel that they have some control over their own environment, and there is nothing more productive of alienation and discontent than the feeling that important decisions are being taken by remote and dictatorial outsiders.

Finally, there is a great deal to be done in developing techniques for quantifying the values of amenity and the costs of dislocation of people's lives.[4] Some work is being done on the refining of techniques for cost/benefit analysis, and there is considerable scope for their use. While the ability to fix levels of monetary compensation does not absolve the authorities from the duty of minimising inconvenience and of refraining from permanent damage to the environment, it would be possible to do much more to reduce resentment and dislocation if proper compensation could be accurately assessed and paid in full.

The techniques of cost/benefit analysis could also help in decision-making in other fields, where the price to be paid for technological advance does not affect only the physical environment but affects people's lives in other ways. They could be developed to deal not only with other problems of amenity, such as noise and pollution, but with changes which involve large-scale movements of workers or alterations in methods and hours of work.

It is not always realised that much of the argument over the costs and benefits of technological change is misconceived. It is of course necessary to be realistic. In some cases, we are actually paying quite a high price now in discomfort and inconvenience for the *lack* of efficient technology. Technology can very often confer great benefits without exacting a high cost from people in terms of amenity and changes in their way of life. There is nearly always *some* price to be paid, and it is important to find out what it is and assess it as accurately as possible, but often the balance of advantage is clearly on the side of technical advance. That this is less clearly realised than it might be is very largely due to the inability of technologists to discriminate between those of their projects which do exact a high price and those which do not; their tendency is to advocate both with equal fervour, and to brush aside objections and queries as irrelevant obscurantism.

This actually breeds suspicion in the cases where it is scarcely justified.

Technologists must never be allowed to get away unchallenged with the proposition, in which many of them clearly believe, that technology is an end in itself. Technology is no more an end in itself than production or work. There is nothing to be said for large-scale organisation and techniques of automation unless, on balance and in the long run, they are means to a worthwhile end. But equally, there is nothing at all to be said for doing things wastefully, expensively and inefficiently, if technique can get them done better without exacting too high a price in terms of the quality of people's lives. However, it must not be the technologists, or their commercial employers, who decide in the long run whether the price is too high or not. This must be done impartially and honestly by others.

The case for pressing on with large-scale technological change will always be urged with passion, and the arguments adduced for particular changes will often seem very strong. But the decisions must never be taken out of their context and without careful study of the relationships of the particular proposals to other things and of the possible secondary effects in the future. Of course it is necessary to estimate the advantages of technological development to the country's economy as a whole, and the competitive disadvantage in the export market which may result from being outdistanced by other countries. But it must also be remembered that the economy is not everything, although clearly a great deal depends on it. It is itself the amalgam of everyone's work and everyone's consumption, but it does not measure everything. There are important aspects of life other than the purely economic.

This is, of course, the essential point, and it needs to be constantly stressed. Unless it is continually emphasised, the contrary argument will win by default; for the advocates of the purely material calculus have already gone far to get their assumptions accepted by the mass of the people. After all, they have spent a very great deal of money, and employed the most sophisticated techniques of communication and persuasion, to get the message across. I do not think people have for the most part wholly accepted the assumptions yet.

They do not yet feel convinced that material prosperity and high standards of consumption represent the whole of the good life; indeed, most of them seem to have a deep instinct against this. Yet they are tending more and more to acquiesce in the patterns of behaviour which the purveyors of consumer goods have worked so hard to impose. The conditioning process is bound in the end to be effective if there are no alternatives and conflicting incentives.

Much more thought and enquiry need to be devoted to the question of size and scale in industry and administration. Far too many people seem to imagine that great size is in itself a good thing, or at the least that it automatically conduces to efficiency. In fact, large-scale organisation is – if anything – rather bad *per se* than good, and it may actually lead to great *in*efficiency. Again, it is a question of calculating and balancing comparative costs and benefits.

Large-scale organisation makes for uniformity rather than variety, and it involves remoteness of the decision-makers from those who are affected by the decisions. This can lead to considerable frustration and loss of confidence.

These things are bad in themselves. But large undertakings are often seriously inefficient, failing even to provide a good service to their customers. The nationalised industries are not the only examples one could quote; some very large industrial corporations have shown signs of becoming less, rather than more, efficient as they grew larger.

Unless the disadvantages of large-scale organisation are offset by substantial decentralisation of control and decision-making, there is often a net loss of efficiency. There is a *social* price to be paid for size, as well. Often it would seem to be easier to mitigate the genuine disadvantages of small-scale organisation than to wrestle with the administrative problems and the checks and balances necessary to offset the disadvantages of great size.

What needs to be done here is to study each proposal for takeover or amalgamation with great care. Where the likely result is to produce real economies of scale, without producing an administrative unit too large to be efficiently managed, there is a *prima facie* case for greater size. When the motive is simply to eliminate competition, with a consequent reduction of consumer choice, there is a strong case for refusing to allow the merger to happen. In the same way the reasons of efficiency generally given to justify the aggregation of large administrative units in government need to be examined with care, to make sure that they do not conceal a bad case of empire-building by officials.

No one really knows how great a reduction in overhead costs you need to compensate for the loss of the loyalty, keenness and community pride which smaller firms can often inspire in their workers – or the loss of intimate contact with the public which the smaller local authority can maintain. These are components of efficiency beyond the measurement – or even the imagination – of cost accountants; but they can markedly affect the efficiency of the total result.

It must, obviously, be realised that there are some industries in which small units are either impossible or at least grossly inefficient. It is no good complaining about large-scale production units in the motor-car industry; without them we should have either no cars at all or else very expensive ones. But this is not to say that every country – even, perhaps, a country the size of the United Kingdom – ought to try to support industries which necessarily involve very large units.

Finally, it does need to be remembered that the scale of production units has a great effect on the nature and conditions of work for those employed in them. The greater the amount of capital invested in a plant, and the more complex the plant is, the more necessary it is to keep it operating continuously and at full capacity. This means a quite different pattern of work and working hours from those generally to be found in smaller firms. It will sometimes – though not always – mean that the work is less interesting and less satisfying, because of the breaking down of processes into detailed tasks, and it may also destroy the kind of small group relationships which often are socially important to the workers.

Much has been written by psychologists and sociologists about the problems of industrial relations and work satisfaction, and many suggestions have been made for improving them. Valuable as some of them are in dealing with the detailed problems, they do not in total add up to anything like a solution of the whole enormous problem of the individual role of the worker in modern industry and of the depersonalisation which has overtaken him. It may be that there is no possibility of reversing these trends, although it seems certain that the resources of technology might be more fruitfully used to try to tackle this problem from the worker end, rather than always demanding conformity by the worker to the organisational needs of production technique.

At any rate, the position of the worker must always be considered a major factor in decisions about the optimum scale of industry. Moreover, it is worth considering whether we do enough to make it possible for those who want to work on their own to do so, and whether it is not worth while to put up with some loss of economies of scale in order to give more satisfaction in work. Also, I am sure that Galbraith is right when he says that there should be much more flexibility in industry in respect of the length of the working day and working week that a man must work in order to be employed in a plant. Flexibility is never popular with technical organisers, since it involves some unpredictability and inefficiency and requires much more complicated planning. But it should be possible for a man to work shorter hours for less money if he wants to, and to take on a second job of a contrasting kind in order to introduce more variety into his life. Here again, changes in the tax system would help.

In the end, worker satisfaction makes an enormous difference to efficiency. It is scarcely to be doubted that many of the unofficial strikes that take place all over industry are the result of a general dissatisfaction with the job – or even a desire for a change and for a little excitement – rather than a particular fight for the (often trivial) cause ostensibly paraded for the strike. Once again, it is a question of balancing comparative costs and benefits.

Jacques Ellul is certainly right when he says, in the quotation from *The Technological Society* at the head of this chapter, that the first essential in overcoming the dangers posed by technique is to recognise the nature of the threat. Left unresisted and uncontrolled, the imperatives of technique will become the universal and accepted determinants of the whole of life. Once the threat is recognised and its enormous implications realistically assessed, then it may be possible to control it. Up till now, too few people have taken it seriously and recognised its full implications – or else the majority have gloomily acquiesced in what seems to be an 'inevitable trend'.

The time has come now to pose the counter-challenge and to resist. Decisions having long-term results can no longer be taken on short-term calculations of advantage and inadequate appreciation of the costs involved. The techniques of fact-finding and measurement, systems of cost/benefit analysis and methods of disseminating information on which judgements can be based, all need to be improved. But the most important need is for a general will to resistance.

Governments, being themselves large-scale organisations and also intimately connected with large-scale industry and technology, cannot be trusted to make the right decisions and to resist dangerous trends unless there is a strong pressure of public opinion driving them along the right path. Once a large number of people realise that resistance is possible, and that there are things involved here which are worth fighting for and which can be won, then the necessary control of and compromise with the imperatives of technique will be achieved. Often it will be necessary to decide, not how we can secure the maximum of efficiency in a particular case, but how much *in*efficiency we can afford to tolerate in the interests of variety, amenity and the general quality of life. In the end, governments and other powerful organisations will be driven to abide by a philosophy which puts individual people and their environment above the collective abstractions of 'society' and the 'national interest', and which recognises that life is more than a dedication to consumption and material welfare.

There are already signs in Britain that more people are recognising the dilemma and are prepared to resist the encroachments of technique on the frontiers of their private lives. One day, perhaps, the technologists will get the message too.

CHAPTER 12

British Political Institutions

It is disconcerting in the extreme to contemplate the possibility that cherished democratic institutions have become empty forms which have no visible connection with the acts of democratic nations, except perhaps to render these acts technically less efficient than they otherwise need have been. But the fact that they have no connection is, paradoxically, a powerful reason for their survival.

John Wilkinson, translator's introduction to *The Technological Society*

It is not institutions, *qua* instruments of public life, that are going badly in Europe; it is the tasks on which to employ them. There are lacking programmes of a scope adequate to the effective capacities that life has come to acquire in each European individual. We have here an optical illusion, which it is important to correct once for all, for it is painful to listen to the stupidities uttered every hour, with regard to Parliaments, for example. . . . The loss of prestige by Parliaments has nothing to do with their notorious defects. . . . It arises from the fact that the European does not know in what to utilise them.

José Ortega y Gasset, *The Revolt of the Masses*

To have common glories in the past, a common will in the present; to have done great things together; to wish to do greater; these are the essential conditions which make up a people. . . . In the past, an inheritance of glories and regrets; in the future, one and the same programme to carry out. . . . The existence of a nation is a daily plebiscite.

J. E. Renan

I suspect that Renan's definition will appeal to most people's imagination, as it does to mine. One feels that it is *right* – that this is how it used to be and ought to be. But can one really feel that it is true of Britain today?

Clearly it is the will to do greater things in the future that is lacking: or perhaps not so much the will, as the belief that it is any longer possible to do great things, either alone or in concert with others. It is this failure of confidence that seems so horrifying to those who bewail our national malaise.

It is true that a failure of confidence can be a mortal

sickness, but there is nothing inevitable about this. A people, like an individual, can regain lost confidence and turn its attention purposefully to the future. The first essential is to have been able to diagnose the malaise. Once we know that the basic failure is one of confidence, we can avoid the more common irrelevancies and set ourselves to determine what are the root causes that have to be tackled.

There are many who attribute our troubles to the failure of politics, or at least of politicians. Among politicians it has become common to attribute everything to a failure of institutions, and to talk as if all would be well if we would modernise them and make them more efficient. Both of these diagnoses miss the point in one way or another. There is no essential difficulty, for those who are not hypnotised by 'inevitable trends', about adapting our institutions to changed needs: but there is little point in trying to adapt them unless we are absolutely sure of what it is that the institutions are supposed to be for. If the modern preoccupation with means – with 'know-how' – continues to stifle all clear thought about ultimate ends, we might just as well leave our institutions as they are.

When the whole business of politics comes to be dismissed by the electorate as a tiresome waste of time, I suppose there is a sense in which it can be said that politics – or politicians – have 'failed'. Nevertheless, it is of vital importance to get the sense right. Politics can be said to have 'failed' only in the sense that one speaks of a supply of mains electricity having 'failed'; in other words, it is perfectly possible to get the thing going again. Politics have not 'failed' in the sense that a bankrupt company is wound up. Yet there are many people who discuss the subject in exactly those terms: nothing could be more dangerous.

It is not the first time that a general disenchantment with politics has become apparent in this country, just as it has happened in other countries. All it means is that politics have failed to keep up with events – or at least with the public reaction to events. If one political party wakes up – and catches up – in time, a period of political stagnation can be followed by a highly creative period of political thought and action.

There is, of course, the danger that a disillusioned people will turn away from democratic politics to an authoritarian alternative, but it does not seem that we have got to that stage yet. Before that is likely to happen, there would have to be an intervening stage during which there was a rapid slide from apathy to moral and political anarchy. Then, since there is a limit to the amount of anarchy most people are prepared to put up with, the danger of an authoritarian reaction would be very real. Clearly the immediate need now is to dispel the prevailing apathy before the apostles of anarchy (and they are not lacking) succeed in their aims.

Not every politician would agree that this is a job for politicians. The argument is apt to follow the 'chicken and egg' cycle. Is it the business of politicians to lead and to inspire, or is their role the more passive one of reflecting and realising the general will of the people?* It is no doubt true that most people vote for politicians in the hope (however faint) that the particular party they support will give them what they want. When it becomes apparent, however, that they have no really clear idea of what they do want, then someone has to assume the more active role of leadership and inspiration. Nevertheless, it is neccessary to point out that this role is not exclusively one for politicians. If a people is bemused and purposeless, without the will to action, it is not only the politicians who have 'failed'. It is the leaders in every walk of life, from the press to the pedagogues and from the pulpit to the parish pump. And indeed, it is apparent that the anarchic belief that 'civilisation can be maintained without intellectual commitment'[1] has spread pretty widely in church, press and common-room. When Renan's 'daily plebiscite' provides no common ground for action, nor even a conviction that action is necessary or possible, then there is not a great deal for politicians to latch on to.

The institutional argument is equally unconvincing. We are often told that the reason why people have lost faith in politics is that nothing seems to work properly. It may be noted in passing that this complaint is not absolutely, but only relatively, justified; it is at least true that performance

* This is, of course, the old controversy of the 1930s, of Baldwin and rearmament, of Chamberlain and peace.

has not fulfilled the promises. Even in these terms, however, the contention is debatable. No doubt most people would feel less frustrated if the public services worked more efficiently, but greater efficiency does not by itself always lead to greater happiness. Indeed, those who are compelled to become efficient may well be much less happy.

What, then, is the purpose of politics, and what are the institutions through which they work? Presumably the purpose of politics is to provide ideas and machinery for the government of the country, and government is simply organisation to enable people to live together and to perform certain common tasks. The avowed purpose of every political system is to provide government for the common good.

Since all government depends – at least in the long run – on the consent of the governed, what the majority of the people want will in the end get done. It will not always be done quickly, since people do not always want the same things and sometimes do not really know what they do want. In the long run it may be better that what the majority wants at any given moment should *not* be done too quickly; there may be great merit in institutions and political machinery which slow down what might otherwise be rash and ultimately disastrous action. The best system of government is that through which the real and enduring wishes of the people are carried out with enough speed to keep the inevitable tensions between government and governed to a minimum. By this test, the British system of government has functioned remarkably well in the past.

A study of history may suggest that the British people has in each age managed to evolve a form of government suited to its current needs, and it is tempting to conclude that this represents a steady and salutary progress towards the 'ideal' system. Of course it does not. Needs change, and the machinery has to change to meet them; but the change required may not necessarily be always in the same ideological direction.

Perhaps the best description of democratic government has been given by George Santayana:

> Political democracy . . . may retain, as notably in England and in all ancient republics, many vestiges of older and less democratic institutions. For under democratic governments the people have not created the state; they merely control it. Their suspicions and jealousies are quieted by assigning to them a voice, perhaps only a veto, in the administration; but the state administered is a prodigious self-created historical engine. Popular votes never established the family, private property, religious practices, or international frontiers. Institutions, ideals, and administrators may all be such as the popular classes could never have produced; but these products of natural aristocracy are suffered to subsist so long as no very urgent protest is raised against them. The people's liberty consists not in their original responsibility for what exists – for they are guiltless of it – but merely in the faculty they have acquired of abolishing any detail that may distress or wound them, and of imposing any new measure, which, seen against the background of existing laws, may commend itself from time to time to their instinct and mind. . . .
>
> Social democracy is a general ethical ideal, looking to human equality and brotherhood, and inconsistent, in its radical form, with such institutions as the family and hereditary property. Democratic government, on the contrary, is merely a means to an end, an expedient for the better and smoother government of certain states at certain junctures. It involves no special ideals of life; it is a question of policy, namely, whether the general interest will be better served by granting all men (and perhaps all women) an equal voice in elections. For political democracy, arising in great and complex states, must necessarily be a government by deputy, and the questions actually submitted to the people can be only very large rough matters of general policy or of confidence in party leaders.[2]

The British system of parliamentary government has grown up in this country through a long and continuous process. It does indeed co-exist, as Santayana noted, with many relics of aristocratic government, and has also come to embrace certain new methods and institutions of a bureaucratic nature which are perhaps *less* 'democratic' than those that preceded them. It does not, however, follow that this process of change – or at least the recent direction of the change – is either inevitable or neccessarily for the best. It is not reasonable to assert that simply *because* certain features of our constitution existed before the days of universal suffrage, they are therefore outdated and should be superseded by something new. Nor is it sensible to assert that anything evolved *since* the advent of mass democracy is for that reason good, and that all older institutions should be modified in the same direction.

Politics, however narrowly defined, now directly affect people's lives to a much greater extent than ever before. To take only the most obvious examples of this relationship, the State employs a substantial proportion of the working population, runs their education and health services, and influences by its financial policies their prosperity and even their housing.

Inevitably, as the attitude of politicians towards the individual has changed, so has the attitude of individuals towards the politicians. The more responsibilities politicians purport to undertake, the more benefits do people hope to secure through political means. As soon as the State goes beyond its narrowest functions of preventing some things and encouraging others, and begins actually to *provide* for needs more particular to the individual than are met by such communal services as defence and sewerage, the vote becomes something that can be used to secure a material benefit for oneself. This is not to say that past generations of electors cast their votes without reflecting on the probable effects which the victory of one party or another would have on their own particular circumstances; but they did not have to make decisions between party programmes offering specific benefits like family allowances or free medicines.

There are two obvious dangers in the development of the sort of blind faith in the efficacy of political action that grew up during the last hundred years. First, it is liable to be (and to some extent has been) replaced by an exaggerated contempt if the results fail to come up to expectations. Secondly, it persuades people that the ballot-box is a short cut to economic progress of a kind that cannot in fact be achieved by the actions of governments. It is perhaps hardly surprising that politicians are not always willing to admit the limitations of their craft. The vote of an elector who wants more money is not to be won by telling him to go out and earn it; it is tempting to promise the benefit, and then pay the bill by mulcting those who would never vote for you anyway.

Let us now examine the machinery through which Britain is at present governed. We must start with the position of the Executive, which consists in effect of Cabinet, Ministers and official administrators and others deputed to carry out government policies.

The Executive is based on Parliament, since the Cabinet consists of M.P.s and peers chosen by the Prime Minister from the party that has a majority in the House of Commons. In so far as policy is initiated anywhere, it is initiated (at least in form) in the Cabinet, although there are certain exceptions to this rule. If a party wins power after having been out of office for a long time, the new government may be committed in advance to a number of policies decided through the machinery of the party as a whole. It is also sometimes possible, later in a Parliament, for policies to be forced on an unwilling Cabinet by the pressure of public opinion, whether it is directly expressed through the results of by-elections, agitation in the party organisation or through M.P.s in party committees in the House. However, although this pressure can sometimes stop an unpopular measure, mitigate the details of an unpopular policy or cause the Government to pull some unpremeditated rabbit out of the fiscal hat in order to bribe the electors to keep quiet, it seldom results in any major change in the direction of policy. Still less is it likely to result in any significantly new policy being initiated, if only because public opinion is not generally in any condition to evolve one.

At the same time, the ability of the Cabinet to initiate policy is circumscribed by its lack of technical knowledge, so that even quite important departures may actually be initiated by departmental officials. The Executive should, for all practical purposes, be considered as consisting of the whole departmental machinery of government, including both the responsible Ministers and their official advisers and executive officers. There can be no doubt at all that the importance of these advisers – the 'bureaucracy', as they are called when anyone wants to be rude about them – has enormously increased in this century. This was inevitable, in view of the huge increase in the sphere of governmental activity. No Cabinet Minister can possibly grasp and supervise all the details of his department's work, let alone understand those of another department. He will often have no very clear idea how a particular objective can be achieved, and sometimes no very clear idea what objective *ought* to be achieved – except in the most general terms. This, of course, makes the 'bureaucrats' very important people indeed: they can not only tell the Ministers what ought to be done, but they can also (and often do) give them the most convincing reasons why the things the Government want to do cannot be done.

The great Government departments do undoubtedly represent a powerful vested interest in opposition to necessary change. There is nothing sinister about this, and the Administrative Class of the Civil Service is not necessarily to be blamed – or at any rate vilified – because it is so. Its members are for the most part of high intelligence, well-educated, conscientious, hard-working and knowledgeable about their jobs. In addition – and this is of obvious importance – they are so free from corruption as to be the envy and marvel of the world. In a sense, ironically, it is their very efficiency and conscientiousness that make them a barrier to radical change. They have evolved, and operate, a machine for running the country *as it is now*. This is not to say that they are not trained to look ahead and to foresee the predictable needs of the future, because of course they know very well that they must be prepared for future eventualities. They study the birth-rate and plan ahead to provide enough school places for the children being born; they study the trends of automobile registrations and the movements of population in order to plan programmes of road building and development; they do their best to stimulate farmers to grow as much of their products as they think the public is going to eat, and no more (a singularly difficult task, as events have proved); they worry about the future cost of retirement pensions (as well they may), about the future demand for scientists and doctors, about the future of trade and employment and a score of other things.

They do all this, and often with surprising efficiency. They try to look ahead, and having done so prepare as best they can to receive what the future is obviously and inescapably going to dump in their laps. To this end they will make the minimum number of essential modifications to the administrative machine itself. The fact remains, however, that the machine itself is basically designed to run the country as it was rather than as it will be. This is obvious, when one reflects that many things about the country have recently changed radically and rapidly, while the essential structure of the machine – despite its expansion and modifications of detail and method – has changed relatively little. It is a good machine, and it does a job. But so complicated is it, and so hard does it find it even to keep up with things as they are, that it tends to mistrust and dislike what it regards as *unnecessary* changes – the officials themselves being the judges of what is necessary. If the machine, as at present constituted, cannot handle something, then that something is – for obvious reasons – undesirable, if not impossible.

When institutions become very large and complex, two things tend to happen. First, it becomes hard to adapt them rapidly or radically to change, and this gives them a vested interest in preserving things as much as possible as they are – this being the situation with which the institutions are designed to cope. Second, it becomes more and more difficult for anyone in them, even at the top, to break away from administration for long enough (and completely enough) to stand outside the institutions and see them whole and in relation to the movement of events in the world around them.

For all these reasons, civil servants tend to make their Ministers cautious and conservative. Since it is an important part of their job to point out the difficulties and dangers of any proposal that is mooted in their hearing, it is small wonder if a nervous and impressionable Minister sometimes begins to feel that it is difficult and dangerous to do anything new at all. Certainly the officials will, if pressed, produce plans for doing anything; but sometimes the course of action under examination is made to appear so fraught with risk – and above all so costly – that the impression given is that it is virtually impossible. Some Ministers can cope with this, announcing firmly at the outset that they intend to have their wishes carried out with no nonsense about why it can't be done; as a rule they do get their wishes carried out, the officials often adapting themselves to a comparatively unfamiliar role with something approaching enthusiasm. But such Ministers are fairly rare, and most of the rest are always in some danger of becoming cautious and platitudinous mouthpieces for conservative officials.

Now this is often extremely frustrating and annoying to imaginative and energetic back-bench Members of Parliament. Departmental officials have at their disposal such a vast array of facts, figures and precedents that they can generally put up (through their Ministerial mouthpiece) what looks like a devastating case against any proposal at all. A Minister who is being hard-pressed by back-benchers urging him to do something about an obvious abuse or need (or even just to do something) will finally turn at bay and with heavy irony invite his critics, if they think they can solve a problem that has so far baffled his expert advisers, to submit their own solution. He adds, quite untruthfully, that he would welcome any constructive proposal and will certainly adopt it if it proves to be workable. Having thus shifted the onus of finding a solution from the shoulders where it belongs to those of his critics (who are probably without the technical qualifications needed to produce a detailed solution, but who know very well that something is wrong and ought to be put right), he can then relax in the certainty that his advisers will be able to shoot down any proposal that is put up to them.

A few years of this is apt to discourage all but the most fanatical or most patient of M.P.s. The fanatical ones are often (though not always) ambitious, and can therefore sometimes be kept in line by the promise of (or threat of withholding) patronage. The patient ones are often amenable to appeals by the Whips for loyalty to the party and its leaders.

If all else fails, the Executive still possesses the enormous strength of a procedural system built up over the years to enable the Government of the day to get its business through Parliament with as little trouble as is decent and to enable it to dodge almost any issue it wants to. There is, too, the time-honoured device of referring any really awkward issue to a Royal Commission or expert committee, which usually results in the problem having the heat taken off it for at least two years. Since the committee will often contain one or more retired departmental officials and probably an ex-Minister, there is a built-in body of expertise determined not to make any rash or awkward recommendations. Reports of Royal Commissions often make excellent text-books or works of reference; frequently they recommend useful reforms; very seldom do they make any radical or imaginative suggestions. That is not what they are appointed for.

All this is not to say that the parliamentary and departmental machinery cannot carry through a great deal of radical legislation very quickly if the occasion arises when it has to do so. This was clearly shown by the record of the Labour Government of 1945–50, when a volume of far-reaching and complicated legislation infinitely greater than had ever been thought possible was drafted and passed. But this was an exceptional situation. When the Labour Party won office in 1945, it had never previously had an absolute majority in the House of Commons, let alone in the country. Founded in 1901, with roots going back beyond that, it had accumulated over half a century a large stock-in-trade of policy measures which it was pledged to carry out. It now had a very large majority in the House, a House of Lords too frightened of being abolished to block Government legislation, and an obvious 'mandate' from the country to do something, even if that something was not the full party programme. The possibility that some of the measures in the policy bag were already rather old-fashioned, having been designed for economic conditions which no longer obtained, did not deter the Labour Government from its determination to carry them out. The leaders believed – wrongly as it turned out – not only that they would not be returned to office if they failed to carry out all their policies, but that the carrying out of all the policies would in fact ensure their return. Assured, in any case, of five years of office, they were in a strong position to force their policies through. This they did, with remarkable success. They knew roughly what they wanted, and their departmental officials (many of whom, in 1945, were in any case in sympathy with their aims) had little choice but to co-operate effectively.

Similarly, the Conservative Government of 1951 was able to secure certain of its most important objectives with some speed. But the more normal situation is that which obtained during the period of the Labour Government of 1950–51 and from about 1955 up to the 1964 election. That is to say, a situation in which the party in office has carried out the most urgent parts of the programme which won it power, including all its specific pledges. Thereafter it tends to coast along with routine legislation, administrative reforms, an occasional bright idea, and enough visible improvements to give it a fair chance of re-election. However much it would like to carry out radical reforms (which by that time is not very much), it is most unlikely to receive any encouragement or breath-taking schemes from its official advisers. That is not what officials are for.

The trouble is that, as a result of all this, almost no one does any long-term thinking of a fundamental or radical nature. The officials are too busy with either the problems of the present or just with administration, besides being by nature cautious. The Ministers are either too busy or have been discouraged by their officials from thinking out of turn. The Opposition is often too pre-occupied with winning the next election on immediate issues. (Oppositions, too, always seem to be more afraid of losing votes than eager to win them, which is the reverse of what you might expect).

The machinery of government is thus capable of carrying out rapid changes at need, but it is not designed to generate them. Indeed, there are those who would argue that it appears to have been designed to inhibit the kind of constructive thinking that does generate them.

But does it follow that constructive thinking, of the kind that leads to action, would necessarily result simply from changing our institutions? There is today a great deal of talk about 'modernising' institutions, and even of 'streamlining' them, whatever that means. It seems to me to spring from two lines of thought, the first dangerous and the second merely futile. The first clamour arises from people who – generally for ideological reasons – want to undertake varous radical changes to which other people are strongly opposed. Since the existence of certain democratic institutions either prevents or slows down their achievement of these aims (which is of course exactly what the institutions are designed to do), their advocates demand the 'reform' of these institutions on the grounds that they are 'holding up progress'. The second argument is generally put forward by those who are dissatisfied with the way things are going, but have no clear idea of what ought to be done. They see that our existing parliamentary and executive institutions are not producing dynamic government of the kind they feel is necessary to cope with current problems, and they have come to believe that changing the institutions would galvanise government. But why should it? What is the point of changing our institutions unless we are absolutely sure what it is that we want the institutions to achieve? If we had a clearer idea of what we wanted to do through them, there might be some purpose in redesigning them to our needs.

It is much more likely that what is wrong is that the creative tension of British politics has been running down and needs winding up again. If there had been any sharply defined and constructive urge shown by governments to make substantial and radical progress along clear lines of policy, then we might know whether our institutions have been thwarting progress or not. A government that had clear and radical ideas about what it wanted to do would not necessarily find it very difficult to adapt institutions to its purposes: so far there has been little indication that the trouble lies in method rather than in lack of ideas.

Only in the Conservative Party, in its recent years of opposition, has any constructive thought about long-term policy been initiated. In the meantime, partly owing to the inertia and conservatism of the Labour Government, Conservative leaders have felt obliged to preach the science-cum-technology gospel adumbrated by Harold Wilson in the early 1960s. This doctrine of economic and institutional efficiency, dedicated to the attainment of higher standards of material prosperity for all, could of course lead to a demand for changes in institutions, ways of life and habits of thought, far more radical than any so far advocated by the parties of the left. If this trend of policy were carried to its extreme conclusion, leading to a total surrender to the imperatives of technique, then the demand for the 'modernisation' of institutions would be a logical consequence. The technocrat would come into his own, and large-scale organisation would proceed with the systematic conditioning of society to meet the needs of technique. However, for reasons which are discussed elsewhere in this book, I do not believe that this is either desirable or likely to happen.

Future political conflict will, however, certainly bring its own pressures to change institutions; and the advocacy of change will be for the purpose of achieving certain specific ends, not – as now – a demand to change institutions because no one can think of anything more constructive to advocate. Meanwhile, many of the demands for institutional change seem to be irrelevant, if not positively misconceived. We may nevertheless briefly consider some of them.

There has been a great deal of talk about the decline of Parliament, and about the need to make it more 'efficient'. The arguments generally fall into two categories. One is concerned with the apparent decline in the influence and power of the back-bench Member of Parliament; the other concentrates on the alleged need to speed up and 'streamline' the actual procedures of Parliament. We may take the first complaint first.

I am sure that the change in the status of the Commons back-bencher is more apparent than real, and I am by no means convinced that his power will not increase rather than diminish over the years. It is even now greater than is often supposed.

This is not a fashionable view, and it is not easy to interpret the historical evidence on which one might compare the Member's present status and powers with those of his predecessors. Writing in 1867, Bagehot concluded in *The English Constitution* that the power of party leaders over their Parliamentary followers was much more 'strict and wisely limited' than it had been fifty years earlier. Writing in 1963 (before he became a Minister and for a time Leader of the House of Commons), Mr. R. H. S. Crossman commented: 'It was not until well after Bagehot's death that this system was fundamentally transformed by the transfer of effective power from the floor of the Commons to the great party machines and the bureaucracy in Whitehall.'[3]

This is both an over-simplification and an exaggeration. 'Effective power', in so far as it resided on the floor of the House of Commons, was always subject to certain controls. Moreover, wherever 'effective power' now resides, it is certainly not in 'the great party machines', and it is extremely doubtful whether it can be said to reside in the 'bureaucracy'. We have seen that the departmental officials are very powerful and influential, but their power can be tamed by a determined Minister; in a 'show-down', they must do what they are told. As to the 'great party machines', I remember asking Mr. Crossman, during a broadcast discussion, what he meant by this phrase. It appeared that he had been using it in a rather special sense. He was not referring to the 'backroom boys' of Transport House, Conservative Central Office and Liberal Party Headquarters, for the offices in Smith Square are not in themselves powerful at all. He was referring to the power and patronage exercised by the party leaderships and constituency organisations acting in concert: this power, he believed, was enough to finish the parliamentary career of a recalcitrant backbencher, so that the ultimate power rested with the 'machines'.

I still do not believe this. It is of course true that if the leader of a party, his Chief Whip *and* a constituency party organisation all decided simultaneously that they had had enough of a particular Member of Parliament, then it would be extremely hard for that Member to be re-elected to Parliament. The point is that they very seldom do act thus in concert. Persistent rebels against party leadership are continually re-adopted as official party candidates, and often their independence makes their local organisations the more anxious to stand by them and the more suspicious of any interference by Westminster. Again, a Member may find himself in trouble with his local party activists and yet be supported by a central leadership which is anxious neither to bring a party split into the open nor to create a martyr. In these circumstances he can generally survive. Indeed, the remarkable thing about the behaviour of the 'great party machines' since the war has been the unwillingness they have shown to use the great powers which in theory they could bring to bear on the individual M.P.

Since the parties are, on the whole, generally run by intelligent men, the reason is not far to seek. The powers are much more apparent than real, and an attempt to use them in any but the most exceptional circumstances would result in trouble. The independence of the back-bench M.P., currently so thoughtlessly dismissed as non-existent, still survives and is jealously guarded. Moreover, M.P.s have stronger sanctions at their disposal than is generally believed. It is true that the House of Commons no longer causes governments to fall – although it still could, and might still – so that it can no longer be said to 'elect the Prime Minister', as Bagehot recognised that it did in the early nineteenth century. But each party leader, which is to say the Prime Minister and his potential successor, is elected by the members of his party in the House of Commons. Moreover they can, and sometimes do, get rid of him. It is true that the party leader has great power, influence and patronage; but it is a delegated, conditional power, not an absolute one. It can and will be removed from him when he ceases to deliver the goods demanded by his followers. He tends nowadays to spend as much time placating as leading.

Moreover the party leader, even when he is the Prime Minister, is continually on trial in the House of Commons before one of the most critical audiences in the world. All Ministers are interrogated by back-bench M.P.s with a severity which they – and their official advisers – take extremely seriously. It is true that they enjoy great advantages in information and preparation, and they are seldom completely defeated in any single engagement. But it is nevertheless true that the back-bench Members of the House of Commons can in the end destroy a really ineffective Minister. Few Ministers with a consistently poor record of performance in the House survive for very long unless they have remarkable compensating virtues.

Every Minister (and every 'Shadow' Minister in Opposition), who aspires to the leadership of his party, is to some extent at the mercy of the back-bench M.P.s of his party. He cannot afford to ignore them. Now this may not be 'power' in the sense that the political scientists define that elusive thing, but it gives M.P.s very considerable strength if they know how to use it. They also have much more influence over policy than used to be recognised. Discussions in party committees, or even informal representations to the party whips, can produce changes of heart in Ministers or party leaders.

What is needed is not a radical reform of Parliamentary or political institutions to 'restore' to the private Member the 'power' he is deemed to have lost. That kind of effect does not, in any case, commonly result from that kind of deliberate institutional change. What is needed is for M.P.s to recognise how great is the power they already possess, and then to learn how to use it more fruitfully. This they will not do until they discover what it is they want to achieve. It is also high time that governments were prepared to face defeat in the Commons on minor details of legislation without regarding this as the end of the world.

There could scarcely be a better example of the futility of the urge to 'reform' institutions without knowing what the institutions are for, than the fashionable campaign to set up 'specialised committees' in Parliament on the United States model. Because the committees of the House and the Senate in Washington are powerful and attract great prestige and publicity, it is thought that to set up similar committees of back-bench M.P.s in the House of Commons will somehow make M.P.s more 'powerful'. In fact, it is just as likely to weaken some of the power they already have. Nobody could ever have imagined that this was a good idea who had seriously considered what was the purpose and function of the American prototypes.[4]

The importance of the committees of Congress derives from the fact that the members of the President's Cabinet, and indeed the whole American executive, are debarred from membership of either House of Congress. It is therefore only in the committees that individual Ministers can be personally interrogated and their policies and objectives probed. The committees therefore serve a unique function and provide a unique opportunity. On the extent to which the head of an American department of state carries a Congressional committee with him may depend whether he gets his policies approved by Congress and his budget passed. Moreover, it is only rarely that a Senator or a Congressman is ambitious to become a member of the Cabinet; not only are the Federal Executive and the Legislature separate at any given moment, but there is not much movement between them over a period of time. The chairmanship of a Congressional committee is an object of ambition in itself, and carries a very real power in the right hands. Members of the committees are not, therefore, subject to the same pulls of ambition or the same personal pressures of Government promise and patronage as the British back-bencher member of a specialised Parliamentary committee is bound to be.*

The danger of the British experiment is that it may actually detract from the power and functions of the House of Commons. Since the House can itself regularly interrogate Ministers and compel them to explain themselves *inside* Parliament, the need for the specialised committees does not exist as it does in the United States. But the committees may well be used by clever Ministers to evade the Parliamentary gauntlet. They have only to cosset a special committee along, lulling it into stupefaction with a mass of dull (and relatively unimportant) information, and then avoid a dangerous debate in the House by claiming that the question has already been fully explored by a committee deputed by the House. I doubt whether the possible uses of these committees (which I recognise) can outweigh their potential dangers.

We may now consider briefly the demand, which has recently been accorded some support by Members of Parliament in all parties, for the 'streamlining' of the procedures of Parliament itself. This should be regarded, it seems to me, with the greatest caution. The traditional rigmarole of Parliamentary forms need not, of course, be regarded as sacrosanct in every detail. Much of it is derived from needs and circumstances

* It is true that recalcitrant members of Congressional committees are open to Executive 'persuasion' through favours to their constituents.

which no longer exist. Equally, however, the forms and procedures have been continually adapted over the years to conform as far as possible with the realities of government today. There is no reason why this process should not continue, but there are dangers in being too radical about it. It is true that some of the details of procedure are time-consuming and apparently irrelevant in a modern context, although even some of these have their uses in emphasising the dignity of Parliament or in reminding legislators of the historical origins of the formal framework within which they function. On balance, there can be no objection to a reasonable simplification of these procedures if useful tradition is not totally destroyed.

Much of the demand for 'reform', however, clearly springs from impatience with the checks and balances of the democratic process itself, and this should be regarded with suspicion. It is tempting for supporters of the Government in office – particularly new and enthusiastic M.P.s who are utterly convinced of the unique merits of the Government's proposed legislation – to regard with indignation the attempts of the Opposition to slow down the passage of legislation so obviously and urgently needed in the interests of the people. Anything which shortens this process, they feel, must be in the public interest; the solution is clearly to 'streamline' outmoded parliamentary procedures. The dangers of yielding to this demand are obvious. The Executive has already very great reserve procedural powers to enable it to get its business through Parliament. 'Timetable motions' (the 'Guillotine' procedure) are sparingly used, but they can always be resorted to in an emergency, and meanwhile the closure device for bringing a particular debate to a conclusion is used with great frequency. Moreover, much recent legislation (particularly in respect of new taxes) has been hastily drafted and in need of close scrutiny and detailed amendment: indeed, the Government itself has often introduced amendments to its own Bills at every stage of their passage through Parliament. Any substantial curtailing of the process of scrutiny would certainly result in some lamentably half-baked legislation reaching the Statute Book, quite apart from the constitutional risk involved in further increasing the already wide powers of the Executive.

What seems to some people a more reasonable excuse for demanding the 'streamlining' of parliamentary procedures is that it would enable Parliament to get through more work. This demand is entirely misconceived. Parliament is already capable, as we have seen, of getting through an immense amount of legislation in a Session when the need (or at least the pressure) is urgent,[5] and it is extremely improbable that more could be dealt with without the quality of the drafting being impaired. But the real objection is one of principle. There is a Parkinson's Law relating to legislation, and indeed to the whole of the Government's parliamentary business. The business expands to fill the time made available for it, and there is precious little sign that the country has been the better for this.* Britain is, if anything, over-governed and over-legislated for, and little good is likely to come of carrying the process much further. In any case, M.P.s are already more fully occupied with legislation than is good for them; they have too little opportunity for constructive thought and discussion.

There is almost certainly a better case for arguing that any major changes in parliamentary practice and procedure should be in the opposite direction. In the House of Commons, the balance between the right of a Government with a working majority to get its business through and the right of the Opposition to scrutinise legislation and seek to amend it has probably been struck at a reasonable equilibrium, and the scales should certainly not be tipped any further towards making things easier for the Executive. What does require serious consideration now is the position and powers of the House of Lords.

The present situation is both absurd and dangerous. Not only have the amending and delaying powers of the second chamber been emasculated, by the Parliament Acts of 1911 and 1949, but until 1968 the Lords feared that their opponents would not hesitate to provoke a constitutional crisis which might well result in the second chamber being reduced to total impotence. Thus, even when they were convinced that it would be right to oppose a particular measure (and perhaps

* It is generally agreed that the 1967 experiment of morning sittings in the Commons was a failure, accomplishing nothing and inconveniencing everyone.

believed that public feeling would support their action), they were for long unable to make up their minds that they ought to act decisively in a particular instance. It seemed that the total effect of having their remaining powers stripped from them might be worse for the country than to let one bad measure through; they were therefore forced to compromise again and again, putting off the moment of truth in the hope that the precisely right occasion would arrive for defiance. In the summer of 1968 they rebelled on an Order in Council about Rhodesian sanctions, after the Labour Government had already threatened to reduce their delaying powers still further.

Useful as the House of Lords still manages to be, since it can muster an impressive array of talent for a major debate and can make useful amendments to minor measures, the fact remains that it is now no longer fulfilling the proper functions of a second chamber. There is a real need for an Upper House with delaying powers that can be effectively used. It is obvious that there are difficulties in trying to restore the powers lost in 1949 – which is what I believe will have to be done – to a chamber with a built-in Conservative majority of hereditary peers. So far, every attempt to reach agreement between the parties on a suitable formula for a reconstituted membership has broken down; early in 1969, a Government Bill embodying a rather absurd proposal was assailed in the Commons by Right and Left alike, and finally killed. At present – although few people have appreciated the truth of the paradox – Labour is getting the best of both worlds. The House of Lords, apparently overwhelmingly Tory, dare not oppose a Labour Government on any matter of importance, so that a Labour majority in the Commons can do what it likes. Any change in constitution and powers, even if it provided for occasional Labour majorities in the Upper House, would leave a Labour Government more at risk than it is now.

A change, if it is to be made, will have to be made by a Conservative Government, and it will probably have to be made without the agreement of the Labour Party. Now that a start has been made with the reconstitution of the composition of the House of Lords through the creation of life peers, there is no insuperable difficulty about finding a formula for a working membership. If it is impossible to secure general agreement, then we shall have to go ahead without it. If the formula is reasonably sensible it will probably work as well as anything else would. The important thing – however illogical and socially and politically 'unjust' such a high-handed solution may seem to some – is to have some kind of a viable second chamber with adequate delaying and amending powers.

It may be asked whether there is any possibility of a lasting solution, since future Labour or radical governments will have ample precedents for tampering afresh with any procedural checks to their efforts to impose rapid change. The answer is that we must make it much more difficult to tamper with the powers of the second chamber in future; unless we do, there is little purpose in having a second chamber at all, and an essential check on the power of the Executive will have been removed. We must make up our minds, it seems to me, that in the end we shall have to resort to the expedient of entrenched powers for the Upper House. This is a most un-English suggestion, and it naturally raises some fundamental questions about the nature and future of our constitution.

It is a commonplace, of course, that the British constitution differs from that of other countries in being unwritten in a precise formula. It is, so to speak, the whole body of public law and custom developed and modified gradually over the centuries. While it may be said to be based on a kind of general pact designed to safeguard the rights of individuals and corporations, it is in no sense a formal contract. Much of it can be, and has been, informally and even imperceptibly modified over the years. There is no body charged with the duty of interpreting and safeguarding it, as the Supreme Court is in the United States. The courts perform this function over some of the field, but in a different way. Further, many of the most important constitutional factors are set down in Acts of Parliament, in particular the Parliament Acts and Representation of the People Acts. While the courts can interpret these, they cannot of course prevent Parliament from repealing or amending them in another statute. And of course the situation since the Parliament Act of 1949 is that the majority party in the House of Commons can make very important changes in the constitution which the House of Lords can do no more than delay for a year. There is thus very little check on extremist actions, which may be both ill-considered and irrevocable, carried out even by a Government that has lost the support of the electorate and is clearly doomed to defeat at the next general election.

Despite the pride with which British politicians and constitutional lawyers have traditionally regarded our amorphous constitution, and the scorn which they have often heaped on the formal constitutions of the United States and other countries,[6] it is becoming possible to argue that our system has not stood the most recent tests very well. In some ways the individual is freer, and the powers of the Executive subject to more salutary checks, in the United States and in Australia, where the safeguards cannot be tampered with so easily. Of course, this has always been strictly true, but the tampering process has become easier here in this century owing to the greater apathy of public opinion. In the past it has generally been possible to argue plausibly, not only that the safeguards were adequate, but that the flexibility of our institutions made for more efficient – and even possibly for more humane – government than was provided by more formal constitutions. It is very doubtful whether this argument is any longer valid.

A reformed second chamber will, I believe, need to be given back at least the delaying powers which the House of Lords possessed between 1911 and 1949. Then we must make it much more difficult for these powers to be once more weakened by a subsequent government intent on getting a particular measure through Parliament quickly. I doubt whether it would be desirable to introduce the device of the referendum into our constitutional system, since there would inevitably be pressure to extend this precedent to other and less important controversies. But it might be desirable to provide that the powers of the second chamber could not be altered (that is to say, either increased or diminished) unless by a two-thirds vote in both Houses of Parliament. This proviso might well be formally extended to cover other important constitutional safeguards, such as the powers and composition of the courts of law, the jury system, and what probably ought to be a stronger and more formal provision for protection and appeal against the executive acts of Ministers, tribunals and public corporations (possibly along the lines of a *Conseil d'État*).

We noted earlier that the present composition and training of the Civil Service does not particularly fit it to be in any sense a vehicle or inspiration for imaginative and constructive thought or for salutary change. Much anxious thought has recently been given – mostly outside the Civil Service itself – to the problem of how it can be made more efficient and flexible without losing the benefit of the undoubted merits it possesses. This culminated in the report of the Fulton Committee, not long after the publication of Mr. Max Nicholson's important book *The System* (subtitled *The Misgovernment of Britain*). It is unnecessary to traverse here the ground covered by Mr. Nicholson, but it may be said that his book represents the extreme case against the Civil Service system as a whole. He finds it – correctly, as I believe – out of touch with the people whose lives it administers, remarkably inefficient in its accounting and contracting, slow to move with the times and incapable of securing and assessing expert professional advice and translating it into constructive action with reasonable speed. Mr. Nicholson also finds that the economic policies of the Treasury have almost invariably been wrong.

This is a formidable indictment, but it is hard to feel that it is substantially exaggerated. Mr. Nicholson's conclusion that an essential prerequisite of any effective reform is the abolition of the Treasury, in its present form and with its present dictatorial powers over other departments, is also persuasively argued. He is clearly on the right lines, too, in saying (as did the Fulton Committee) that the career structure and exclusiveness of the Administrative Class need to be changed. There should be much more fluidity in the movement of suitable men and women both into and out of the service. Administration – at least as it is at present understood in the Civil Service, with its almost complete lack of specialised training in anything – should not necessarily be considered a safe career for a whole working life. It is possible to feel a little chary of sharing wholeheartedly Mr. Nicholson's and the Fulton Committee's faith in the virtues of being governed almost exclusively by highly-trained experts. Such men are apt to be too enthusiastic in their urge to impose the imperatives of technique on everyone else, and liable to be carried away by their enthusiasms to the point at which they frequently fail to appreciate (or at least give proper weight to) the possible secondary social and human effects of their actions. There is something to be said for assigning some place to the humane judgement of the aloof 'Oxbridge' graduates of whom Mr Nicholson is so scornful and whom the Fulton Committee stigmatised as 'amateurs'. Certainly they are inadequate if they are left to do the whole job by themselves; but they can provide a necessary and effective counterpoise to the ruthless enthusiasms of the expert manager or the besotted technologist.

It is scarcely necessary to repeat that none of these reforms would solve our problems by itself. Nor would all of them together have any effect unless the political inspiration is present to use the more efficient institutions in a constructive way for the right purposes. The reform of institutions is a quite secondary priority. But once we are on the right track politically, we may as well get this right too.

Enthusiastic proponents of the panacea of institutional reform all agree that our system of local government requires drastically 'streamlining'. Unfortunately, they seldom agree on the lines which the reformed system should follow. Most of them have been carried away by blind worship of the virtues of large-scale administration, and think in terms of regional units of one kind or another.

It is, of course, easy to show that some of our present units are too small to be perfectly efficient in some respects. There are obviously economies of scale to be secured by carrying out certain functions – particularly where purchasing or contracting is involved – through pretty large units. However, there are also certain grave disadvantages involved in trying to govern people through large and remote organisations. The relationship between our existing large local authorities and the individuals living within their boundaries is none too close today, and there have to be very good reasons indeed for weakening the links still further. Indeed, there is reason to believe that the right trend would be one which devolved as many functions as possible to the authorities in the most intimate contact with local inhabitants. Regional government is an admirable idea if the purpose is to devolve some of the functions of central government to the regions, but there are serious dangers involved in swallowing up all the smaller units and their functions into large bureaucratic headquarters.*

A particularly naive objection often raised against the smaller local authorities is that they must be inefficient because they cannot afford to pay the salaries of first-class officials. We know, of course, that many excellent officials are enticed away from smaller to larger local authorities by the promise of much larger salaries. Only too often the result is that a man with a special gift for getting on with local people, and who runs a small authority smoothly and well, ends up in an office in a large city hall where he scarcely meets anyone but other officials. And a moment's reflection should show that relative salary scales have absolutely nothing useful to say about the optimum size and functions of a local government unit. These should be assessed on a reasonable balance between economies of scale and the risk of remoteness from the governed.

If we follow our philosophical principle of considering the personal role and involvement of the individual and the safeguarding of his physical environment as our first priorities, then we have some guidelines to work by when considering the future of local government. We should have a predisposition towards small units wherever possible, and towards maximum devolution wherever the main units have to be large.

But this is a subject for a book in itself, and it is time to move on from the institutions of government to the political parties through which most of government is carried on.

* It should perhaps be noted that this book is going to the press before the publication of the Redcliff-Maud Report on local government.

CHAPTER 13

The British Political Parties

Democracy, which is a charming form of government, full of variety and disorder. . . .

Plato, *The Republic* (tr. Jowett)

The House of Commons thrives on criticism, it is perfectly impervious to newspaper abuse or taunts from any quarter, and it is capable of digesting almost anything or almost any body of gentlemen, whatever be the views with which they arrive.

Sir Winston Churchill

The Conservative Party has changed much and many times since its first Tory origins became discernible in the 17th century. From being the party of the Stuart kings and the Anglican High Church, it became the party of the English landed gentry. For a time, while retaining its connection with the landed interest, it became the party of opposition to the unbridled *laisser-faire* of the new capitalism of the industrial revolution. This made it a reforming party, but it was discernibly a conservative party for all that. It was trying to conserve some of the paternalist traditions of the past and to mitigate the inhumanity of the industrial juggernaut. It was also, of course, trying to preserve the status and privileges of 'the gentlemen of England' as a ruling class, against the rising power of the new capitalist middle class. Those of its members who belonged to this class split off from it under Peel and became Liberals. Gradually the Whig grandees joined the Tories, who were from time to time reinforced by, and had painfully to digest, other 'right-wing' sections of the Liberal Party, and later (on a much smaller scale) of the Labour Party. Despite a narrow escape at the time of the Coalition crisis of 1922, the Tories have not suffered a leftward split since 1846.

The fascinating thing about the Conservative Party today is that it still contains within itself, perfectly preserved and visible like the contents of archaeological strata, specimens from nearly all its historical changes and of all its acquisitions from the left. It still comprehends virtually the entire 'landed interest', and preserves in something still recognisable as the vestiges of their former splendour the territorial magnates of the 'Grand Whiggery'. It can show here and there a romantic of Disraeli's 'Young England' period, and quite a number of social-reforming Tory Democrats of the age of the later Disraeli and Lord Randolph Churchill. It contains specimens of all the types of businessmen acquired from the Liberals, including even a few who still believe in perfect competition and would like to see no State intervention in the economy at all. It has preserved followers of nearly all the principles of Joseph Chamberlain, although it is doubtful whether any one individual could be found who holds them all at once. It contains exponents of all the different periods and forms of protectionist doctrines; Tory radicals and right-wing Fabians; militant patriots who believe that Britain would still rule the waves if it were not for the weakness and incompetence of her governments; Little Englanders; Laudian Anglo-Catholics and Birmingham Unitarians; royalists who still deprecate the Parliamentary usurpation of the prerogative powers of the Sovereign: and, like all parties, a few amiable and by no means useless eccentrics.

Obviously this heterogeneous collection of seemingly incompatible elements generates many tensions within the party; but the party, like the Church of England, has adapted itself to a comprehensive tolerance. Like the ostrich (which it occasionally resembles in certain other respects), it can digest almost anything and turn it to some account. Its immunity from actual fission since 1846 has not made it careless of the dangers; on the contrary, watching the fates of its successive left-wing opponents has given it a highly developed sense of self-preservation, so that it closes its ranks at the first sign of real danger.*

This, then, is the Conservative Party. What it believes in, what is its philosophy, and what it is now trying to conserve, are matters more difficult to determine. Until recently, the conventional view of the respective position of the political

* Or did, until the leadership 'crises' of 1963 and 1965.

parties was at least approximately correct, and the parties recognisably conformed to it. The Conservative Party was a party of moderate and gradual reform, dedicated to the maintenance of certain traditions and institutions. The Labour Party was dedicated to the interests of manual workers, to a measure of socialism, and to certain radical social changes. The Liberal Party was somewhere out to the left of the Conservatives, although nobody was at any given moment quite sure where.

Now, however, the situation has become confused. After the 1964 election, the Labour Party showed signs of settling down to a strangely conservative maintenance of the *status quo*, while the Conservative leaders began talking with great spirit about the need for radical change in methods and institutions – particularly the need for technological change. What is the elector to make of this?

Politics require a creative tension between two parties of different philosophies and attitudes; we need a conservative party and a radical party existing side by side and alternating in government. But is it really possible for the historic Conservative Party and the Labour Party to change roles without chaos ensuing?

The Labour Party outside Parliament is a less heterogeneous collection of people than the Conservative Party, for the overwhelming majority of its members and supporters are working-class trade unionists. The solidarity of this core has hitherto been proof against any risk of a split arising out of differences inside the working-class 'movement'. Yet the party is by no means completely homogeneous; and whereas the very multiplicity of the tensions arising in the Conservative Party, from the wide variety of its component types, tends to make cohesion easier as the tensions cancel one another out, what divisions there are in the Labour Party tend to be sharper, more open and less easily resolved. Like the Conservative Party, it can show a fair range of fossilised specimens from the strata of its past – non-conformist pacifist radicals, republicans, militant Clydesiders, Marxists, Fabian socialists and so on. But there are two main tensions within the party, and they do not wholly coincide. One is the division, older than the party itself, between the working-class trade unionists on the one hand and the middle-class intellectual reformers on the other. The solidarity of the working-class core of the 'movement' is based on the traditional loyalties (more than a century old) of the older basic industries – the miners' lodges, the spinners and weavers and the dockworkers. The tradition of middle-class reformism is probably almost as old as civilisation itself, although it has been continuously visible only since the Reformation.

The second tension within the Labour Party is that between the socialists and the rest: between those who consider that the party's main objective, which is to advance the interests of the workers, can be pursued along whatever lines seem at a given time to be most promising, and those who believe that it can in the long run only be secured through socialism. Most of the keen socialists are intellectuals rather than trade unionists, but by no means all. Some are both.

The Labour Party is not at present a vehicle for economic expansion and change. It was designed to meet a situation that no longer exists. It came after the period of capitalist expansion (for which it would not, of course, have been at all suitable itself), and was largely aimed at dealing with the abuses created by it. It offered a method of redistributing wealth and incomes, and might perhaps have provided greater economic stability within this country than we actually had between the wars. It is, nevertheless, doubtful whether a socialist system run by the Labour Party could have encouraged even the volume of redistribution of labour between the contracting older industries and the developing new ones that did take place in the inter-war years. Probably the influence of the vested interests of the older trade unions would have slowed the process down considerably. Certainly it seems extremely unlikely – to put it no higher – that a socialist system in this country would have made us any more competitive with our exports, any more expansionist in our economic philosophy, or any better adapted to meet the needs of the changing world than we actually are. Some socialists will object to this, and it is true that the theory provides for such needs; but actual experience of the operations of those industries that have been nationalised, and of the policies of economic planners under a Labour Government, does not suggest that socialism has any potential as a vehicle for dynamic economic change. It tends always to look at tomorrow's problems in terms of yesterday's theories.

If socialism offers little hope in this respect, still less does the Labour Party's solid core of trade unionism. In one important respect this is immensely conservative, for it is deeply rooted in the past. I have already referred to the vested interests of the workers in the older staple industries, which are certainly a strong brake on rapid redistribution of labour. Even more important is the craft basis of many unions, with roots traceable back to the middle ages. That this results in some industrial inefficiency, in resistance to technical improvements and in a higher level of production and distribution costs than could be achieved even without reducing individual earnings is surely beyond doubt. The effects have often been exaggerated, and of course there are plausible arguments (such as those based on industrial safety) for some of the craft rules. Nevertheless, it cannot seriously be argued that they do not act as a brake on technological advance.

The effects can be retarding even when unions are not pulling in different directions, as the craft unions often do. For one thing, the general objective of the trade union movement is to advance the specific interests of the worker in his capacity as producer. These do not necessarily always coincide with the best long-term interests of the country as a whole, although of course high wages and full employment are in themselves good for the country if too many other essentials are not sacrificed to them. In general, subject to the maintenance of full employment, the unions aim at securing higher earnings and shorter hours of work for their members. To the extent that these are achieved, production costs are likely to rise unless one (or both) of two things accompanies them: either the workers must do more work in each hour, or new processes (which generally involve new capital investment) must be found to enable them to produce more in each hour. If it happens that the new processes involve an actual saving of labour, then some workers may be displaced by them, and this the unions will generally oppose. The unions are the main cause – although employers have often connived at it – of the appalling over-manning of so many industrial processes.

While trade unionists have, in their capacity of consumers, an interest in keeping the cost of goods down, they seldom display an overriding desire to keep costs down in their own industries. As a result, there tends to be a fairly steady price inflation, which trade unionists counter by forcing up their own wages. This is not to say that there are not plenty of trade union leaders who see the need to increase productivity and keep costs competitive. But the motive to reduce costs is seldom strong enough or sharp enough to override the immediate considerations of their members' interests. There is a tendency to insist that price reductions can be made in other ways – by a reduction in profits, or by improvements in distribution. This is sometimes true, but the result is generally that nothing gets done at all. It has sometimes appeared as if employers and workers had agreed to combine against the consumer, both sides being apparently convinced that there is virtually no limit to the possibility of passing on rising wage costs in higher prices. And of course it can be argued that in a closed economy there *would* be virtually no limit. Unfortunately, however, ours is not a closed economy.

The Labour Party is therefore in a difficult position. The organised workers represent the overwhelming majority of its support, and it cannot therefore pursue for very long any policy that appears – even on a short-sighted view – to conflict with the interests of any substantial section of these workers. At the same time the support it can secure from organised labour is not enough by itself to achieve a majority in Parliament. It must win a fair number of middle-class votes, and these are not to be won if the policies the party pursues are too narrowly sectional in the interests of the workers. It cannot be radical in its economic policies because almost any radical policies would be sure to conflict at some point with the conservatism and the vested interests of the trade unions. It sometimes seems as if the Labour Party is inhibited from having any consistent policies at all.

The Liberal Party was once the traditional vehicle for radical change. The question is whether it can ever fill this role again.

There is no need to recapitulate the history of the party in any detail. It was a radical party which reached the zenith of its inspiration and success with its overwhelming electoral victory in 1906. Thereafter the Labour Party ate steadily into its working-class support; it split and split again, until in the 1950s it was a ghost, polling fewer than 750,000 votes in an electorate of thirty million. Yet there were those who would not let it disappear: some of these were elderly Liberals nostalgic for the great old days, others the young who wanted only something different. Then, in the later years of Conservative Government, the Liberals began to profit from the Labour Party's failure to attract support away from an administration with which the people had perhaps become excessively familiar. Their by-election successes were the result. Since 1966 their support has dwindled again, perhaps fatally.

Have the Liberals a future? And, if so, what? The first question to be considered is fundamental. Is there room for three parties in the British Parliamentary system? I think one must conclude that, with our present electoral system, it is extremely unlikely that three parties could co-exist permanently; moreover, it seems probable that it would produce no very satisfactory situation if they could. Apart from a few rapidly atrophying limbs severed by internal crisis from the main body of one party or another, three parties of comparable size have existed together only during the period when the Labour Party was supplanting the Liberals as the party of the Left. (I do not count the Irish Nationalists, who were something rather special and improbable.) The fact that it has never happened before does not, of course, necessarily mean that a situation *could* not arise in which three parties might exist in some sort of equilibrium. It does, however, provide a pretty strong argument against it, unless the factors that prevented it before have ceased to exist. And it would appear that at present they are still very much in existence. If the essential political struggle is between the forces of radical reform and those favouring a gradual development by means of changes made piecemeal and decided on largely empirical grounds, then two radical parties, or two conservative parties, would never find it easy to exist together for very long. Once one of them began to forge ahead of the other, even as the result of some quite ephemeral issue, the logic of politics would tend to accentuate its success and draw to it not only those who like to back a winner but also the many who rightly believe that only through a *successful* political party can anything practically useful be achieved.

There remains, of course, the possibility that the Liberals could exist as a third party in the centre, between the other two, as a kind of compromise for moderates, especially those who dislike the Tories for historical reasons and Labour for its occasional support of socialist doctrines. But is this really a feasible proposition today? Certainly it is what a lot of voters would like – or think at certain times that they would like – and certainly it is what many Liberals would like to be. But surely it is precisely in the middle that there is, in either the short or the long run, no room at all for a third party to manœuvre in Britain today. There are plenty of people on what must (for lack of any more conveniently descriptive term) be called the 'right wing' of the Labour Party who are far more conservative, far less radical, even far more reactionary, than on the 'left wing' of the Conservative Party. The two larger parties do, in fact, overlap on the political spectrum; and not only in terms of individual members, but of policies too.

Moreover, quite apart from the improbability of three parties being able to co-exist with policies sufficiently different to make them viable, there is the fact that the whole parliamentary and electoral system is against it. Even the physical construction of the House of Commons is against it, divided as it is into *two* confronting rows of benches for Government and *an* Opposition, with no cross-benches inside the Bar of the House. The procedure for debate is primarily arranged to allow two parties to oppose each other. The electoral system, too, works effectively – in the sense that it almost invariably produces a Government with a working majority of seats in the House of Commons – with two parties. Certainly it tends to exaggerate swings of opinion, and it can produce a sizable majority in the Commons even when two parties are almost evenly balanced in the country: this is indeed what it is designed to do. When there are three parties, however, the results are liable to be confused: no clear-cut results may emerge. This may not only be bad for government, but it is unlikely for long to satisfy the electors. And if it does not satisfy the electors, they will certainly kill one of the three parties, or at least reduce it to virtual impotence.

It can be argued that a three-party system is theoretically possible. Nevertheless I am quite sure that it is, for more than a relatively short transitional period, impracticable in this country – *with our present parliamentary and electoral system.* At this point it may well be asked whether there is anything completely sacrosanct about this system. In changing times, surely institutions of this kind can themselves change? Certainly they can, and almost certainly will. They have been gradually adapted to changing circumstances and needs over the centuries, and as the pace of change quickens no doubt constitutional changes will need to be made more quickly and more often. The present point, however, is comparatively narrow. Do we want this particular change for this particular purpose?

It is easy to argue this question in the wrong way. Those who start from the conviction that it is necessary or desirable to have three parties are naturally not impressed by the objection that the present electoral system makes it extremely difficult, if not impossible. They simply reply that the system can and should be changed. But the real question remains: not whether the system should be changed to allow three parties to co-exist, but whether we want three parties enough to make it worth while to change the system.

To many people it is self-evident that three parties must be better than two, largely on the grounds that it would give the electors a wider choice. The two major parties, they maintain, have become stale, they have had a monopoly of politics for too long, they need some competition. It may well be asked, however, whether the conclusion necessarily follows from the premises. It is true that the long and virtually unchallenged supremacy of the Conservative Party after 1951 produced a political situation that was the reverse of dynamic. Certainly the period of Conservative rule lasted too long for the health of the party system. But did it necessarily require a third party to break the deadlock? Could not the required results have been achieved either through the rejuvenation of the Labour Party or through its supersession by the Liberals as the party of the left? In any case, what were the objections to the two great parties? If it is true – and I am sure it is – that there is no room for a centre party between them, then the objections must have been based on a conviction that the Conservative Party was not conservative enough or the Labour Party not radical enough, or both. There are, indeed, people who hold such views in respect of each of the two parties, but surely they do not prove that what is wanted is a *third* party? The argument is surely one for the reform of one or both of the existing parties; and while a third party might act as a catalyst for this process, or even in time supplant one of the others, it does not in the least follow that the reform necessitates (or would even follow from) the creation of a situation in which three parties could permanently co-exist.

Further, there is one obvious question: why *three* parties? If it is desirable to give the electors a wider choice; if the two great parties of Labour and Conservatism are not enough; then why stop at three? Why not produce a situation in which there could be four, or five, or even dozens of parties? This would not be to the Liberals' taste, of course, but it is at least possible that any change in the electoral system that would permit three parties to co-exist would also allow more than three. Does anyone really believe that a multi-party system in this country would work better than the two-party system has done? I hardly imagine so. A comparison of the working of the two-party systems in Britain and the United States with the record of multi-party systems in other countries is almost, if not quite, conclusive. It is extremely unlikely that the British would long tolerate the compromises, the frustrations and the frequent changes of administration and policy that a multi-party system, which can scarcely exist for long without multiple coalitions, would involve.

It is possible, though not easy, to devise a system of voting that would favour the maintenance of three parties without encouraging the growth of more. But there is surely not the faintest justification for doing so. The present system of single-member constituencies, with a single vote and election of the candidate who receives the most votes in a single ballot, has been fairly conclusively shown to favour a two-party system in the long run. Its chief advantages are simplicity and the fact that it tends to produce clear-cut results and good working majorities in the House of Commons. These are considerable advantages. If anything, the system tends slightly to anticipate and exaggerate swings of opinion in the country. This, nowadays, is also no bad thing. The chief criticism of the system is that it virtually disfranchises many of the supporters of any minor party. Two million Liberals were in 1959 unable to return more than six members of Parliament, instead of the forty or so that would represent their proportion of the total electorate. This may be held to be 'undemocratic'. Yet it is scarcely more undemocratic than the fact that there are no Communists in the House of Commons, to say nothing of Fascists, small shopkeepers and people who believe the earth is flat. A system designed to give the Liberals what they believe to be their democratic right must also in justice open the door to every minority group that can muster a few hundred thousands of votes. Now whether or not this would be desirable – and I am quite sure that it would not – the people of Britain simply would not tolerate such a shambles for any length of time.

It is, however, not inconceivable that a situation might arise, if a Liberal revival proved sufficiently durable, in which the two main parties found themselves more or less deadlocked with equal numbers in the Commons and the balance of power was held by a small body of Liberal M.P.s. In this case it is again not impossible that one or other of the major parties (and it would be more likely to be the Labour Party than the Conservatives, if only because the Labour Party is in the long run more vulnerable) might promise amendment of the electoral system in order to secure Liberal support to form a government. They would, I think, be foolish to do it, but they might; and in that case, we might find ourselves for some time with three parties. Nevertheless, I do not believe that it would last, and I believe that the party that was originally responsible for the change would incur considerable unpopularity as a result.

It is also extremely improbable that the country would for long tolerate a situation in which a minority party continually held the balance of power and dictated terms to the Government. Sooner or later – probably sooner – the minority party would disappear, unless it had managed to secure a majority and displace one of the other two parties in the meantime. And this brings us to the question: if I am right in believing that there is no future in the long run for the Liberals as a third party, is there any chance of their survival in the only other possible way – the supplanting of one of the other two?

It does not seem in the least likely that the Liberals will be able to supplant the Conservative Party. Indeed, the only possible way to do this would be for them to *become* the conservative party. This would be an extremely tricky and hazardous operation, because in the short run it would probably result in the Liberals losing the hard core of their own support – the elderly radicals to whom Toryism has always been the arch-enemy, together with the new young radicals who are against the Establishment.

It seems, then, that the only hope for the survival of the Liberals on terms which might one day enable them to form a government is for them to reverse the process that took place during the first half of this century by replacing the Labour Party as the left-wing opposition to the Conservatives. There are many reasons for supposing that it is unlikely to happen, and several for believing it to be undesirable.

One great danger that we should face during an interim period while the Liberal Party was gaining ground at the expense of Labour, is the risk that the Liberals would gradually win away from the Labour Party all its most intelligent and enlightened 'progressives' and all its middle-class radicals, leaving the most reactionary forces of trade union labour entrenched in the last ditch in a mood of sullen resentment and suspicion. Then, instead of the breaking down of class barriers, instead of the narrowing of the gap between the 'two sides of industry', instead of the spirit of co-operation and shared adventure that the new Liberals preach, we might be faced with a period of real – but nevertheless utterly pointless – strife.

At present the Liberal Party has made almost no impression on the solid working-class support of Labour. It has scarcely fought elections in Labour strongholds, nor has it put forward any policies likely to appeal specifically to organised Labour. This is all to the good in the sense that it leaves the Liberals free of commitments to particular interests and free to become a 'classless' party of the left. But, whereas a party committed exclusively to the interests of organised labour would scarcely meet the needs of the whole country today, it is nevertheless true that a left-wing party cannot hope to win an electoral majority unless it can secure the support of a large proportion of manual workers. This the Liberals are very far from having achieved; indeed, they can scarcely be said to have tried.

One can hardly feel any confidence that the Liberal Party will succeed, or even long survive. Indeed, it is noticeable that the arguments for its preservation increasingly take the form of urging that it acts as a useful pressure group in ideas, and prevents the other two parties from becoming either too dull or too silly. This is not, however, something that requires a political party, expensively fighting elections in hopeless constituencies. It is even doubtful whether the Liberals are any longer producing any significant new ideas; certainly, the corpus of their policies makes no great sense. Whether the party's continued existence has a salutary effect on the two larger parties is also debatable. It can no doubt be said to some extent to keep them on their toes, at least in the sense that they have to make allowances for the Liberals in calculating their electoral strategies. Nevertheless, it can equally be argued that their existence is actually slowing down the process of adjustment to modern problems and to the new mood of the electorate. It may well be true that the Liberal leaven would work more powerfully and usefully if Liberals were to decamp to one or both of the two main parties and exert their pressures from within.

It is difficult to make any confident pronouncement about the prospects of the nationalist parties in Scotland and Wales, other than that they are likely to continue doing well in by-elections. How far they will retain their present support at general elections remains to be seen. In the end, I think, they will gain the substance of their demands, for some measure of regional decentralisation is the only antidote to the centralising tendencies that have been alienating the inhabitants of provincial areas, and Scotland and Wales are obvious candidates for a substantial measure of devolution and limited internal self government. If these concessions are made – as I think they will be – then the nationalist parties will presumably continue for a time to play a political role in their own countries, although they will be unlikely to have much influence at Westminster.

CHAPTER 14

The Politics of Consensus

The best and safest way for you, therefore, my dear brethren, is to [submit] all your deeds past to a new reckoning, to re-examine the cause ye have taken in hand, and to try it even point by point, argument by argument, with all the diligent exactness ye can, to lay aside the gall of that bitterness wherein your minds have hitherto over-abounded, and with meekness to search the truth.

Richard Hooker, *The Laws of Ecclesiastical Polity*

You had that action and counteraction, which, in the natural and in the political world, from the reciprocal struggle of discordant powers draws out the harmony of the universe.

Edmund Burke, *Reflections on the Revolution in France*

It was the opinion of A. J. Balfour – and his dictum has become a cliché of British political thought – that parliamentary government cannot long survive unless both political parties are in substantial agreement about basic constitutional conventions and about the ultimate objectives of policy. Only if they were so agreed, he thought, could the parties oppose one another constructively over methods and administrative details. If they were not, their conflict would sooner or later break the constitutional framework in which it was set. But of course the theory was one naturally congenial to Balfour, who recoiled from bitter strife and from anything savouring of ideological dogmatism. Besides, he regarded Parliament as a debating club for gentlemen.

In one sense, parties are always in agreement about ultimate objectives, since they all purport to be devoted to the welfare of individual men and women. Even in a totalitarian regime, it is difficult to pretend that there is either purpose or virtue in serving the State for its own sake alone, with no thought for the ultimate function of the State in serving the interests of its citizens. The ostensible objectives of fascist and communist regimes are not wholly different in kind from those of liberal democratic governments. Even the romantic nonsense of Nazism, the glorification of *ein Volk, ein Reich*, to which all short-term individual interests had to be sacrificed, was at least based on the assumption that in the end all Germans would be richer and happier when the 'historic mission' was accomplished. With Marxists the objective is quite explicit; the ends may be forgotten, or overlaid by the impatience of leaders or the corrupting distractions of power, but individual welfare (at least in the material sense) is the aim of policy.

It might seem that this 'ultimate objective' fulfils the Balfourian condition, since controversy can thenceforward confine itself to the means of achieving individual welfare. Indeed it appears that this is the assumption on which British politics are now proceeding. Yet for much of our history it was not so, and it is open to grave doubt whether it ought to be so now. For the assumption implies a tacit, and much more fundamental assumption – that both sides are agreed on the essentials of human welfare.

One of the basic, genuinely creative tensions in British politics is removed by this tacit agreement. It by-passes the main philosophical conflict. The plain fact is that until quite recently political parties were *not* agreed as to what constituted the welfare, and conduced to the ultimate happiness, of human beings. Or perhaps it would be more accurate to say that there were always in politics, although not necessarily rigidly segregated by party lines, men who held two essentially different opinions about this. Put like that, of course, it may still be true; but there can be little doubt that the accepted assumptions of party leaderships seem now to have transcended the disagreement.

Briefly, the conflict – however much and often blurred by expediency or muddleheadedness – was between a purely material concept of welfare and another which was sceptical of the material calculus. It was at no time easy to say exactly what the non-materialist school wished to substitute for this calculus, which is probably why it is in decline. It is only too apt to go off into vague talk about 'spiritual values', or to become bogged down in that interminably sterile argument on the theme of political v. economic 'freedom.'

This lack of precision, the inability to frame repugnance to pure materialism in terms of an attractive 'practical' policy, is almost certainly unavoidable. It is inherent in the nature of politics. One can follow the struggle to express it in the writings of Burke, Coleridge and innumerable others. It is the instinctive recoil of the philosopher from the facile assumptions of economics: the conviction that life is not really *like* that; that it is all made to sound too simple; that there is more to the needs of men and women than material prosperity, and that the politician who ignores or denies this may do incalculable harm.

The present political 'consensus' derives from the primacy of economics, which has usurped almost the entire field of politics. On the efficient functioning of the economy the *whole* of the 'good life' for the individual is deemed to depend, with the result that what we now call 'government' has become largely preoccupied with the conditioning or regulation of the economy. To the extent that this obsession rules it, the traditional conception of the nature of government is contracted, and politics are diverted from many of their legitimate concerns. The obsessive preoccupation with the economy in its turn derives from the increasing assumption by the State of responsibilities which were formerly privately borne, and by the definition of 'welfare' in terms of cash benefits and 'social security'.

The philosophy, if such it can be called, has of course an element of practical truth in it. It is obviously true that men and women cannot make much of their lives in conditions of poverty and unemployment, and that some measure of governmental supervision is required to prevent these miseries. But it seems to me that there is a very narrow dividing line, hard to define or position with accuracy, between the sphere of regulation to this end and a total political concern with the material prosperity of individual citizens.

This is much more than the difference between two opposed conceptions of 'social security' – the belief in the minimum or 'safety-net' level of benefits and the full Welfare State theory of universal provision of all social services at the highest possible level. It is a difference of emphasis and approach of the most fundamental kind. The current consensus goes far beyond the Beveridge ideal of 'a new war against Want, Disease, Ignorance and Squalor',[1] the aim of which was still to *remove* the material factors inhibiting the good life. It asserts that, even when these have been removed, the continued upward projection of the curve of economic prosperity will *of itself* make the good life even better.

Now it is necessary to emphasise that this is really an assertion of fundamental importance, and moreover an assertion that is novel. It is founded on important assumptions, and it has important practical results for government and politics. Although perhaps few of those who adhere to the consensus would actually say so – or even know that this was the implication of their policies – they have clearly accepted the assumption of 'technique' that the most important thing in human life is increasing consumption. Not only must production continually increase to meet the artificially stimulated demand for 'consumer goods', but the urge to consumption must continually be more powerfully stimulated in order to maintain that 'growth' of production (i.e. of the economy) which the technologist requires for the efficient exploitation of his techniques. To the State is allotted the task of stimulating 'growth', which requires both an inflationary economic climate and a steady rise in the cash benefits of the social services.

This seems to me to be the significant, indeed the essential, feature of what are now called the 'politics of consensus'. It has perhaps been imperfectly recognised by those who dislike the increasingly materialist calculus of modern 'society', which explains the bewilderment, frustration and even the incoherence in protest of those in all political parties who retain an instinctive idealism in their politics. On the other hand, it is very clearly recognised by the enthusiasts of 'technique', who are almost invariably in favour of the politics of consensus, only transferring their political allegiance from time to time as one party or another seems more likely to further the cause of technology and growth.

We have already considered the modern phenomenon of self-fulfilling determinist theories and promises. It is clearly evident in the field we are now examining. The agreed aim generates its own 'inevitable' necessities, and it becomes increasingly hard to believe that there are any sensible alternatives to the kind of political action they demand. The range of political action itself, together with the whole field of political discussion, is thus narrowed. 'Consensus' becomes more and more of a reality over a widening field. Economic 'growth' becomes the overriding end.

Meanwhile there are other tendencies making for a diminution in political controversy. One is the modern power of party 'machines'. Although, as we have seen, there is a great deal of exaggeration in common complaints about this, it is still an important factor. The Conservative and Labour parties are both coalitions of men holding quite widely differing political beliefs; as a result, continuous efforts are made by party leaders and managers to conceal conflicts inside parties and to display only the unity suggested by party votes in the House of Commons. This process of concealment, which involves confining the controversy to private party meetings, is not always successful. Sometimes the split goes too deep to be kept from the public and the conflict erupts in public or in Parliament. This happened to the Conservatives over the American loan terms after the war, over the abolition of Resale Price Maintenance in 1964, over Rhodesia in 1965 and over the Race Relations Act of 1968. The Labour Party split openly over the rearmament of Western Germany, over the imposition of charges in the National Health Service, over the proposal to drop the 'Clause 4' commitment to nationalisation from the party constitution, over the war in South Vietnam, and over the prices and incomes 'freeze' of 1966–8. Moreover, the concealment of intra-party differences has become much harder since newspaper lobby correspondents have applied themselves seriously to the business of finding out and reporting what happens at the 'private' party meetings.

Even so, the need to settle on compromise policies for each of two essentially 'coalition' parties has resulted in the narrowing of differences between parties; whatever politicians may say on platforms, what their parties do in office tends increasingly towards the politics of the centre.

This has caused many people to complain bitterly of the unreality and futility of party politics, and indeed of parliamentary government. It is perhaps not surprising that among them are many of the same people who have in the past been heard loudly demanding an end to party strife in the national interest. It has often been said that the British people do not like coalitions, but this has never stopped a great many of them demanding a 'national government' whenever they have no clear idea of what a government ought to be doing. There was another upsurge of this during 1966–7. The critics who demand an 'end to party strife' are generally of two kinds: the one logical and dangerous, the other foolish but fairly harmless.

The first kind of critics regard themselves as plain, sensible men of affairs, and as such have no patience with politics or politicians. They look upon parliamentary government as a pointless waste of time, and feel strongly that the politicians should agree on a sensible course of action and then get on with it. At the same time they are sure that a handful of intelligent businessmen would make a better job of it. Yet when the differences between the parties do in fact narrow, the critics become more rather than less impatient. If, they say, it is bad for the country to be deeply divided on great issues, it is merely a silly waste of time to bicker about small details. The plain truth is that most of these critics – though few have any idea of it and all would deny it indignantly – are at heart fascists. Sooner or later, if pressed in conversation, they will say that 'we should all be better off under a benevolent dictator'. Asked how a dictator is persuaded to stay benevolent, they talk evasively of General de Gaulle. Unfortunately, they have no idea at all of what politics are about.

The second kind of critics believe themselves to be sincere democrats and actuated by the best motives. They deplore political strife, but are quick to deny any sympathy with the idea of single-party government. No, they say, of course we must have parties, because that is essential to democracy, but the parties must not indulge in *too much* controversy. The problems involved are too serious for that. We see, they go on, much that is good in the policies of *all* parties: what is needed is for men of good will (like us) to come together and agree on a basic programme for the good of the country. All parties will then suppport it, and the country will be saved.

Nothing will ever dint the armour of self-righteousness in which these amateur statesmen (who include many writers of leading articles in 'independent' newspapers) have encased themselves. They are the Pharisees of politics. Calling themselves 'progressive', they do their utmost to weaken the forces making for any kind of progress. Priding themselves on their independence, they support no decision that is not a compromise and invariably oppose the kind of independence that stands out boldly for a cause. Having neither power nor responsibility, they are instinctively hostile to any effective power and to anyone who shows signs of being willing to shoulder responsibility. Their ideal statesman is one who sees both sides of every question and never gets to the heart of the matter at all. Their ideal system would be government by political eunuchs. Like the crypto-fascists, they know nothing about politics at all.

Unfortunately, however, their argument has a sort of superficial reasonableness that appeals to other people who know nothing about politics and have never thought deeply about the problems involved. Of course political controversy often appears sterile, and often is so in fact. Obviously it would be useful to secure the agreement of all political parties to a programme of action that would 'solve' the country's most serious problems. Unhappily, the outsiders who are confident that they see clearly what this programme should contain are generally the ones who have least appreciation of the nature and complexity of the problems, and no idea at all of the political difficulties of securing agreement on the remedies. A political synthesis is extremely hard to achieve. It is impossible to combine the salient features of the programmes of all parties, because the policies (at least the policies concerned with methods) by which each party sets most store are almost certain to be mutually incompatible. On the other hand a centre coalition is unlikely to agree on any 'middle way' that amounts to more than a few pious platitudes and an agreement to go on administering the existing system with a few very minor adjustments. Moreover such a coalition would not in the least abate political controversy; indeed, it would almost certainly exacerbate it. The coalition would be continually assailed, in increasingly violent terms, by extremists on both right and left who refuse to compromise their beliefs; in the end it could probably survive only by the unconstitutional suppression of opposition.

The whole 'coalition' thesis is founded on two monumental fallacies. The first is that correct courses of action are more likely to be found when there is less, rather than more, controversial discussion about the problems. The second is that the right policies must necessarily lie somewhere in between the policies of contending parties, which is simply not true.

There is one obvious historical example to serve as proof. At the time of the formation of the so-called National Government in 1931, to deal with the rapidly worsening slump, it was clear that there was no salvation in a middle way between the policies of the three parties. The Conservative policy was deflation and tariff protection of industry, the Liberal policy was Free Trade, and the Labour Party had made it abundantly clear that it had no policy at all. The Conservative policy was adopted: aided by improving terms of trade and a measure of inflation in the United States, it appeared to work. A fairly steady improvement took place from the end of 1933 until 1937. But few economists now would doubt that the right prescription for the 1931 situation was one which lay in the political spectrum well to the *left* of the policies of all the parties. It was what later came to be known as the 'Keynesian solution', which at the time was being canvassed by Professor G. D. H. Cole and other left-wing economists and was given in part a political airing by Lloyd George.

Similarly, when parties appear to have reached a consensus of policy and the policy fails to work, it is a reasonable conclusion that the right answer lies outside the consensus altogether. It is unlikely to lie in burrowing even deeper into the centre.

Finally, it must be emphasised that the most dangerous consensus of all is the tacit agreement which stifles discussion about the *ends* of policy.* If the parties agree on the *means* to be pursued to a given end, the experiment can be tried and some estimate made of its success; if it fails, another can be tried. But if everyone is determined to pursue the wrong end, it may be impossible ever to get on the right lines at all. Agreement on ends is an excellent ideal, but it is necessary to be very sure that the end agreed on is the best. This sounds so obvious as to be pointless, but it is not. For the fatuous assumption underlying the belief of so many people in the virtue of coalition and 'pulling together' is that any agreement must be better than none – even when it is to do the wrong things. The best way to avoid the danger of premature and erroneous conclusions is full, open and wide-ranging discussion – in other words, political controversy.

It has been maintained by some political scientists that democratic politics can be effectively pursued only if the political parties represent large interests and groups in the country between which some working accommodation has to be arranged. This is certainly true to the extent that democratic politics do not seem to work in those under-developed countries where there is no middle class and no counter-balancing of interests. But it is an inadequate guide to politics in a complex and sophisticated society.

It is clear that the political parties in Britain can no longer be analysed in terms of single interest groups. The Liberal Party represents no interests. The Labour Party, while it certainly stands for the interests of organised manual workers, neither commands the allegiance of all of them nor is exclus-

* I hope it is not necessary to waste time in refuting the frequently heard cry that 'we have a coalition, and all work together, to win a war, so we ought to be able to do it in a peacetime crisis'. A moment's reflection should show that the analogy is meaningless: first, because dealing with an economic crisis involves making genuinely political decisions about which there ought to be political controversy, while the fighting of a war (as distinct from beginning and ending it) does not; secondly, because it is desirable in war to secure, democratically, agreement between parties to impose temporary totalitarian measures. Of course, it may well be true that what many of the advocates of peacetime coalitions really want is the imposition of totalitarian measures 'in the national interest'.

ively dedicated to their interests; it is also the only effective vehicle for the views of intellectual middle-class radicals. The Conservative Party is very far from representing only the interests of industry and commerce – indeed in some respects it does not represent them at all. Since it also represents the landed and agricultural interests, it has a conflict of interests on its hands from the start. But it also seeks – not always with success – to represent the interests of the individual against the State and big business, and at the same time to appeal to those who are of a naturally conservative cast of mind. It is probable that the present political line-up involves altogether too many inherent contradictions to be permanently viable.

We have seen that the tensions *within* the two main parties have been increasing of late years. They must ultimately be resolved, and not until they are will the political controversy *between* parties become meaningful again.

The Labour Party cannot indefinitely hold together politicians who are dedicated to intellectual theories of planning, and to large-scale administration and the interests of technique, and also representatives of traditional types of manual craft workers and labourers who are dedicated to the conservative preservation of an industrial structure regarded by technocrats as obsolete. It is equally difficult to see how the Conservative Party can for ever survive the tensions generated by the confrontation of its conservative and individualist elements with its current preoccupation with 'big government' and massive technological change.

I believe there is likely to be a gradual, long-term shift in policies and alignments, rather than any sudden change. For one thing, the Labour Party is bound to try to continue walking its uncomfortable tightrope for the present, because its members are convinced that any split in it would put it effectively out of office for a generation.

That the Conservatives will suffer considerable internal tensions is obvious. There is always the danger that the party will fall too much under the influence of the all-out apostles of technique, and that the philosophical principles we have seen to be essential will receive too little attention. Those Conservatives who reject the primacy of the material calculus and who insist on tempering the imperatives of technique with an overriding concern for the interests of the individual and his environment will need to use all their influence to ensure that the spread of technique and the growth of 'big government' are held in check.

However, it seems to me likely that the two parties will in the end resume their traditional roles in politics. The Conservative Party is historically and temperamentally quite unsuited to undertake the permanent role of radical rather than gradualist reformers, and the underlying assumptions of the extreme technocrats are essentially repugnant to most conservatives. On the other hand, the radical and technocratic elements in the Labour Party are almost certain in the end to achieve a dominant influence; the conservative influence of the old craft trade unions is obviously something that cannot be dominant for ever.

We shall thus, I believe, return – perhaps after one quite radically reforming Conservative Government – * to our customary confrontation: between a conservative Tory party, with a strong bias towards tradition and gradual reform, and a radical reforming left-wing party dedicated to technocracy rather than socialism (although it will remain markedly collectivist in its outlook). The radical party will retain Labour's theoretical attachment to the principles of egalitarianism, which will be opposed on philosophical grounds by Conservatives. There will also be a constant tension of opposed philosophies of social welfare.

The result is likely to be that the country will return to its normal 20th century pattern of occasional bursts of radical reform under a radical government, with long intervening periods of conservative rule.

There is, it seems to me, only one possible alternative to this situation. That is that the two leading parties will simply exchange roles. The conservative forces within the Labour Party would gain control, and turn it into a party dedicated to the maintenance of the *status quo*, while the Conservative Party would become a largely technocratic party dedicated to material prosperity and 'big government'. This is not an

* The next Conservative Government seems certain to make substantial changes in trade union law and the tax system, for example.

impossible contingency, although it would involve a considerable realignment of forces and shifting of personal political allegiances. It is, however, unlikely, since it would involve the Tories in such severe internal conflict that they would almost tear themselves apart. It would also be extremely bad for the country, since significant interests would be left unrepresented and the underlying tensions would be likely to increase rather than diminish.

CHAPTER 15

The Meaning of Conservatism Today

The common problem, yours, mine, everyone's,
Is not to fancy what were fair in life
Provided it could be, – but, finding first
What may be, then find how to make it fair
Up to our means – a very different thing!
No abstract intellectual plan of life
Quite irrespective of life's plainest laws,
But one, a man, who is man and nothing more,
May lead within a world which (by your leave)
Is Rome or London – not Fool's-paradise.

Robert Browning,
Bishop Blougram's Apology

A depressing doctrine, it will be said. . . . But in the main the depression springs from the exclusion of hopes that were false and the discovery that guides, reputed to be of superhuman wisdom and skill, are, in fact, of a somewhat different character. If the doctrine deprives us of a model to be laid up in heaven to which we should approximate our behaviour, at least it does not lead us into a morass where every choice is equally good or equally to be deplored.

Michael Oakeshott, *Political Education*

'There was indeed a considerable shouting about what they called Conservative principles,' wrote Disraeli ten years after the publication of Peel's Tamworth Manifesto; 'but the awkward question naturally arose, what will you conserve?'[1] It is a problem that has bothered many people ever since, including Conservatives. Indeed, at regular intervals suggestions are made for changing the name of the party to something 'more modern'. Since the same people also petition the party leader every few years for a 're-statement of Conservative principles', it is not surprising that the search for a new name is fruitless. People who do not know what their principles are will be unlikely to agree on any name that is not meaningless.

The name 'Conservative', in these cosmopolitan days, has

acquired an aura that is thought to be unfortunate. It suggests Mr. Goldwater in America, and ineffectual reactionaries on the continent of Europe. It is not modern, it is not progressive, it is not *sympathetic*. Thus far have even nominal Conservatives been taken in by the left-wing confidence trick. Many of them have not yet realised that the wheel is almost come full circle. To be modern and progressive is already rather old-fashioned. It is the implications of the modern world, of progress, that are felt by an increasing number of people to be unsympathetic. As progress takes people into a more and more unfamiliar world, the vanishing guides and landmarks are increasingly missed; the few that remain begin to seem more precious than they did. In short, it is becoming easier to see what ought to be conserved, both in the physical environment and in our culture and social organisation. Indeed, it is even possible that in the latter field people are actually beginning to feel reactionary yearnings to have some of their vanished guides and standards restored.

To meet these needs is essentially, and solely, a task for the Conservative Party. In no other party is there any significant body of opinion that either recognises the needs or would feel a strong urge to meet them if it did. If it does not appear to everyone that even the Conservative Party is at present dedicated to this task, the reply must be that before long it will have to rededicate itself to it, for in the end it has no alternative. The pressures will be too strong.

What is involved in this is something that goes rather beyond the historic role of Conservatism, although that is an essential part of it. The consciousness of continuity, of operating within a tradition that is both moral and humane, imposing certain imperatives which are rather instinctively felt than precisely apprehended, shapes the approach of Conservatives to social and economic problems. Suspicious of rapid change that is deliberately brought about at the dictates of ideologies – even when it is the ideology of 'economic growth' and making money – Conservatives look at innovations critically, but in no rigidly hostile spirit. They seek to understand what is happening, and to balance the probable benefits of particular innovations against probable costs and the risk of undesirable secondary effects. 'Change', said Disraeli, 'is constant', and change is simply the aggregate of innovations which have been tested and accepted. It would in any case be strange for true Conservatives to oppose innovations on principle, for Conservatives believe in variety rather than uniformity, and innovation is essential to the maintenance of variety.

It is this instinctive feeling that diversity is essential to humanity which makes ideological egalitarianism a bitter and dangerous enemy to be fought by Conservatives to the death. Without diversity there can be no excellence, and the quality of life is impoverished. The mentality which seeks to level this quality down to a proletarian mediocrity is anathema to the Conservative. This is why there can in the end be no compromise with those who wish to destroy independent schools, private professional practice and the institution of private property, or to diminish academic excellence in the 'interests' of those who cannot attain it. This is a tough creed, no doubt, but a core of toughness is essential in a philosophy or creed if people are to look to it to give direction to their lives. We have suffered too much from the diffuse benevolence that takes no account of cost, of priorities or of secondary social effects. The time comes when the facts of life have to be stripped of the fuzzy verbiage that has been allowed to obscure them, so that people can see them sharp and clear and decide what *they themselves* want to do about them.

Certain decisions have to be taken. Conservatives have not been able to perceive the contradictions in their own present position. They attack socialists for their readiness to curb economic growth in the interests of an artificial equality; and certainly it is true that in those sectors of the economy where the classical theory is allowed to operate it is only the incentive of inequality which stimulates any progress at all. Enforced equality is fatal not only to the enterprise which creates material wealth, but to the achievement of any heights of distinction in culture and learning. So far, so good. Yet the standardisation prescribed by industrial technology and large-scale administrative technique is also a kind of enforced equality, ultimately just as fatal to the genuine progress that is based on selection from infinite variety.

Much of progress is the result of what *appear* to be accidents; whether they are is a question for the metaphysicians and the psychologists, and matters little for our purpose. 'The growth of civilisation rests largely on the individuals' making the best use of whatever accidents they encounter, of the essentially unpredictable advantages that one kind of knowledge will in new circumstances confer on one individual over others.'[2] Moreover, human beings themselves are essentially unpredictable; therein lies much of their humanity, distinguishing them from conditioned automata. To the Conservative, then, the variety, unpredictability and inequality of human beings are the source of all progress that is worth while. To the technocrat, on the other hand, 'the individual is a brake on progress':[3] the fact that he is 'ceaselessly tempted to make unpredictable choices' makes him 'a source of error' rather than the source of that variety on which true progress depends. It follows that no Conservative can yield unreservedly to the imperatives of technique.

There is, as we have seen in earlier chapters, a dilemma here. How are we to preserve variety when the operations of a more or less free market appear to be moving consistently to destroy it? Ought we even to try? Is it not possible that any effort to intervene will produce either chaos or inefficiency without compensating advantages? This, at least, is the classic liberal argument, and it is the argument of the 'Powellites'. Moreover, taking the long view, they may well be right. The situation probably will sort itself out in time. The inherent inefficiency of centralisation and excessive size of units, together with the resistance of industrial workers to the kind of changes in their way of life demanded by technique, may *in the end* produce either a breakdown in the system or a reaction to greater variety and smaller-scale operations. The question is, how much damage – and how much of it permanent – will have been done before the error is corrected? The damage, to people and to the environment, may well be greater than that inflicted by the 19th century industrial revolution. The question for Conservatives is whether they dare risk it. And, if they feel the risk is too great, how is it to be averted?

Although some of the decisions to be taken are concerned

with new problems, the dilemma itself is not new. Conservatives have always sought a 'middle way' between the inhumanity of total *laisser-faire* and the inhumanity of collectivism, one which will retain the incentives and discipline of the competitive market while mitigating the social damage it can do. Of recent years, however, they seem to have lost confidence in the search, and for the worst reasons. They have unconsciously accepted the assumptions of their opponents, and these assumptions are entirely false.

The first of these assumptions is that a political philosophy, to be respectable, must constitute a complete and logical system which will cover and account for everything. This is a heresy of the political left. Both the theory of *laisser-faire* and the collectivist theory, each of which was in its time embraced by the left, purport to be complete and logical systems. Confronted with one of these, persuasively argued, it is easy to lose confidence in a policy which seems less defensible intellectually, and to feel impelled to seek the security of a system. Conservatives opposed the policies of *laisser-faire* for perfectly sound reasons when they were dominant. Now, when collectivist policies are in the ascendant, they are inclined to be attracted by the intellectual arguments for *laisser-faire*.

The second, and more dangerous, assumption is that a pragmatic policy, if it does not appear to work perfectly in all circumstances, must be wrong. This is completely fallacious. It *may* be wrong; but, if there is no other policy which would work better, it may equally well be right. In this case, Conservatives have allowed not only the public but themselves to be taken in by a simple confidence trick. When something goes wrong under a Conservative Government, their opponents announce triumphantly that Tory policies do not work. When things go even more wrong under a Labour Government, socialists are apt to say, 'Well, of course it can't be the policies that are wrong, because we know the theory is sound and covers everything. We have just been blown a little off course – the sort of thing that might happen to anyone, with all these currency speculators and wild-cat strikers about. But it will be all right in the end, once the theory gets a chance to work out in practice.' For the most part, they are allowed to get away with it, against all the odds. In fact, it is the theory itself which is wrong, and no policies based on it will ever work satisfactorily. Surely a theory which is supposed to cover everything ought at least to have enabled *one* Labour Government to operate without continuous economic crises?

Conservatives have to take one major decision, and to take it fairly soon. This is simply to make a conscious and explicit effort to control and discipline technological advance, or on the other hand to allow it free rein and accept the imperatives it will impose on people and on their environment. It does not seem to me that in the end Conservatives have any alternative but to come down in favour of control, great as are the difficulties involved in this choice. If individual men and women are the most important political end, together with the environment in which they live; if production exists rather to serve them than to sustain itself; and if variety rather than large-scale uniformity is important in itself; then the effects of encroaching technique must somehow be mitigated. In all these things Conservatives must believe, and therefore they must accept the implications.

The arguments which are commonly advanced by Conservatives against the firm control of technological development and of the trend towards ever larger industrial and administrative units are of two kinds. One consists of the simple statement that large units are 'more efficient' than small ones. This is, as we have seen, a proposition which can by no means be accepted without qualification. It is not always true on any terms or by any definition. Sometimes very large units are not even efficient by the simple test of unit costs and profitability. Sometimes it is uncertain whether the real savings in production or administrative costs will not in the long run be balanced by the loss of workers' loyalty or of contact with customers served or electors being governed. Sometimes the units simply become too large to be properly administered, so that the service to customers or electors deteriorates. In short, there is no certainty about this at all. Large units *may* be more efficient in some circumstances – indeed, some undoubtedly are – but it is impossible to say with certainty that they always are.

Now if this is so, then the whole of the first argument falls to the ground. If each case has to be taken on its merits, and possible savings balanced against other, less easily measurable, costs, then the argument for an empirical policy aimed at achieving ends less narrow than the immediate objective of material prosperity becomes much stronger. It cannot, at any rate, be ruled out of court on theoretical grounds.

The second Conservative objection to control takes the form of questioning whether it can ever be possible to make the 'right' decisions in trying to exercise the control. Who is to say, the argument runs, that this or that size of firm would be better than another, or that it would be 'right' to allow this commercial venture and prevent that? No outside observer, whether he be politician or departmental 'expert', can possibly be certain of being right; indeed, he is much less likely to be right over a period than the combined judgements of those in the industry who are venturing their own money and will tend to organise themselves and their businesses in the most efficient way.

This is, of course, the classical argument of the 'invisible hand'. It raises, as we have seen, certain questions: not least the question of what is 'the good of society as a whole' to which the complicated processes of the market are supposed to conduce. Moreover, it is based on a system-theory, designed to pander to the quite un-Conservative yearning for a theory which will cover everything. That many Conservatives feel this to be inconsistent with their fundamental beliefs is shown by the attempts which have been made to modify the theory. Most leading Conservatives have always accepted the general proposition that economic decisions – other than the main strategic fiscal and monetary decisions to be made by government – should be left to the operation of a free market. They have, however, generally qualified this proposition in two respects. First, they admit that it may be necessary to force the operators to compete freely, by prohibiting certain kinds of monopolistic or inter-company agreements and practices. Secondly, they accept that it is desirable in certain circumstances to intervene for purely social reasons, for example to prevent great hardship to individuals and localities when structural changes are taking place in an industry.

This is perfectly reasonable: but, once the desirability – or even the possibility – of making exceptions of this kind is admitted, can there be logically any end to the number or kinds of exceptions that can be made? This thought has clearly begun to worry leading Conservatives, so that quite recently they have begun to move away from 'interventionism' in the direction of greater reliance on the unrestricted operation of the market. This seems to have been due in part to the influence of the 'Powellites', and partly to the exciting promises of the technocrats, holding out the hope of enormous benefits to humanity if they are only left free to 'get on with the job'.* This is a retrograde movement, and for Conservatives clearly wrong. For both technique (in its widest sense) and the unrestricted market theory of *laisser-faire* are essentially ideologies, and Conservatives cannot without inconsistency embrace ideologies.

The fact is that Conservatives *must* admit the desirability – even the necessity – of interfering for social reasons in the operations of a free market economy. Indeed, they have always been ready to intervene (though not always soon enough) in the interests of individual men and women against the theoretical claims of economists and industrialists. Moreover, it can be clearly demonstrated that such intervention is necessary. Despite the enormous economic growth set off by the Industrial Revolution, and the resulting rise in average living standards, no one can now possibly claim that the incidental suffering of many men, women and children should not have been more effectively mitigated by State intervention, or that the immense damage done to the physical environment was other than criminal. Again, it is now clear that the contemporary arguments of liberal economists and industrialists against State intervention were often absurd. Not only Cobden and Bright but even Peel, a humane and moderate man, opposed the Ten Hours Bill on the grounds that to limit the working hours of young people to ten hours a day would result not only in the collapse of manufacturing industry but in the impoverishment of the workers themselves. Conservatives should never be afraid to champion the cause

* It may also have been due in some measure to the awful warning of Mr Aubrey Jones and the Prices and Incomes Board.

of intervention against theoretical arguments of this kind,* and should always be chary of being taken in by them themselves.

Now of course, if it is consonant with Conservative principles to intervene in the operations of the free market to prevent men, women and children from being inhumanly exploited and their physical environment from being blighted, it is perfectly legitimate to intervene for the purpose of protecting them from some of the ravages of unrestricted technique. I do not underestimate the dangers, or the difficulty of knowing where to draw the line. Every effort must no doubt be made to keep intervention to a minimum, and to interfere as little as possible with the detailed operation of the market. But there are certain trends and developments which Conservatives simply cannot allow to proceed absolutely unchecked to their logical conclusion, which is the total triumph of technique and the total conditioning of human beings to its requirements. These trends are *not* inevitable, and Conservatives must never allow the theoreticians to convince them that they are. Indeed it is clear that, for example, tax changes to encourage *small-scale* enterprise would actually help the market system to work more freely.

Above all, Conservatives must not be afraid to admit that the decisions they take will sometimes be wrong and the effects of them unfortunate. After all, when the mistakes of their opponents are plain for all to see, it does seem rather absurd to try to compete with them in promising perfection. In the long run, the imperfections of a policy which will be largely empirical will be less than the physical and social ravages likely to be caused by ideological adherence to the logical imperatives of technique.

To forestall some of the objections which will be raised against this demand for interference with 'inevitable trends', it is probably necessary to repeat once more that what has been said above is in no sense a plea for 'socialist planning'; nor is it a futile Luddite attempt to 'halt the march of technological advance'; nor does it envisage a return to some mythical Merrie Englande full of cottage industries. It is no

* Even when they are advanced by contemporaries to prove the necessity for the importation of cheap coloured labour.

more than a simple statement that free human beings have a right to decide whether technique shall be their servant, used to create conditions of life which they themselves have chosen for their own convenience, or whether it shall be their master, conditioning them to work and consume in ways convenient to technicians and moulding society into a pattern in which individuals and families count for little or nothing. It is a demand that the technological revolution shall not be allowed to repeat, after its own fashion and on a larger scale, the inhumanity and physical destruction of the Industrial Revolution. In particular, it is insistent that the short-term benefits of cheapness and speed shall not always be allowed to prevail over the long-term well-being of people and their environment; also that technology shall be forced, as its industrial predecessors were not, to clear up its own mess as it goes along, devoting a greater part of its knowledge and skills to the reduction of noise, pollution and unsightliness.

All this is scarcely consistent with the neo-classical theories of the Powellites. But it is no more consistent with the theories of the collectivists, since these tend to encourage centralisation and the increasing power of administrative technique. It is a recipe for a moderate and non-doctrinaire Conservatism which knows what it is that it is trying to conserve – which puts people above processes, the interests of those who need to be served above the interests of those who exist to serve them, and the trusteeship of the physical environment above the immediate requirements of technique. The results can never be completely successful, for there is no magic solution for the problems of a technological age and a complex society, but they are likely to be more constructive and less destructive than what is happening at present. Change will be continuous, but it will tend to follow a general direction derived from a philosophical conception of the aims and needs of the community. It will, if you like to call it so, be planned change – which is no more than to say that it will be in some measure the result of conscious and deliberate choice.

Many of the choices will be agonisingly difficult to make. The argument for very rapid and far-reaching technological change will often seem overwhelmingly strong. If we limit it, shall we be able to compete with other countries in overseas markets? Is control consistent with membership of the Common Market? Is it right to deny people the immediate benefits of new processes and methods? Yet always the necessary questions must be asked, the long view taken and the benefits and the costs weighed against each other. It will be necessary to remember, too, that this is not only a problem for Britain. It is one that will soon be facing every advanced industrial country; and if Britain can show the way to others, by pioneering methods of dealing with the problems, she will have achieved a new leadership in which she may regain some of her confidence and pride.

This, then, is the chief task which gives a new meaning to the idea of Conservatism, and it is a task which only the Conservative party can perform. At first sight, perhaps, it looks a 'soft' rather than a 'tough' policy, involving much paternalistic interference to protect people from the rigours of the world. In fact, it is a very tough policy indeed, and will on occasions be far from popular. Commercial interests will try ceaselessly to persuade people that technique would make them happier if it were allowed to ride free, and sometimes they will succeed. Not everyone is prepared happily to forego immediate satisfactions to avoid long-term troubles – still less to sacrifice their own comfort for the interests of posterity. There are just as many people prepared to put up with ugliness and desecration as there are people prepared to inflict it for a quick profit.

The preservation of quality demands a certain toughness in the defenders, and it will mean requiring some toughness from the people. They will be required to resume some of the responsibilities which modern theory and modern public authorities have tended to erode – responsibilities in government, as well as in the support and control of families. Elimination or concentration of subsidies, encouragement of private rather than public provision of welfare services, a much less permissive attitude towards adult crime and juvenile indiscipline, an insistence on the legal validity of labour agreements – all these policies are based on the same philosophical principles, and all tend in the same direction, which is the restoration of individual responsibility. Finally, Conservatives will seek always to put the preservation of quality above the enforcement of equality.

All this requires considerable faith, even boldness, on the part of those who decide to put these policies into effect. Yet in the past, when Conservatives have been impelled under the influence of great leaders to 'trust the people', they have not been disappointed with the results. The task is to restore people's confidence in themselves, and it may be that this can be achieved only by leaders who have implicit confidence in the people. Once the facts of life are clearly recognised, the artificiality and pretensions of our present 'society' may be replaced by a greater sense of realism and a tougher approach to our besetting problems. To those who maintain that this is all high-flown nonsense, and that the overriding task is to solve the economic problem, on which all else depends, I would pose one question: is it not at least possible that without the changes I have outlined the economic problem *cannot* be solved? For myself, I believe that these changes would make a solution very much easier.

People will only do great things if they see the possibility of great things to do. Once they see the possibility of creative action – *their own* action – they may regain the confidence that has begun to desert them. When they have regained, through the resumption of responsibility and the pride of action, their own self-confidence, they will recover a confidence in their country. When they have rediscovered a role for themselves in their country, they will rediscover a role for their country in the world.

Reference Notes

INTRODUCTION

1. Edmund Leach, *A Runaway World*, the Reith Lectures (1967).
2. Jacques Ellul, *The Technological Society* (1954), trans. John Wilkinson (1964).
3. J. H. Newman, *Essay in Aid of a Grammar of Assent* (1870).
4. *The Letters of Junius* (No. XVI, 1769).

CHAPTER 1

1. René Descartes, *Meditationes de Prima Philosophia* (1641).
2. T. H. Green, *Prolegomena to Ethics* (1883).
3. J. H. Newman, preface to *Via Media* (1877).
4. Newman, *Essay in Aid of a Grammar of Assent* (1870).
5. A. N. Whitehead, *Science and the Modern World.*
6. Hannah Arendt, *The Human Condition* (1958).
7. Arendt, *Between Past and Future* (1961).
8. Arendt, *The Human Condition* (1958).
9. *Daily Telegraph*, 31st August, 1966.

CHAPTER 2

1. Hannah Arendt, *The Human Condition* (1958).
2. F. W. Maitland, *The Constitutional History of England* (1908).
3. F. A. Hayek, *The Constitution of Liberty* (1960).
4. Edmund Burke, *Tracts Relative to the Laws against Popery in Ireland.*
5. Arthur D. Innes, *England Under the Tudors* (1905).
6. Judith N. Shklar, *Political Theory and Ideology* (1966).
7. F. Engels, in a letter to Mehring (1893), quoted in Shklar, *op. cit.*
8. Karl Marx and F. Engels, *Manifesto of the Communist Party* (1848).
9. The significance of Hobbes's thought is well summarised by Christopher Hill in *Puritanism and Revolution* (1958).
10. C. R. Morris, *Locke, Berkeley, Hume* (1931).
11. John Locke, *Second Treatise of Civil Government* (1690).
12. For a suggestive – albeit tendentious – study by a Marxist of the social implications of Locke's views, see C. B. Macpherson, 'The Social Bearings of Locke's Political Theory', reprinted from *The Western Political Quarterly* in Shklar, *op. cit.*
13. Hannah Arendt, *The Human Condition* (1958).

14. *Ibid.*
15. Enoch Powell, M.P., *A Nation Not Afraid* (ed. John Wood, 1965).
16. Gunnar Myrdal, *The Political Element in the Development of Economic Theory* (1953).
17. *Ibid.*
18. See Mary P. Mack, *Jeremy Bentham, 1748–92* (1962).
19. T. D. Weldon, *The Vocabulary of Politics* (1953).
20. Mr. Weldon's thesis has been concisely criticised by Alfred Cobban, *In Search of Humanity* (1960).
21. See especially. Russell Kirk, *The Conservative Mind* (1953).
22. Edmund Burke, *Reflections on the Revolution in France* (1790).
23. James McAuley, *The End of Modernity* (1959).
24. Quoted by Alfred Cobban, *In Search of Humanity* (1960) from P.-M. Masson, *La Religion de J.-J. Rousseau* (1916).

CHAPTER 3

1. Rudyard Kipling, *The Gods of the Copybook Headings* (1919).
2. For example, John Buchan (the first Lord Tweedsmuir) was reflecting uneasily along these lines in his last years. See esp. *Memory Hold-the-Door* (1940), pp. 288–90.
3. Herbert Spencer, *Essays* (1857).
4. Hannah Arendt, *Between Past and Future* (1961).
5. J. P. Corbett, *Europe and the Social Order* (1959).
6. Rex Warner, *Pericles the Athenian* (1963).
7. Hannah Arendt, *The Human Condition* (1958).
8. *Ibid.*
9. *Ibid.*
10. Alfred Cobban, *In Search of Humanity* (1960).

CHAPTER 4

1. Pierre Teilhard de Chardin, *The Phenomenon of Man* (English edn. 1959).
2. From the passage already quoted in Chapter 3 from Hannah Arendt, *Between Past and Future* (1961).
3. Arendt, *op. cit.*

CHAPTER 5

1. Sir James Jeans, *Physics and Philosophy* (1942).
2. Jacques Ellul, *The Technological Society* (trans. John Wilkinson, 1965).
3. *Ibid.*
4. *Ibid.*
5. *Ibid.*

6. Kurt Baier, *The Moral Point of View* (1960).
7. This proposition is neatly, simply and impressively sustained in Kurt Baier, *op. cit.*
8. Ellul, *op. cit.*
9. F. A. Hayek, *The Constitution of Liberty* (1960).
10. Michael Oakeshott, *Rationalism in Politics* (1962).
11. Edmund Leach, *A Runaway World*, the Reith Lectures (1967).
12. Oakeshott, *op. cit.*
13. Samuel Butler, *Erewhon* (revised edn., 1901).
14. Alfred Cobban, *In Search of Humanity* (1960).
15. E. J. Mishan, *The Costs of Economic Growth* (1967).
16. J. M. Keynes, *The End of Laisser-faire* (1926).

CHAPTER 6

1. Jacques Barzun, *The House of Intellect* (1959).
2. *Ibid.*

CHAPTER 7

1. Denis de Rougemont, *Passion and Society* (tr. Montgomery Belgion, 2nd edn. 1956).
2. Morris Ginsberg, *On Justice in Society* (1965).
3. Alan Gewirth, 'Political Justice', in *Social Justice* (ed. Richard B. Brandt, 1962).
4. William K. Frankena, 'The Concept of Social Justice', in *Social Justice* (see *supra*).
5. *Ibid.*
6. *Ibid.*
7. *Ibid.*
8. Gregory Vlastos, 'Justice and Equality', in *Social Justice* (*supra*).
9. Ginsberg, *op. cit.*
10. Walter Bagehot, *Physics and Politics* (1869).
11. C. A. R. Crosland, *The Future of Socialism* (revised edn. 1964).
12. Ginsberg, *op. cit.*

CHAPTER 8

1. C. A. R. Crosland, *The Future of Socialism* (revised edn. 1964).
2. *Ibid.*

CHAPTER 9

1. François Lafitte, in *The New Outline of Modern Knowledge* (1956).

2. See esp. E. G. West, *Education and the State* (1965), and other publications of the Institute of Economic Affairs.

CHAPTER 10

1. J. M. Keynes, *The General Theory of Employment, Interest and Money* (1936).
2. J. K. Galbraith, esp. Chapter VIII of *The Affluent Society* (1958), and Chapters III and VI–VIII of *The New Industrial State* (1967).

CHAPTER 11

1. Cf. the splendid diatribes in Jacques Barzun's *The House of Intellect* (1959).
2. J. K. Galbraith, *The New Industrial State* (1967).
3. Jacques Ellul, *The Technological Society* (trans. John Wilkinson, 1963).
4. There is some interesting pioneering work in E. J. Mishan, *The Costs of Economic Growth* (1967).

CHAPTER 12

1. James McAuley, *The End of Modernity* (1959).
2. George Santayana, *The Life of Reason.*
3. R. H. S. Crossman, introductory essay to a new edition of Walter Bagehot's *The English Constitution* (1963).
4. This is argued in relation to Australia (and the arguments apply, *mutatis mutandis,* to Britain also) in Chapter 11 of Sir Robert Menzies' memoirs, *Afternoon Light* (1967). See also Ronald Butt, *The Power of Parliament* (1967).
5. This point is well made by Max Nicholson, in *The System* (1967).
6. It is salutary now to read Bagehot, in *The English Constitution* (1867), on the constitution of the United States. His criticisms, whether or not they were valid at the time, have not worn well in the century since they were written.

CHAPTER 14

1. William H. Beveridge, *Full Employment in a Free Society* (1944).

CHAPTER 15

1. Benjamin Disraeli, *Coningsby* (1844).
2. F. A. Hayek, *The Constitution of Liberty* (1960).
3. Jacques Ellul, *The Technological Society* (1954), tr. John Wilkinson (1964).

Index